AUTOMOBILE QUARTERLY'S

# Great Cars & Grand Marques

**BONANZA BOOKS**

New York

# AUTOMOBILE QUARTERLY'S *Great Cars*

## EDITED, AND WITH AN INTROD

# & Grand Marques

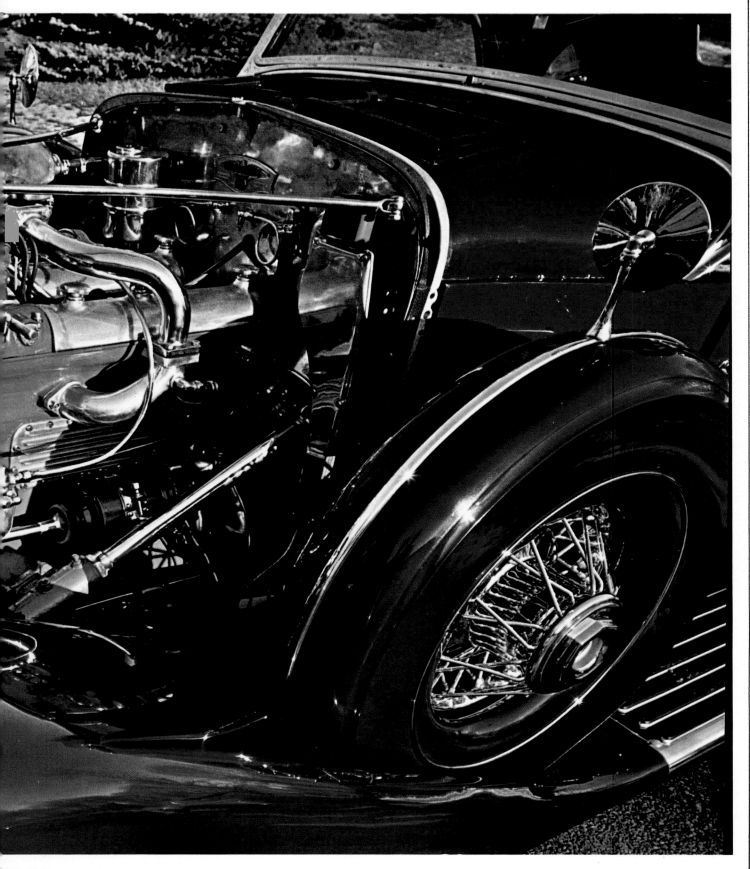

CTION, BY BEVERLY RAE KIMES

# Staff for this Book

## AUTOMOBILE QUARTERLY PUBLICATIONS

Publisher and President: L. Scott Bailey
Editor: Beverly Rae Kimes
Senior Editor: Stan Grayson
Art Director: Theodore R.F. Hall
Assistant Art Director: Edmond Fenech
Production Editor: Ian C. Bowers

## CONTRIBUTING AUTHORS

Griffith Borgeson, Arthur W. Einstein, Jr., Allan Girdler,
Stan Grayson, Peter Helck, Maurice D. Hendry, Beverly Rae Kimes,
Dennis May, Sam Medway, David Owen, Simon Read, Don Vorderman, W.C. Williams

Typesetting by Kutztown Publishing Company, Kutztown, Pennsylvania
Color separations by Graphic Arts Corporation, Toledo, Ohio

This edition is published by Bonanza Books,
a division of Crown Publishers, Inc.,
by arrangement with Automobile Quarterly Publications.
a b c d e f g h
BONANZA 1979 EDITION

Printed and bound in Hong Kong
by South China Printing Co.

# Contents

# Introduction

There are doubtless those abroad in the land who consider car people johnny-one-notes. An enthusiasm for automobiles, it is thought by some, is a mania narrowly confined, a diversion of limited scope enjoyed by people whose emotions are revved by getting their hands rather dirty and their wallets quite depleted—all in pursuit of a recreation which is at best ephemeral.

We think that's silly.

Few realities have more permanence than the automobile. In less than a century, it has reshaped society in its image, just imagine a world without it. It has been the focus of industrial battles as bitterly—and sometimes viciously—fought as Culloden. It has been the object of intrigues as intricately woven as a Gobelin tapestry. It has been the prop for humor as broad as the Keystone Cops. It has been the catalyst in sporting confrontations as electrically charged as lightning— with machines almost as fast. It has been the medium upon which fantastic glories of rolling sculpture have been wrought. It has been the reason for engineering tours de force ofttimes exquisite in either their sophistication or their simplification. It is as contemporary as the latest far-out idea and as rooted in antiquity as the self-propelled notions appearing on the walls of ancient Egyptian monuments. The automobile is history, it is art, it is technology, it is sport. It is all this...and more.

Car people know this.

To truly appreciate an automobile, one must have a sense of the aesthetic, an acquaintanceship with technology, a feeling for history, a liking for drama—even a sense of humor. It is for such people that this volume has been produced. We like this book. We had an enormous good time doing it. We knew we would. Firstly, two hundred forty pages, every one of them in full color, was as mouth-watering a prospect as those dreams a lot of us had as children of being locked in a candy factory. At AUTOMOBILE Quarterly, we've always relished color; an automobile is, we think, best shown as close to reality as possible. Without color, a dimension is lost. And to be utterly frank about it, we like the flamboyance of color.

We like to ooh and aah, and occasionally wow, as we flip through big pages with big pictures of magnificent motorcars. We doubt we shall ever become so blasé as not to enjoy the automobile purely as spectacle. And when the spectacle spans—as it does here—decades numbering eight, cars numbering into the hundreds and in a variety quite as multiferous, we admit to an excitement only equaled perhaps by the Fourth of July in a Bicentennial year. We had fun too deciding what to call the book.

Why not be audacious? Why not say great and grand? We know full well that such adjectives are diversely reserved by car people for motorcars of their own individual preference, some equating the terms with expanse or expense. What is great to one automobile enthusiast might be a mass of unnecessary complexity to another, and even the most obvious marques about which superlatives are flung have rarely enjoyed fulsome unanimity of opinion. For our part, we remain catholic in this regard. Erecting rigid parameters would make for a small corral—and lots of fascinating cars would be left out. A great car to us is one of compelling interest for reasons that might variously be aesthetic, technological or historical. Sometimes greatness is simply to have tried in the face of insuperable odds. Sometimes it is an exquisite rendering of all those things poets have said through the ages about charm. Sometimes it might be something we're not even sure we can define. Maybe it's just that we like cars so much.

The automobile—as we noted in the credo to our first issue nearly fifteen years ago—is an extreme passion with us, and we've elected not to dilute it by being unnecessarily arbitrary. We can become as enthused about a Kelsey Motorette with three wheels and ten horsepower as we can about a Duesenberg with four of the former and over three hundred of the latter. Those are but two of the marques covered in this volume, there are dozens more. And that was the most fun of all—selecting the stories to appear herein. A pastiche, that was our aim, one that would reflect our special view of the automobile, as expressed by our editors and the stable of writers, artists and photographers who feel about cars as we do and who have been long-time comrades of AQ. The selection process proved to be most revealing— and a bit of a surprise. With AUTOMOBILE Quarterly magazine —for both our readers and ourselves alike—the results of all efforts are neatly spaced, every quarter of the year. Here our task was to choose and consolidate in one volume a representation of a decade and more of publishing— and in the editing and revising and preparation project, we were provided a fresh look at our world of the automobile. What impressed us most was the interplay of history, the threads of commonality or contrast which weave through the various marques and which tend to braid themselves together when the subjects are placed in the proximity of one volume. They are subtle sometimes, but we think you'll enjoy spotting them as much as we did, as you move from story to story. For example, James Scripps-Booth's worrying that his board of directors was moving the Scripps-Booth precariously into Biddle territory—without realizing, of course, that the Biddle was having considerable troubles of its own. Or the problem that Eddie Rickenbacker in Detroit and Louis Delage in Paris shared in trying to put across an idea that the public wasn't sure it was yet ready to accept. Or the safety consciousness of Vincenzo Lancia in the Twenties with the Lambda as juxtaposed with BMW's thoughts along similar lines in the Seventies with the Turbo. And there are threads of the glory that was Packard's during the good years, the elegance that was Delage's, the tradition that has always been Lancia's. The romance that Victor Riley found when he fixed his sights on building some ruddy good sporting cars, the quandary Everett Cameron had in fixing a site for the building of his motorcar. There's the cachet that was the Amilcar's during the Twenties, the colossus conjured with mere mention of the name Duesenberg. The breakthrough that was the step-down Hudson's during the early postwar period…or was it? There's the delicious contrast between what Rudyard Kipling had to say about the Locomobile after a thirteen-mile trek through Sussex and what Henry Ford exclaimed when he saw one blasting its way down the roads of Long Island en route to America's first victory in an international race. Then, the poor Prunel whose best-ever sporting finish was a second at Wentworth Woodhouse… amid a two-car entry; the high and mighty E.R.A., veritable champion of obsolete engineering practices which, relative to the number built, managed to cop more victories than any other racing car ever had or would; and the thundering years of the Auto Union and Mercedes Grand Prix cars, an era such as the world had never before seen, and never will again. We might lament the past, of course, mourn the fact that the Hudson is no more, the Bentley isn't what it used to be. We don't have the automobile's grand afterthought, the radiator mascot, anymore, nor are they writing songs like they used to about the motorcar—and Pierce-Arrow had the right idea about automobile advertising some sixty years ago. We can wonder why the critics were so hard on Alexander Winton at the turn of the century, heave hindsight sighs for the cars that should have survived but didn't—and we now know why; wax enthusiastic in the recollection that one never had to worry about being ordinary in a 300 SL and declare stolidly that the best way to get from Kansas City to Dallas in time for tech was towing your racer behind a Chrysler 300. And that, metaphorically, a standing quarter in the 427 Cobra is being shot from a cannon. There are many more cars and many more stories in the pages that follow, in our mélange of motorcar lore. The question is often asked, what draws men to cars? We hope this volume in some measure might answer it. It is the bewildering variety in form and purpose that the automobile has taken through the years, the engrossing stories which lay behind it, the magic that it can have, the frequently larger-than-life posture it has assumed, the clamorous victories it has enjoyed, the resounding defeats it has suffered, the phenomenal fact of what it is and what it has been. Please join with us now in our adventure which is the automobile. We think you'll have a good time too.

*Beverly Rae Kimes*
*Editor, AUTOMOBILE Quarterly*

# THE MASCOT

*An Afterthought, But Certainly One of the Automobile's Grandest...*

It was bound to happen. With a mode of transport as individual as the automobile, it was inevitable that man would wish to make a motorcar uniquely his own, to personalize it, to differentiate it in some way from that of his neighbor. One suspects that as early as the first day after the first automobile was shown to the public, someone somewhere must have been thinking about a line of accessories to adorn it. A gargantuan industry would grow up devoted to this cause—providing through the years varying niceties from acetylene headlamps, bulb horns, robe rails, fender braces, luggage trunks, demountable rim wheel outfits, clamp-on bumpers, folding glass windshields to mag wheels, hood scoops, steering wheel knobs, giant plush dice, lamp stone guards, ski clamps, air horns blowing the strains of the "Wedding March" or "Lisbon Antigua." And, of course, all manner of performance packages from Rajo heads for the Model T to velocity stacks for the Beetle. But surely man's ingenuity has been exercised to the fullest via the radiator cap mascot.

Indeed it was almost certainly the mascot that man first imagined as an accessory to the automotive idea. Way back in 1827, when the idea of personalized motor transport was but a fantasy, an English visionary drew a three-wheeled steam carriage he called a Docudep: Perched upon its tiller bar pivot was a golden bird with outstretched wings—the first recorded use discovered to date of a mascot on a motorized vehicle, if only imaginatively. When the reality came, again it was an Englishman to whom is granted the distinction of first having thought of a mascot for his vehicle. On the dash of his 1896 four-cylinder Daimler, Lord Montagu of Beaulieu placed a bronze statuette of St. Christopher, patron of travelers. (It's still there, the vehicle on display at the National Motor Museum in Hampshire established by the present Lord Montagu.)

The mascot idea quickly caught fire. By the turn of the century, it had traveled across both the Channel and the Atlantic Ocean. Examples could be purchased in fine jewelry shops and a few accessory stores—or appropriated elsewhere. In the United States, many a flagpole would be found without its ubiquitous eagle. The earliest dated "genuine" American mascot design was a small, gnome-like fellow called "Gobbo,

*Buick's Mercury of 1931-1932.*

God of Good Luck" whose likeness was copyrighted by L.V. Aronson in March of 1909. A prolific designer of mascots, Mr. Aronson was also responsible for the graceful diving girl or "Speed Nymph" which hit the marketplace in 1910 and was soon copied by uncounted numbers of English and French mascot makers.

Meanwhile, in France, sculptors were coming up with lots of ideas of their own as well—animals, birds, nudes and semi-nudes. And occasionally a touch of the macabre: One design shown in a 1913 French catalogue was entitled "Hara-Kiri" and depicted a Japanese gentleman committing exactly that.

Two years later, in Paris, a jeweler and designer by the name of Rene Lalique created his first mascot—a dragonfly with its wings folded. His medium was glass, and the twenty-seven Lalique designs which followed were sculpted of the same translucent substance, each an exquisite work of art. Other glass and crystal makers, both in Europe and America, copied Lalique, but for all the flattery imitation proverbially represents, the results suffered sadly in comparison. There was only one René Lalique and he designed his last automotive mascot in the late Thirties—though certain of them may still be purchased in Lalique shops today, as paperweights. During those fabulous days when they resided atop the radiator of a grand classic, they could be acquired with an especially designed base incorporating a small light bulb for illumination of the mascot at night. This, of course, contributed not at all to the function performed by the headlights, though it must have piqued the curiosity of drivers in oncoming cars.

Others would find more practical purpose for that space atop the radiator. Sometime along about 1912, someone thought it might be nice for a driver to know the status of the water temperature in his radiator. Thus

"Indian Javelot," circa 1930, designed by F. Bazin.

was born the motometer or calormeter. While manufactured in a large number of designs, it initially was a pedestrian thing, differing only in face plate. By the 1920's however, Boyce and other manufacturers began offering mini-mascots to be attached to the top of the gauges, while mascot designers offered a variety of figures to which a motometer could be affixed. Unfortunately, the more advanced automobile manufacturers soon decided to install temperature indicators on their cars' instrument panels, leaving the top of the radiator cap for their own mascot or one of the owner's choosing—and gauge manufacturers recognized that they might soon find themselves out of hot water. For a while, they solved that by producing mascots themselves with temperature tubes cleverly concealed within the design—girl vaulting over temperature pillar, for example. As late as 1934, one could buy a Ford greyhound mascot with a tiny temperature tube tucked between its rear legs.

*Devil from a 1912 Léon Bollée, above; Lalique's "Archer," below.*

*From the late Twenties, a devil from France.*

Historically, motorcar manufacturers preferred at first to remain aloof of the mascot. Vulcan had offered its blacksmith since 1902, Rolls-Royce its "Spirit of Ecstacy" since 1911, but these were isolated cases. The flood of "approved" mascots by manufacturers didn't come until the Twenties—the Star dancing nude on Star of David and the Farman Icarus in 1922; the Lorraine-Dietrich stork and the Chrysler winged hat of Hermes in 1924; the Minerva goddess of wisdom in 1925; the Cadillac herald and Pontiac Indian in 1926; the Buick goddess and the Vauxhall griffin in 1927; the DeSoto warrior in 1928—and dozens upon dozens of others. Soon thereafter most automakers offered an approved mascot as standard

On the facing page, mascots by René Lalique, his eagle's head, his pheasant, his hawk's head, his cock's head. Lalique's falcon, for an early Duesenberg, above left.
The eagle used by Marmon for its eight-cylinder cars from the years 1927-1928, right above. "Eagle on a Globe" by Brau, which adorned the Messier in 1928, below left.
An example of personal expression in mascots, dated circa 1930 and from England, adapted from an owner's coat of arms for his Rolls-Royce, right below.

*Clockwise, from above: "Speed Nymph" by Aronson, 1910; Lalique's "Spirit of the Wind";
a very French and very stylized mascot from the late Twenties; Lalique's famous "Femme Nu";
a cherubic lass leaping over a stone-tablet-concealed motometer, from I. Florman, 1923;
"Girl in Updraft" by Dit-Mar, a variation on the "Speed Nymph" theme from the late Twenties.*

equipment or a deluxe accessory.

Once the subject was decided upon, of course, the manufacturer didn't
always consider the matter settled. Mascots were frequently varied.
Pierce-Arrow's archer, for example, gained weight, removed his clothes
and made himself a bit more comfortable as the years went by. Nor was a
manufacturer's allegiance to a mascot necessarily as long-lived as the car:
The last roar of the Franklin lion was heard several years before the
marque met its demise.

Motorcar owners, by the bye, did not necessarily ascribe to the mascot
selected for them by the manufacturer of their vehicles. Ofttimes they
preferred one of their own which more specifically reflected their taste,
their lifestyle—or their station. England's Elizabeth II has a fondness for
St. George and the dragon, the Queen Mother a figure of Britannia sitting
on a globe. George VI's choice was the Imperial crown and lion; the
Emperor of Japan selected an exquisite chrysanthemum blossom. Rudolf

*"The Kid" and "Old Bill" and the Vulcan's blacksmith from the post-World War I era as used on lorr*

Valentino had his cobra, as did several other motorcar owners who wished perhaps to emulate moviedom's Sheik. Jackie Coogan had "The Kid," produced in France in 1925. Doris Duke affixed a "Hawaiian Surf Rider" atop the Peerless she used at her retreat at Waikiki. One of the Madams Corning had a glass Pegasus—symbolic of her horse stables—mounted on her Rolls-Royce in upstate New York. And in England, another Rolls-Royce owner—a droll gentleman, he—preferred a stainless steel joint removed from his own hip to the "Spirit of Ecstacy." On its base, he had engraved, "A loyal supporter."

Probably because enthusiasts today collect the finest examples, the mascot is thought of generally as an expensive adornment. Historically, this simply was not the case. Mascot quality ranged from fine works of art wrought in bronze and silver to the cheap and nasty. The advent of that miraculous metal known as "pot" and the die casting industry opened the door to the proliferation of the decoration. By the mid-Thirties, mascots could be purchased for as little as thirty-five cents. These creations, as one might expect, were almost always crude and ungainly representations.

*Pontiac's Indian from 1929, Lalique's frog and his greyhound, like all Lalique ornaments, available unlighted or in models to be illuminated from below.*

Often they were direct copies of the designs found on better cars. The Packard goddess of speed, for example, could be had in a hundred inexpensive designs ranging from flagrant imitations of the winged mythical creature with wheel to figures of undetermined sex holding aloft torches, flames, lightning bolts, ad infinitum, ad nauseam.

One would wish not to appear unnecessarily snobbish about this. Certainly it should be recognized that even the meannest of mascots did provide its owner some measure of personal expression—courtesy of a giant die casting industry that included such companies as Ternstedt of Detroit, Jarvis of Grand Rapids and Stant of Connersville (Indiana) which supplied automakers with inexpensive mascots by the hundreds of thousands. And, like the cars for which they were designed, these mascots showed some change of aspect—the omnipresent American facelift—as year passed year.

Streamlining spelled the death of the individualism represented by the mascot. By the mid-Thirties, meaningless blobs of metal replaced it and by 1942, except in a few instances, the mascot was gone. A couple of decades later, it would be revealed—by those gentlemen who advise powers-that-be in the United States Government on matters concerning safety—that the mascot hadn't been good for us anyway. We might get hurt by it. But not so much as by its loss.

There is something in man—or so one would hope—that abhors the absence of the distinctive. And that's precisely what a mascot represents. Interestingly, there has been a revival of the idea of late. General Motors' styling chief Bill Mitchell was quoted a couple of years back as saying, "I can't stand a hood that looks like a turkey roaster or a bed pan." Still, this return to the classic tradition of the mascot is rather meaningless, since the contemporary variation is merely an extension of the trim, designed in, and not the grand afterthought that the individualized mascot once was. Among contemporary production cars, the traditional mascot survives only on the likes of Rolls-Royce, Mercedes and the Excalibur produced in Milwaukee by Brooks Stevens. True, the occasional taxicab might sprout a cheap accessory horse and sulky or some such. It's not the same. It's not like it used to be. These pages certainly show why. ⊕

# MIGHTY MODEL J

## A Discourse on the Car For Which "He Drives a Duesenberg" Was All That Needed To Be Said

There has probably been more nonsense written about the Model J Duesenberg than about any other car. American enthusiasts of the marque have generally been standing too close to see it clearly. English journalists seem to know absolutely nothing about it, and few Continental and Scandinavian journalists have ever even seen one. Only a few writers—most notably the late Ken Purdy, whom anyone who ever cared about a motorcar shall always remember—seem to have realized what a remarkably superior machine it was—in an era which witnessed the most uncompromising cars the world is ever likely to see.

Blatantly put, the Model J was the most superlative automobile ever built. During its prime years, it surpassed the finest cars of Europe—Hispano-Suiza, Isotta Fraschini, Rolls-Royce, Mercedes-Benz—not to mention everything else built in the United States. There was simply nothing on wheels that could equal its combination of technical sophistication, power output, performance, smoothness and superlative road manners, all dressed in a bewildering array of coachwork which ranged from blisteringly fast two-seaters to sedans, touring and town cars of awesome opulence and elegance. The Duesenberg was, in a word, stupendous.

About that power output: Fred Duesenberg claimed 265 horsepower for the unsupercharged J, at 4250 rpm. An awful lot of ink has been caused to flow in an effort to prove the J's did not in fact deliver this much at the flywheel, and in all likelihood many of them probably didn't. Power output varied considerably from car to car, and unless a customer specifically asked that his engine be tuned for maximum output—a very complicated and time-consuming business which was done at added cost—the car would most likely be delivered with something less than the advertised 265 horsepower. A power curve for a very early production engine (1929) was acquired by John Bond back in 1939 which showed 208 hp at 3600 rpm. However, this engine was subsequently scrapped by Lycoming and never even delivered to Duesenberg, which clearly indicates what both thought of it. But, if one does project that early power curve upward to the 4250 rpm limit, one arrives at a figure of around 245-250 hp with the rather modest 5.2 to one compression ratio which was standard for the Model J. That's pretty good for an engine they decided to throw away.

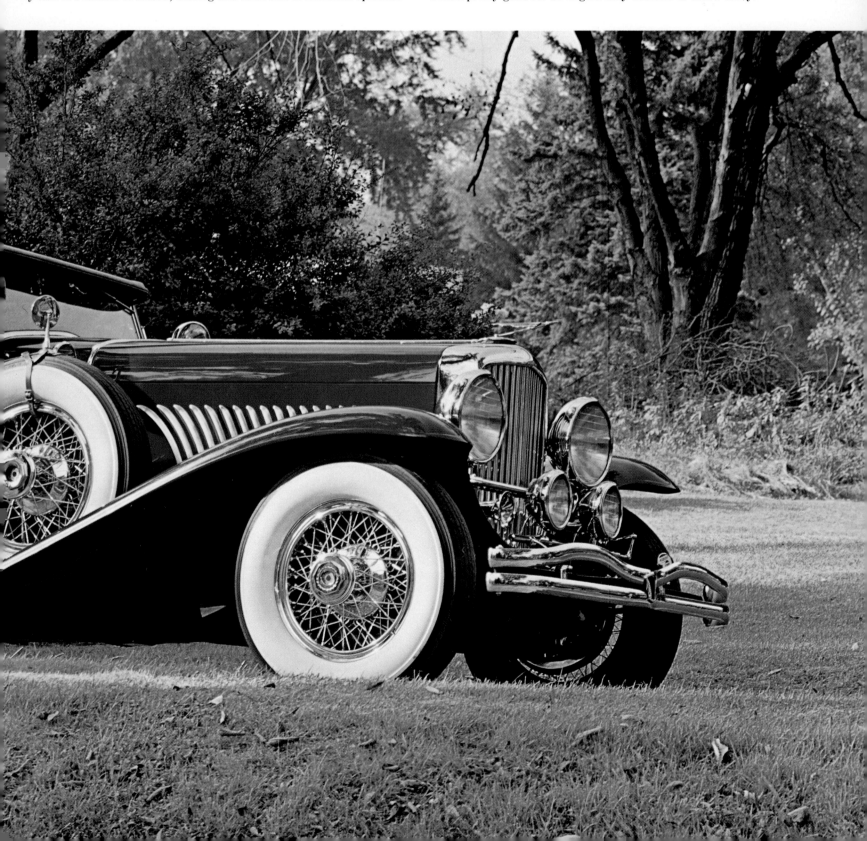

So, strictly speaking, let's say that though 265 hp was altogether possible, most of the standard production Model J's produced around 250 hp. How did this compare with Europe's best? Hispano-Suiza was building its T68 then, which had a 9.4-liter, twelve-cylinder engine that developed a surprisingly modest 190 hp with a 5.0 to one compression ratio and 220 hp at 6.0 to one. Compared with the Duesenberg, this particular Hispano was unpleasantly trucky, as was the 770K Mercedes (200 hp). The 8B Isotta was a far more pleasant car to drive, as were the lovely D8 Delages of the period, but of course neither had anything like the output or the performance of the mighty J. Suffice it to say, then, that Fred Duesenberg was building the most powerful production car in the world.

The Model J was formally introduced on December 1st, 1928. This was opening day of the New York auto salon, and except for the comparatively small audience of motoring magazine readers, it caught the public completely by surprise. The habit of being second best is a difficult one to shake off psychologically, and there were many who found it hard to believe that this magnificent new chassis with the European name and an $8500 price

tag—coachwork was extra, and ranged from $3500 up—was created in homespun Indiana.

But there it was, the result of an alliance between Errett Lobban Cord the empire builder and Fred Duesenberg the automotive perfectionist, both of whom, from the very beginning, had promised insiders that the J would be "the world's finest motor car." Certainly the Model J chassis lacked nothing.

Even today that straight-eight engine is an awesome thing to look upon. It is fully four feet long from fan to flywheel. The block, finished in Duesenberg's traditional apple green enamel, was relieved by a multitude of nickel, chrome or stainless steel fittings and flanked on each side by huge manifolds. Above all this sat that giant cylinder head with its thirty-two valves, sixteen to a side, nestled beneath the chain-driven twin overhead cams. It embodied most of the features of Duesenberg's enormously successful racing engines, twin cams, thirty-two valves and all, but scaled up to Jovian proportions.

The rest of the chassis was of equal refinement and heroic scale. The

frame was eight and a half inches deep at maximum and nearly a quarter of an inch thick. The brakes, hydraulic and of an exclusive Duesenberg design, were fifteen inches in diameter and three inches wide—a vacuum boost was standard equipment within the first year. The gear lever, instead of coming straight out from the top of the box, was set forward and emerged just behind the clutch. This placed all foot controls on the toe board rather than on the floor, leaving that area completely open.

The car lubricated itself. Every seventy-five miles, the chassis lubrication points were fed under pressure supplied by the oil pump. A green light on the dashboard informed the driver that this Bijur system was operating. A red one told him the reservoir contained sufficient oil. Still another light would appear every 1400 miles, suggesting that the battery be checked. Oddly, this automatic lubrication system has since been removed from a number of Model J's, some previous owners being either mystified or intimidated by it. It's a shame, because like everything else on the car, if it's kept in halfway decent condition it works perfectly.

Although this was the heyday of what might be called the Cast Iron Age,

aluminum alloy was to be found everywhere on the Model J. To quote from a contemporary brochure: "Although involving considerable extra expense aluminum alloy parts are used wherever possible to secure moderate weight, and all are heat-treated to give double strength. The list includes: Pistons, connecting-rods, dash, instrument board, instrument board supports, steering column bracket, differential housing, differential housing cover, pinion housing, tail lamp bracket, torque tube yoke, torque tube brackets, flywheel housing, engine oil pan, timing chain covers, camshaft covers, water jacket covers, all brake shoes, spare wheel supports, gas tank filler body."

One could go on for pages recording the extraordinary qualities of these cars, but it should be sufficient to state only that, in its time, the Duesenberg had no equal, and there has certainly been nothing approaching it since.

And the performance! For sheer overkill, we'll concentrate on the Duesenberg to which was added a supercharger and which was introduced in May of 1932. It is a pretty fast car today that will reach 100 mph from a    21 standing start in seventeen seconds. Chances are your full-size family sedan won't come anywhere near that figure. The supercharged Model SJ Duesenberg did it easily. It was—and remains—the fastest luxury car ever built, and it's all the more remarkable that it set such a standard nearly a half century ago.

What about 104 mph in second gear? Or 140 mph in top? If you're old enough to have been aware of the cars of the Thirties, you'll recall how staggering these figures were, and how the nation marveled when Ab Jenkins took the Duesenberg Special, an essentially stock 142½-inch SJ chassis with a special roadster body, to Bonneville in 1935 and averaged some 135.47 mph for twenty-four hours, 152.145 for one hour and was hitting nearly 160 mph as he went over the finish line. Yes, the SJ Duesenberg had teeth all right, yet like the unsupercharged J, it was exceptionally quiet at low-to-medium revolutions, and produced but a pleasant burble at higher speeds. With an open exhaust, however, an SJ did make a deafening racket that could only appeal to the hardiest enthusiast—and then not for very long.

On these pages. Above left: 1935 Model J Convertible Coupe by Rollston. Above right: 1936 Model J N Convertible Coupe, one of four built, by Rollston, with supercharger added.

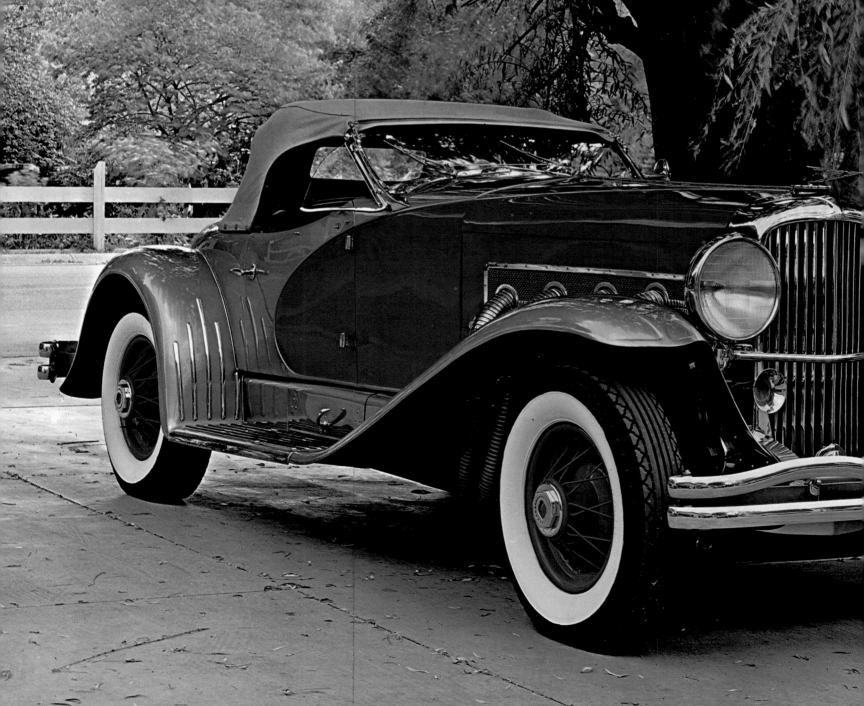

*Below: 1935 SSJ Speedster by LaGrande, built for Clark Gable. On the pages following. Left: 1930 Boattail Speedster by Murphy. Right: 1934 Convertible Sedan by Brunn.*

While on the subject of exhaust systems, you might recall that there was once a time when any car with "flexible" external pipes was supposed to be supercharged, even though the meaning of the term was not too clear to most people. This arose, of course, from the presence of these devices on the flanks of various Auburns, Cords and Duesenbergs during the Thirties, and Mercedes, who had popularized the practice in the Twenties, all of which could be had with supercharging. The external pipes weren't always necessary, of course (except on the Duesenberg), but the novelty became a custom, and a rather nice one, we think.

Eventually, the familiar four-pipe outside exhaust system of the SJ was made optionally available on unsupercharged J's, and many of them were so fitted. However, there is the story of the fellow with the early SJ Torpedo Phaeton who insisted on keeping his one-piece eight-pipe external exhaust system, even after the newer type had been introduced. "I would have nothing else," he once wrote to Fred Duesenberg. "At night it glows red in the dark."

There were a few departures from the standard J configuration. As the supercharged engine was a bit heavier, all SJ's had front springs with a slightly higher rate, along with another pair of dampers. Tubular steel connecting rods replaced the drop forged aluminum alloy ones and, of course, there was the water-heated centrifugal supercharger, placed atop a stalk that rises out of the right side of the crankcase. It's an awkward-looking arrangement, but it surely did work. At 4000 engine revolutions per minute, the blower was delivering the mixture to the intake manifold on the opposite side at about five pounds per square inch. That's not much pressure, but the result of it was as much as 400 horsepower.

To return to the horsepower controversy for a moment, there are on record some comments made by Augie Duesenberg concerning the preparation of the Duesenberg Special for Ab Jenkins. Augie said that after exhaustive changes they could "only" get the equivalent of 320 horsepower. Then someone suggested the ram's-horn manifold. Power immediately jumped to 400, and it was in that condition in which the car made its record-breaking runs. The last half-dozen or so SJ's were also fitted with the ram's horns, and Duesenberg experts assure us that they too are vastly more powerful than the standard SJ's, also probably packing about 400 horsepower.

It *had* to be close to that to produce the stupendous performance which was demonstrated time and time again by the SJ. It was after all a big, heavy car—the chassis alone weighed two and a quarter tons—yet it was faster than most contemporary sports cars and handled beautifully. Even so, at the factory, they never regarded the SJ as being a sports car. They saw it simply as a large, exceptionally well-engineered touring chassis that also happened to be bloody fast.

The J and SJ were not the only Duesenberg variations, however. One winter's day in 1935, Gary Cooper strolled into the Duesenberg showroom in Los Angeles. A customer since 1930, Cooper still owned the first Derham Tourster, in pale green and yellow, which he was presently having altered a bit. Maybe he was hankering for something even a bit more sporty. It's not recorded what else was on the floor that day, but what inevitably caught his eye was a shortened, supercharged SJ display chassis. Of only 125 inches in wheelbase, it was the shortest J yet built and as such had a performance potential above and beyond any road-going Duesenberg ever made. The temptation must have been irresistible. Cooper, incidentally, had just recently finished *Lives of a Bengal Lancer* and was about to begin the feature which would catapult him to superstardom, *Mr. Deeds Goes to Town.* He was definitely Duesenberg material.

The abbreviated chassis was returned to Indianapolis and work was begun on a stark, open two-seater body for it at Auburn Central in Connersville, Indiana, the coachbuilding arm of the Auburn-Cord-Duesenberg conglomerate (sometimes known to the public by its more glamorous name "LaGrande"). When completed, the body was duly fitted back in Indianapolis.

Of course, Cooper's new charger created something of a mild sensation among the movie colony folk, one of whom, a certain Clark Gable, decided

he would be unable to relax until he had one too. Gable had also recently completed a blockbuster, *Mutiny on the Bounty,* and was not about to be upstaged by his friend Coop. He had also been a Duesenberg owner for some years, and currently had a JN Rollston convertible coupe (about which more soon) that had been restyled for him by Bohman & Schwartz. The car was handed back to Duesenberg in exchange for the second, very short wheelbase chassis which was similarly bodied, also by LaGrande.

The SSJ is not an officially recognized factory designation for these cars, but it seemed to make sense (Short, Supercharged model J), and since only two were ever made, it doesn't unduly upset the Duesenberg chronology. Though there's no record that such a thing ever occurred, a friendly drag race between these two cars would have been something to see—and hear.

Strictly speaking, only ten JN's were built, one of them the aforementioned Clark Gable car. These were produced by Rollston in 1935: four convertible coupes, three convertible sedans and three sedans, these last on the longer 153½-inch wheelbase. All had the skirted fenders and smaller bullet-shaped taillights which Duesenberg had been supplying for some time, but these two items together do not a JN make. Smaller seventeen-inch wheels (with fatter tires) were also fitted, occasionally with discs

which were optionally available, but the true mark of a JN was the wider body, now dropped down outside the main frame members and recognizable by the deeper doors, the narrower running boards and the missing battery access hatch. It was hardly what you would call a new model, but *was* different from all the other J's, so JN it became.

As far as we have been able to determine, Rollston built only two JN-type bodies for supercharged SJ chassis; one of those four convertible coupes and one of the convertible sedans—each thus becoming an SJN. On J-564 chassis, the convertible coupe was apparently given by a Duesenberg fancier to his wife, who died some years later. The gentleman later took on another, newer model wife and presented the car to her. Then he died and his second wife married her late husband's nephew, both of whom enjoy the car to this day. Duesenbergs were larger than life, bordering on the unreal sometimes, and frequently so were the people who owned them.

There weren't many such people. The Model J's enormous cost and limited production—which bracketed neatly the worst years of the Great Depression—saw to it that only Established Money, movie stars and persons of comparable celebrity were potential customers. Alfonso XIII, King of Spain, was an early J owner, as was young Prince Nicolas of Roumania.

There was William Randolph Hearst and Marion Davies, Howard Hughes and Tommy Manville, Jimmy Walker and Paul Whiteman, the already mentioned Gary Cooper and Clark Gable. Diplomats and gangsters, debutantes and political bosses, robber barons and religious leaders—the Duesenberg's appeal was universal, and in an odd way established a certain kinship among the unlikeliest of people who had reached the top in their particular calling: "He drives a Duesenberg" was the only line which appeared in those memorable Model J advertisements. Nothing else needed to be said.

Approximately 470 to 480 Model J's were built, including the SJ, JN and SSJ variations. A healthy percentage of them survive and are today commanding the highest prices ever paid for any automobile. The hundred thousand dollar mark was broached ages ago, and it's been more than doubled since. We don't suppose there is any point in arguing whether a car is worth the cost of a country mansion. There are postage stamps and even paperweights that can't be bought for that much. It's simply the result of the fact that there are more aspiring Duesenberg collectors today than there are Duesenbergs. If that had been the case during the mid-Thirties, this greatest of all American automobiles just might have survived. ✣

# PIONEERING FROM PAWTUCKET, R.I. TO PUTEAUX ON THE SEINE

*Portraits from the Piquant Gallery –a Collection of Cars That Tried Very Hard, and Could...For a While*

Herodotus cautioned about great deeds being usually wrought at great risk, and Virgil counselled to compare great things with small—and this volume is about great cars. The adjective seems displaced somehow in reference to the piquant vehicles gracing these pages, particularly when a glance at the marque names, like as not, breeds only unfamiliarity. Still, even the mighty Duesenberg wouldn't have ensued had not somebody somewhere blazed an automotive trail several decades before. The Daimlers and Benzes of the world, of course, thrust greatness upon themselves through sheer force of accomplishment—but during those early borning years of the automobile, the minions who tried and failed surely contributed something too. That their great risks resulted not always in great deeds perhaps illustrates the wisdom of Virgil's admonition. For by their sheer numbers, the pioneers demonstrated one very important point: faith. And true believers—successful or not—have a way of inspiring others. How many more tried—and succeeded—because so many had opened the way before is immeasurable. But surely the figure might be an impressive one—quite sufficient to justify recalling fondly, if perhaps with a bit of whimsy, those who contributed to the history of the automobile in a small way.

Georges Filipinetti thought so. A racing enthusiast—his Scuderia Filipinetti sports and Formula One cars were campaigned throughout Europe and in 1972, a year before his death, he received Switzerland's most prestigious auto racing award, the "Gold Piston" trophy—he was a man of consummate taste and eclectic interests. Trained as an engineer, he used the fortunes he amassed through business and investments to support —among other things—the search for a polio vaccine, and to create a prize in memory of the great Polish pianist and one-time president of the Polish Republic, Ignace Paderewski. He was president of the Swiss Institute of Antique Arms, his collection of arms and armor being displayed in many of the one hundred twenty-four rooms of the museum he created in his Chateau de Grandson, at the tip of Lake Neuchatel, due north of Lausanne. Displayed there also are twenty-seven beautifully restored automobiles, among them the ten pictured here. Doubtless it was Filipinetti's wide-ranging sympathies which played a part in his amassing

of cars that perhaps otherwise would have been lost in the mists of history.

Take the Egg, for instance. Rudolf Egg was twenty-seven years old when he built his first car—and all of twenty-nine when he produced the charmer herein, powered by a one-cylinder three-horsepower Benz engine, in 1895. The year next, in association with a fellow Swiss conveniently named Egli, he began manufacturing Switzerland's first production cars, in Zurich. Egg & Egli used de Dion engines a while—and even sold licenses to other firms (J. Weber & Company in Uster and Zürcher Patent Motorwagen-Fabrik Rapid in Zurich) to produce their vehicles. The little cars would, company brochures stated, travel at the sprightly pace of forty kilometers an hour on level ground and a full ten up a twenty-percent grade—which may have been exaggerating some—and would do it at a cost not exceeding two centimes per kilometer. Unfortunately, shortly after the turn of the century, Rudolf's plans for his Egg were, shall we say, scrambled, when his factory burned to the ground. The Rapid quickly ceased production thereafter, and in Uster, J. Weber & Company had meantime decided to go its own way, with another car sporting the novelty of shaft drive. Production of all Egg-derived vehicles totaled no more than a hundred units, in industry terms scarcely enough for an omelette. But Rudolf Egg was undeterred. He moved to Wollishofen and created a new company, Motorwagen-Fabrik Excelsior, the initial example of this new marque being shown at the first Exposition Nationale de l'Automobile in Geneva in 1905. It was a curved dash Oldsmobile look-alike, and was produced into 1907, when—as sympathetic histories like to phrase it—"lack of demand led to production being stopped." Thereafter, Rudolf Egg wasn't sure what he should try next, until he met Fritz Moser, in whose factory a four-cylinder light car was manufactured during the World War I years. Egg and Moser collaborated on another car when peace came, which lived for a while into the Twenties. Rudolf Egg died before the next war came.

The Delahaye survived for a few years after it, for nearly a half century before—and there are few who would not affix the label great to this grand French marque. Still, at the turn of the century, the Delahaye was but one of many companies which had erstwhile produced something altogether

*On the opening pages, from the left: the Egg from 1895, the Dumont from 1901, the Clément from 1900. On these pages, clockwise from above left: the Delahaye from 1898*

different—since 1845, brick-making machinery—and was now trying to make a name for itself in the automobile business, if very quietly. Baudry de Saunier put it so nicely in 1900: "She was born and bred in Touraine without much commotion. She recently moved to Paris. She has her faithful followers who never cheat on her and bring their friends. She is well considered in her area of tourism." As for racing, that was something else again. Emile Delahaye did take himself to the Paris-Marseilles-Paris in 1896, but he wasn't a happy participant. Mid-race, a formidable storm arose which felled a gigantic tree on the road ahead of him. A resourceful man, he borrowed a saw, cut through the tree in two places, removed the middle and drove on through. He lost a couple of hours in the process, finished tenth—and decided competition had lost its allure. Although others would campaign the Delahaye admirably in the Paris-Dieppe and elsewhere, the car was, during this period, never a "queen of the automobile battles." She was too discreet, it was said. And soon she was doing too well in the marketplace to necessitate entering the fray to prove herself. Six hundred Delahayes were built in the half decade from 1894 to 1899, but shortly thereafter production was raised to a handsome twenty cars a month. Emile Delahaye retired in 1901, and some fifty-three years later—after a career that saw a legion of sporting successes and some of the most breathtaking classic cars the world had ever seen—so did the Delahaye.

"For the length of life we have yet to see the car likely to attain a greater or more honourable old age" wrote an enthusiastic journalist of the little vehicle Adolphe Clément was producing at Levallois Perret on the Seine. He had already made two fortunes in the allied areas of bicycle and pneumatic tire manufacture—and was now hoping to make a third in his new endeavor. And why not? His addition of the name "Bayard"—after the French hero remembered as the "Chevalier sans peur et sans reproche" and whose statue loomed large near Clément's Mézières factory—seemed to bring good luck, and Cléments with or without the Bayard sobriquet were widely regarded as among the quietest cars built anywhere. For three

years the company had been riding as high as the driver of the 1900 de Dion (two-and-a-quarter horsepower) engined Clément voiturette did, this model having represented the marque's initial entry into the sporting arena, with a remarkable second-place finish in the 1900 Paris-Rouen-Paris. But Cléments would prove even more remarkable than that, a 10/12 hp variation averaging forty-six miles to the gallon in the Irish Trials of 1905, and one George Brand finishing the Tourist Trophy on the Isle of Man on less gasoline than any other of the dozens of competitors. Moreover, another proud owner told everyone who would listen that he had driven his Clément fifty thousand miles, "a distance approximately equivalent to twice round the world . . . without the slightest mishap except a broken wheel, the consequence of severe impact with a spur-stone, occasioned by a bad side-slip." These were impressive statistics all, but there would be one more—and it would be a sad one. Adolphe Clément would retire from the company he founded in 1914, and eight years later the Clément would represent but one more number added to the roster of cars that were no more.

The French were quite marvelous at compiling figures. For 1901, some 5386 motorcars were declared for taxation, of which 1149 were in the birthplace of motoring, Paris, the remainder in the provinces, these figures being further divided into 2893 cars seating three or more, 2493 with room for just one or two. The "total nominal force" of all the cars was estimated to be 26,427 horsepower, of which the 1901 Dumont, produced by Fabrique d'Automobiles Dumont & Cie at 247 rue Péreire, contributed about five. And there is little else, alas, that is known about this de Dion-engined car with wood chassis, belt drive, an opportunity for its engine to see where it was going, and whose life was short but demeanor delightful. No doubt it didn't see 1902's April in Paris.

In the rue de la Folie-Regnault in Paris they were crafted, and that is precisely the word for it. Manufactured would be *une insulte*. The little Rochet-Petit of 1901 featured a one-cylinder four-and-a-half horsepower Aster engine with *bloc en bronze* rear mounted direct to the axle, a four-

*the Rochet-Petit from 1901, the Prunel from 1903, the Vinot & Deguingand from 1901.*

speed and reverse transmission and numerous examples of a slavish dedication to detail. One of the latter was fulsomely described by Baudry de Saunier: "The lever on the outside of the car on the right side disengages, then brakes the back wheels. A pedal at the left disengages, then brakes the differential, while another at the right only disengages. It could happen, in rare cases, that you would have urgent need of both hands for steering and an equally urgent need to stop quickly. Your left toes work desperately on the left pedal, but this is not enough! The fingers of your right hand cannot fly to their duties quickly enough! In the Rochet, a third pedal, also at the right, is offered for your inactive foot. And it is precisely this pedal which has the same effect on the wheel brakes as does the hand lever. You are saved." Such lavishness which seemed to "establish that automobiles are terrible beasts and must be muzzled at every opportunity and which unjustly does not produce simplifications," de Saunier went on, "this lavishness, while superfluous, pleases me infinitely." And it also perhaps hastened the Rochet's demise. Before the end of 1905, the company which "should have the best future"—again de Saunier's words—decided that, although that might be true, it would not be in the automobile business, and returned full-time to the manufacture of the bicycles for which it had long been famous.

Meantime, Société des Usines Prunel at Puteaux on the Seine was producing some very pleasant cars powered by a variety of engines —Herald, Pieper, de Dion and Aster, as the car from 1903 pictured here —but having a dreadful time of it in the sport. The brothers Prunel did not, perforce, produce a performance car. It was out in the first round of the Paris-Vienna on June 16th of 1902, a voiturette performing similarly in the Circuit des Ardennes on July 31st, though one of the light cars made it to the fourth of six laps, averaging 24.4 mph all the while. In 1903 it was ninth in the voiturette class of the ill-fated Paris-Madrid on May 24th, and in the June 23rd running of that year's Ardennes Circuit brought itself up to fourth among voiturettes. The day before, in the heavy car class race at Ardennes, one of the messrs. Prunel had decided that what was wrong was

The state of the automotive art during the wee years of the Twentieth Century as attained by three diverse manufacturers in France, America and Switzerland respectively. From the wine country of Bordeaux, the 1906 Larroumet & Lagarde built in Agen, the Va Bon Train, the marque's most popular model, which translates most appropriately into "it goes good"—which doubtless it did, particularly with its quite modern, for a three-wheeler, convenience of a steering wheel. The Cameron built in 1904 in Providence, Rhode Island, having moved

not the Prunel but the drivers who had been behind its wheel. So he had a go at it himself—and was out on the first lap. The marque's top finish perhaps was across the Channel, at the Wentworth Woodhouse Speed Trials of October 1st, 1904: a second place, *miserabile dictu*, amid a two-car entry. A gentleman by the name of Whitworth—his first name seems to have been misplaced through the years—stormed up the half-mile course in 1 minute 58 seconds and flew down it in 1 minute 13 3/5 seconds, for a combined average forty seconds slower than the winning de Dion-Bouton. No banners, needless to say, were placed outside the Prunel works, but the brothers satisfied themselves as long as they could—and that was 1900 to 1907—with a modest production of a modest car. With fortunes flagging, they took on the sponsorship of other marques in their factory: the Gnome in 1905, the Gracile in 1906 and the J.P. in 1907. Might as well keep busy. And after the bell irrevocably tolled in 1907, they spent a half decade preparing themselves for one last fling, which they called the Phénix and produced from 1912 to 1914.

Also from Puteaux and enjoying a happier longevity—from 1901 to 1926—than the Prunel was the Vinot & Deguingand, whose life began with little liter-and-a-half, twin-engined, five-and-a-half horsepower, belt-and-chain driven two-seaters like the one pictured. The car was also called *La Silencieuse* and was distinguished by its vertical gate gear change. Vinots did rather better in competition too. After the Blackpool Speed Trials in October of 1904 where an A.G. Clay piloted a fourteen-horsepower car to what can only be described as a disappointing forty-fourth place finish, things speeded up somewhat. In the Scottish Reliability Trials of 1905, a twenty-horsepower Vinot earned 1000 marks for reliability and was one of fourteen cars out of a field of better than forty deserving of a nonstop certificate. And, in the Tourist Trophy race on the Isle of Man on September 14th, a fourteen-horsepower Vinot provided the marque's finest performance, Norman Littlejohn driving to a third-place finish, with an average of 37.9 miles an hour and 23.3 miles a gallon. Pleased with their performance in both motor sport and the marketplace, Vinot *et* Deguingand expanded in 1909, acquiring the Société Gladiator of Pré-St. Gervais and moving it to Puteaux, and producing two utterly similar lines of cars. They rethought that decision at the close of World War I, moved themselves to Nanterre and discontinued the Gladiator line altogether, henceforth only

Vinot & Deguingands issuing from the factory. Unfortunately, like a number of other French marques whose reputations were solid in prewar years, the people at Nanterre found keeping up with a now fast-paced industry difficult. The last vestige of the company was seen in 1928, under the Deguingand name, a two-stroke cyclecar designed by Marcel Violet, at a time when the cyclecar idea had fallen into utter disfavor. Even before the Great Depression could do its evil, the Vinot & Deguingand company went under, its factory being acquired by SA des Automobiles Donnet, which survived a few years into the Thirties, the works subsequently taken over by Simca.

The Larroumet & Lagarde, on the other hand, remained in one place for the whole of its life: a little village called Agen in the Bordeaux region of France. The messrs. L & L were, like so many other aspiring automobile manufacturers, cycle producers initially, being listed as same in the 1900 edition of *Guide Michelin*. Three years later, they produced their first motorized vehicle, a tricycle with a single-cylinder engine of the de Dion genre, but significantly larger. By 1905 they were building four-seaters of the "voiturette populaire" variety, as well as a three-wheeler delectably called "Va Bon Train." The latter, with its front-mounted, water-cooled, eight-horsepower engine of Larroumet & Lagarde manufacture and a two-speed clutch by Bozier, was the model most favored in the marketplace—although it was sometimes confused with the "La Nef," which was built by the messrs. Lacroix *et* Laville, who also located themselves in Agen. A look at the two vehicles together, however, quickly pointed up a prominent difference. While the "La Nef" was tiller controlled, the "Va Bon Train" had gone modern and utilized a steering wheel, certainly unusual for a three-wheeler of that era. But the unusual wasn't sufficient for

*there from Pawtucket, these but two of many homes this marque would see during its checkered nearly-two-decades in the automobile arena, a well-crafted car despite its factory wanderings, this early example sporting the novelty of a wire mesh radiator grille which nicely displayed the handsome Cameron brass cooling fan. And the Turicum, translated "Zurich" in Latin, which city was the marque's first home, though by 1909 when this look-of-a-Model T friction drive roadster was built, the company had outgrown its birthplace and moved to Uster.*

Larroumet & Lagarde to prosper, and its founders reluctantly closed their shop, probably around 1910, the year their names disappeared from the pages of *Guide Michelin.* The other messrs. L & L had given up some time previous.

The interesting thing about Everett S. Cameron was that he was ever reluctant to give up. He was a Yankee, and he had a lot of progressive ideas for the car he wanted to build: a front-mounted engine, wheel steering, shaft drive, his own design sliding gear transmission and differential. The problem was he could never figure out where to build it. Initially, he thought Pawtucket, Rhode Island, where under the aegis of the United Motor Corporation, he began production in 1902. By 1904, however, when the two-cylinder air-cooled model pictured appeared, he had changed his mind. Everett Cameron was sure he had a winner—a tough car (it had an oak frame) with a novel identifying gimmick (an open mesh radiator through which could be seen the car's well-crafted four-bladed cooling fan)—and, to increase production, he needed more financing. He found James S. Brown, who had a successful machine company in Providence—and the Cameron forthwith moved there. Unfortunately, by the summer of '06, Brown had second thoughts himself, and they didn't include the Cameron. So the undaunted Everett S. got some friends together in his native Brockton, Massachusetts (where, incidentally, he had experimented with a three-cylinder radial-engined steam car around the turn of the century, before concluding the gasoline car held more promise) and came up with the Cameron Car Company and about $100,000 capitalization. Then he procured another plant in Beverly, announced plans for 1909 for 2000 cars at the two sites, and found time to tell his sales manager to fire off a letter to the editor of *The Horseless Age* who had reported with regard

to the recent Nassau Sweepstakes on Long Island that "the Cameron, which suffered somewhat from tire and mechanical troubles, was second." "We beg to correct this," the Cameron people said, "and advise that our car did not stop for a single second on any account whatever"—and enclosed a circular ("if you will take the trouble to notice . . . ") giving an account of the event. Events for the Cameron—which had passed from its original conception to Franklin resemblance to something utterly conventional now—began to move quickly. By 1909 the marque was in New London, Connecticut. By September of 1910, ground had been broken for a factory at Attica, Ohio—within a year, creditors were suing for overdue notes. After filing for bankruptcy in March of 1912, a new company made a fresh start in the former factory of the Mathushek Piano Company in West Haven, Connecticut, then moved to New Haven in 1914 where the ignominy of an involuntary bankruptcy quickly followed. By 1917 the Cameron people pulled themselves together in a new venture in Norwalk, Connecticut, and the Cameron car stayed there a while, moving ultimately to Stamford. Finally, in 1921, someone apparently decided enough was enough, and the company abandoned both Connecticut and the Cameron, bought the Dauch Manufacturing Company and summarily retired to Sandusky, Ohio—to build tractors.

Probably there were times too when, an ocean away, Martin Fischer wondered whether the automobile business was worth it. A skilled Swiss watchmaker and the inventor of the Magneta clock, he built his first car in 1904, named it Turicum (the Latin for Zurich), gave up time for motion and, with his friend Paul Vorbrodt, started an automobile company. Initially successful, they outgrew their factory and by 1906 the car named for Zurich moved to Uster. There was a quaint Model T look about the Turicum, but a more appropriate American reference might be that it was the Swiss Cartercar, for from the second vehicle built, all Turicums featured friction drive. Ultimately, the Turicum suffered the Cartercar's fate—failure, prior to the beginning of World War I. So, a bit later, did the car named after himself that Martin Fischer had returned to Zurich to build in 1909.

A few failures early in life, Thomas Huxley once suggested, could produce the greatest practical benefit. As for us all, that was doubtless true for the automobile too. ✿

# THE SPORTING RILEYS

*Return With Us
To Those Stirring Days
When Automobile Manufacturing
Wasn't Like Sausage Making*

*Redwing: From 1923 sporting coachwork was available on the 1500 cc chassis, invariably delivered with red fenders and polished but unpainted aluminum bodies, hence the name.*

"I can only continue in business as long as it holds some promise of romance. Races, trials, round the world expeditions—this is the romantic side of the motor industry. When it's no more, I shall retire. I couldn't stand it if it were mere manufacturing, like sausage making."

Thus declared Victor Riley, managing director of Riley (Coventry) Ltd., some forty-five years ago. As good as his word, he quit before the British Motor Corporation swallowed Riley in 1952, ultimately severing the marque's last links with its hotly combatant past, and putting its cars on a par with the sausage for individuality.

But in his declining years (Victor died in 1958, aged eighty-two), "V.R." at least could draw solace from his memories: of an era when Rileys won the Brooklands Five-Hundred twice in the series' nine-year history, beating the Indianapolis winner's speed by almost 8 mph in 1936; sensationally and unprecedentedly placed 1½-liter cars second and third overall at Le Mans in '34; scooped Britain's *Grande Epreuve,* the Tourist Trophy, three times in five years; were chosen as racing and/or record breaking implements, of their own free volition, by no fewer than four Land Speed Recordmen, past, present or destined—Eldridge, Campbell, Eyston, Cobb; gave Britain, a nation with a rightful pride in its small cars, its first-ever light car class victory in the Monte Carlo Rally, twenty years after the event's inception.

Apogee of the family firm, a phenomenon that today is almost out of print in the automotive industry, the Riley company in the inter-wars years revolved around William Riley, chairman, founder and patriarch, and all five of his sons, Victor, Stanley, Allan, Percy and Cecil, in positions of graduated seniority. *L'état c'est nous.* (There was a Rupert Riley; no relation, but presumably this name was enough to get his foot in the door.)

Differ as they might in other areas of Riley policy, the kinsmen saw eye to eye on one thing: They liked their cars to be fast, capable of being made faster, and sufficiently durable to cope with the sternest rigors of any competition work the mind could conceive.

It was the technically brilliant Percy Riley who cast the die that predestined the marque for greatness in motor sport. In 1926 he designed a small sedan called the Monaco Nine. The numeral denoted its horsepower in terms of the arbitrary taxation formula operating in prewar Britain. Actually the original Nine's 1089 cc engine, with its four 60.3 by 95.2 millimeter cylinders, two-bearing crank, single carburetor and separate head, block and crankcase, developed around 28 bhp at 4200 rpm. This, though it would be nothing to write to *The Times* about today, was then a presentable output for an eleven-hundred powerplant putatively born to propel middle class, lowish income families around England's green and pleasant land with a roof over their heads.

But it was the Nine's top end that sent go-culturists into a brown study. At a time when most British touring car engines had side valves, and the valves of the rockerbox minority were as vertical as parading Grenadiers, Percy Riley angled his ohv's at 90 degrees and operated them via very

*Imp: Introduced in 1933 as a somewhat bland two/four-seater, this Riley underwent an almost immediate redesign to become one of the best looking sports cars ever built anywhere.*

*Dixon Nine (above): the amazing two-liter six that averaged 130 mph around Brooklands.*

short and light pushrods from twin camshafts mounted high on each side of the block. This, as far as the valve angle and hemispherical head shape was concerned, was in line with contemporary motorcycle practice, which up to then started where car techniques stopped.

Yet if the Nine had the performance potential it appeared to have, why didn't they build a sports car around it? Three years earlier, using far stodgier material, viz, a 65.8 by 110 mm (1498 cc) sidevalver, Riley had indeed created a rather flashy-looking aluminum-bodied sports car, the Redwing. This one was, as the phrase goes, fairly horsedrawn, so maybe V,R.'s Senior Wardenship of the Worshipful Company of Coachmakers and Coach Harness Makers had a remote symbolism.

Whether the Riley hierarchy caught on to the sporting possibilities of Percy's *coup d'éclat* before or after the Monaco's launch is neither here nor there, but if the latter, it didn't take them long. In the winter of 1926-1927, a firm styled Thomas Inventions Development Company Ltd., headed by Land Speed Record three-timer J.G. Parry Thomas, was commissioned to evolve a *totus porcus* sports car powered by a better breathing, faster revving edition of the Nine engine. Thomas was killed, alas, while shooting for his fourth LSR before the project was completed, leaving it to Reid Railton and two associates, Ken Thomson and Ken Taylor, to round out the job. Fruit of their labors was the ever memorable Brooklands Riley, grandsire of the many and varied sports and racing machines that were to punctuate the non-sausage-making chapters of the Riley story.

Between 1926 and 1957, when in the sacred name of Rationalization the current four-cylinder 2.4-liter version of Percy Riley's hemi-headed opus was ditched by British Motor Corporation and replaced by parallel-valved, single-cam Wolseley clockwork, Rileys of every type and caliber

*Brooklands Nine (left): begun by Parry Thomas, and finished by Reid Railton, in 1927.*

had those distinctive eaves-level camshafts in duplicate, crossflow porting and 90 degree valves. The process of Rationalization, incidentally, incurred a loss of 9 bhp, in spite of a 196 cc gain in displacement and the addition of two extra cylinders.

The Brooklands Model didn't belie its name, it was originally built *at* Brooklands—by the new firm of Thomson and Taylor Ltd., under contract to Riley—and you could race it at Brooklands, or elsewhere, without altering a thing. If you were hardy enough and willing to risk the police hounding that the car's mere appearance provoked, you could drive it on the road, *mit* passenger as long as he/she breathed in as you breathed out and vice versa. The shortened, stiffened chassis, with its rear springs located alongside rather than below the main longerons, placed the aluminum two-seater body so low that an average-to-tall occupant, draping his arm overboard through the deep cutaways that did duty as ever open doors, could lay the palm of his hand flat on the pavement.

All but the first batch of Nine engines were built with their cylinder blocks in unit with the crankcase. The Brooklands Model shared this feature and also had dual sidedraft Solex carburetors, a higher compression ratio and mechanical as distinct from thermosyphon water circulation. Output was up to 41 bhp at 5200 rpm. Further tuned for serious racing, but still with a c.r. appropriate to aviation grade gas or a gasoline/benzol mix, 55 bhp was within reach. On alcohol, the best recorded power by an unblown Brooklands engine was 99 horse.

Perennially popular with Class G (1100 cc) racing folk, mostly amateurs, the Brooklands Nine enjoyed a long and successful career. Among its best remembered Continental performances was the winning of the sideshow voiturette event at the 1931 German Grand Prix by Dudley

Froy of Britain, who made hay when a faster but less sturdy supercharged Amilcar blew up.

Riley Nines, racing and touring types both, were as a matter of fact extremely rugged little automobiles, capable of maintaining their maximum speed, or something close to it, for impressive durations and mileages. This was well demonstrated at Montlhéry autodrome in 1929 when a Monaco sedan shared by Ernest Eldridge, Reid Railton and Ken Thomson broke the International Class G record for 1000 miles at 65.83 mph. The elapsed time included an interval for kicking things straight after Thomson had spun on the ice-coated concrete, plunged off onto the rough infield, overturned twice, righted. Sole damage was some cracked window glass and two strips of body fabric torn off. The following year, again at Montlhéry, a Monaco, with an oversize fuel tank but otherwise "absolutely standard," averaged 64.36 mph for forty-eight hours, another international class record. Captain George Eyston and E.A.D. Eldridge were the drivers.

Meanwhile, casting shadows ahead of Riley's coming outright Tourist Trophy victories, a team of Nines—developed versions of the Brooklands Model—placed one-two-three in class in the 1929 T.T. at Ards, Northern Ireland; *un*placed was John Cobb, who used up one of his nine lives bouncing his Nine off a telegraph pole. Rileys, indeed, became a T.T. byword in the Nine's early-Thirties heyday, dominating Class G three years in a row before finally copping overall honors (Whitcroft first, Eyston second, both driving Nines) in 1932.

Also in Ireland (the republican bit) in 1930, the Saorstat Cup race, part of the Irish Grand Prix program, had fallen to French-born, wild driving Victor Gillow and his modified Brooklands Riley. His speed, incidentally, was 5½ mph faster than the supercharged 1750 Alfa that had won the

*Brooklands Nine (right): a sporting legend into the Fifties, when it was still winning races.*

event during the previous year.

Here we should dispose of the fallacy that the legendary Fred Dixon, whose part in Riley racing history will be capsuled later, was the first man to rig a Riley engine with a separate carb per intake port. This system, actually originated in the U.S., one thinks, by Fred Offenhauser, was used on Rileys pre-Dixon not only by George Eyston but also by the Riley company itself, on the 1931 T.T. Nines. These had four motorcycle-type Amal instruments, sharing two float chambers, Eyston first used *his* quad carb setup later in 1931 when he broke the International Class G one-hour record at 108.11 mph, and five other records concurrently.

Although Percy Riley normally showed a far-reaching grasp of breathing problems, he could nod fit to beat Homer on occasion. The paleolithic induction arrangements of his first hemi six, introduced late in 1928, exemplified these lapses. This unit, effectively a Nine with two extra cylinders added, inspired the euphemistic comment from *The Motor* that "the mixture distribution is very interesting; the carburetor is fitted at the rear of a single straight six-branch pipe." Struggling upstream towards the foremost cylinders, the poor old mixture must have felt as lost as the Babes in the Wood.

Mention of this six, although it didn't immediately find a place in any sports or racing Riley, is relevant insofar as, after downrating to 1486 cc to get inside the Class F limit by reducing bore size to 54.5 mm, it became the power source for the Brooklands Six of 1932 *et. seq.* Neighboring inlet ports were now siamesed and fed by triple SU carburetors, compression ratio was 8.2 to one—high for those days. Side members of the entirely new chassis passed under the back axle and were five and a half inches deep amidships. As on the corresponding Nine, there was no provision for luggage. A tail

*M.P.H. (below): the prototype of this model, built in '34, as a larger version of the popular Imp.*

*Ulster Imp: Replicas of the famed Tourist Trophy cars were available on both the Imp and Sprite chassis, the name deriving from the area in Ireland where the races were run.*

fin, perhaps inspired by the LSR cars of the day, but which actually covered the vertically mounted spare wheel, made the car look faster than it turned out to be; Riley people were quoted as "expecting a maximum of 130 mph." If it wasn't quite that quick—and it wasn't—at least it would go a long way between stops, the gas tank being twenty-six-gallons.

Few if any rival British makes matched Riley during the Thirties for feats of endurance, many of them including a speed element. In 1935 a team of three Australian girls traveled clear from Sydney, as far as possible overland, to Palermo, Sicily, their *starting* point for the Monte Carlo Rally. One of the memsahibs, Joan Richmond, had visited Europe before. In 1932, co-driving with Elsie Wisdom, wife of racing driver and automotive writer Tom Wisdom, she'd won the Junior Car Club Brooklands Thousand Miles Race outright in a Nine. This was the first race she ever drove and most of the competition was male.

The same year in another hemisphere, a Nine broke the 410-mile Durban-Johannesburg record by five minutes at 53.4 mph, "despite the fact that the car turned completely over en route." Yet another Nine, of a special type designed for army use, slashed no less than 1 hour 28 minutes off the 956-mile Cape Town to Johannesburg record, starting with 21,000 miles on the odometer.

Then there was that light car (1100 cc) class win in the 1931 Monte Carlo Rally, recalled earlier. The small Rileys of this period were not exactly mobile featherbeds, but it seems that didn't unman Leverett and Dennison, the successful Monte partners. "They sometimes go seventeen hours without stopping for food . . . and drive in tremendous spells of twenty-four hours or more." Also in '31, Donald Healey and Mrs. Montague Johnston, each driving a Riley six in the German 10,000 Kilometers

Trial, covered the course without losing a single mark. A year earlier, C.E. Shippam and J.B. Dixon had piled adventure upon adventure in the course of an 18,000 mile around-the-world trip in a Nine. It was this exploit that inspired V.R.'s romance versus sausage-making soliloquy.

The brief allusion to Le Mans 1934 in our opener told the truth but not quite the whole truth. Yes indeed, 1½-liter Rileys did finish two-three on general classification, J. Selileau and G. de la Roche, Fred Dixon and Cyril Paul, respectively, but it went further than this. An impudent Nine was fifth overall (Von der Becke and Peacock), another sixth (Newsome and Maclure), another twelfth (Trevoux and Carriere), yet another thirteenth (Mrs. Kay Petre and Miss Dorothy Champney). This was Champney's first race and the guts it betokened—plus other factors peradventure—inspired Victor Riley to ask her hand in marriage. He got it. To complete one of all time's most sensational Le Mans sweeps, Rileys, needless to say, also won their class, placing one-two-three on Performance Index and first in the Biennial Cup contest.

To backtrack again, it was in the months preceding the 1932 T.T. that the Nine engine underwent one of its most extensive updatings. The general layout remained the same but, among other things, the all-important crank was substantially beefed up. Erring on the safe side, Percy Riley, who not only had overall design responsibility but was boss of the firm's separately located engine factory, took it upon himself to build eight powerplants to the new T.T. specification—three more than had been officially bespoken. This decision contained the seeds of history.

While the T.T. preparations were in train, V.R. received a visit from a man he knew well by repute but had never met before: Fred W. Dixon, a motorcycle racing celebrity from Middlesborough, Yorkshire, and in-

*Grebe Replica: Its principal claim to fame being its fathering of the formidable M.P.H., no genuine Grebes exist today, this excellent replica being built from assorted Riley parts.*

cidentally a Riley dealer in a small way of business. By guile, before his interview with V.R., Fred had pumped the interesting news of the "surplus" T.T. engines out of Percy Riley—tidings that were to be helpful to his ambition to break into car racing.

Brooklands Rileys, as it chanced, were at this time in short, nay, nonexistent, supply: Not even Victor Riley could conjure one up to please a man whom he'd long admired from afar and who sold Rileys as part of his livelihood. So how would it be, countered Fred, if he, Dixon, procured a used Brooklands model from somewhere? Would V.R. then come across with a T.T. engine for it? Not being privy to his brother's precautionary over-budgeting, Victor was reluctant to commit himself but said that *if* a spare T.T. engine should become available, Fred could have it.

Dixon beat it to London and the showrooms of another Riley dealer, none other than the mercurial Victor Gillow, and haggled his way into possession of the exhaustively tuned and funnied Brooklands Nine that had won its owner the 1930 Saorstat Cup and other respectable guerdons. This done, he reimportuned Victor Riley, who, knowing now what Fred had known for weeks about the T.T. engine inventory, had one of the spares gift wrapped and released to the gruff little Yorkshireman.

It would be romantic to be able to record that Dixon, who combined the hell-raising bent of a Curtis Turner with the engineering talent of a Frank Lockhart, beat the factory Riley cars and drivers the first time he ever raced on four wheels. He didn't but he could have.

Inside the T.T.'s first hour, this self-entered outsider was leading not only his own class but, on handicap, the entire field. Same at the second and third hour stages. Repeatedly, as he reeled off the laps of the 13.7-mile Ards Circuit, near Belfast, his pit brandished SLOWER signals. Not because

he aspired to an overkill win but because he'd been working nonstop on his car throughout the previous night and day and feared the effect a change of tempo might have on his concentration, Fred ignored these whoa-backs. Then, disastrously, his pit crew inadvertently gave him a signal that simply didn't make sense. While his mind was grappling with the problem, Riley No. 20 shot off the road at fateful Quarry Corner, just beyond the pit area, leapt a trackside bank and stream, felled a healthy tree and landed on all four wheels in a field. Dixon was unhurt, apart from slight posterior bruising, while his riding mechanic Len Ainsley suffered facial injuries.

Although he was a driver of great natural talent, this alone did not of course account for the snook he'd cocked at his supposed superiors at Ards. In the three months period between his acquirement of his car from Gillow and D-Day, he'd completely rebuilt it—the engine excepted—according to a raft of radical ideas that had long been fermenting in his fertile brain. Spelt out in detail, these would hog the whole allotted space here, but by far the most significant single modification involved Dixon's simple but effective interpretation of the stressed skin principle. He junked the original body entirely, replacing it with a manually formed Duralumin shell that was bolted along its bottom edge to the main chassis members at closely spaced intervals, and also to three T-section dural hoops straddling the car at strategic points. This not only gave the structure unheard-of torsional stiffness, but also reduced its weight! Typical of his native cunning was his reconciliation of the spare-wheel-must-be-carried rule with the minute space available for one in No. 20's tapered tail. Finding nothing in the T.T. regulations about the *size* of spare wheels, or whether they had to be inflated, he took one off a derelict Austin Seven, let the air out and just managed to shoehorn it in.

Fred's T.T. Riley formed the basis of his famous track-racing eleven-hundred, the single-seater Red Mongrel. Built in the fall of 1932—and the grabber in October of Class G records from 50 to 200 kilometers, the last at 100.67 mph—this car was a crowning example of a lone-handed empiricist's success in defeating air resistance without aid from wind tunnels or other scientific kickshaws. Apart from its absolutely minimal frontal area and demonstrably "good" external shape, the Mongrel's internal aerodynamics were way ahead of their time. Contrary to contemporary racing practice, the intake slot to the very low mounted radiator was of precisely calculated area. Also there were no hood louvers whatever, for a double reason: One, the unbreached lid permitted no eddy-making air efflux at a point where it would detract most from slipperiness; two, denied an exit by the usual upwards route, air from the radiator—warm but still with considerable cooling potential left—was forced *down*wards around the walls of the heat-abhorring crankcase. Thence it made its final getaway through a tunnel formed by a dural undertray like the T.T. car's.

In contrast with the engine he'd used in the 1932 T.T., which was "standard"—in the qualified sense that it was a replica of the factory team's equipment—the Mongrel's engine was pure Dixon in practically everything but its cylinder block and basic Percy Riley configuration: pistons, valves, cams, porting, manifolding, carburetion—these owed nothing, nett, to Riley thinking. Primarily the Dixon legend rested on his pastmastership of respiration, and it was the Red Mongrel, the world's fastest unsupercharged eleven-hundred of its day, on which he first practiced his one-carb-per-pot arts. Incidentally, to discourage rivals, or merely academically inquisitive persons, from poking their noses into his secrets, he always secured the hoods of his track Rileys with dual padlocks

*Appleton Special (right): the puissant bolide which established new International Class G marks.*

when leaving them even momentarily unattended in the Brooklands paddocks.

The Riley six-cylinder engines, for a variety of displacements from 1½ through 2 liters, were scarcely less successful in racing and record breaking than the Nines, even though their production life was much shorter. The works-entered fifteen-hundreds that placed two-three on Performance Index at Le Mans in 1934 were sixes, so were the Rileys with which Eyston and divers partners set some of the most remarkable Class F records of the Thirties. These included a thousand miles at 102 mph average, in 1934 . . . a speed that no other British car, regardless of size, has equalled to this date. The Riley company, though, or anyway Victor Riley personally, privately took a dim view of the six engine.

It was around this time, September of 1934, that the firm introduced two new production sports two-seaters, the eleven-hundred Imp and the six-cylinder M.P.H. These shared the same very attractive shape while naturally differing in size and amenities. The regular M.P.H. was of 1633 cc (1726 in 1935) but—and this was significant—Riley also offered a 1½-liter (1496 cc) version of it for customers who wanted to fit into an established engine size class with competition in view. Standard transmission for the Imp and M.P.H. both was Preselectagear, a variation on the so-called self-change theme, but a normal four-speed box with a "silent third" ratio was an option in each case. A subsequent development of the M.P.H. was the even prettier Sprite two-seater, a 1½-liter four, again with the option of preselector or "crash" boxes.

As far as racing was concerned, not the least distinction of the 1500 cc four-cylinder Riley was that it gave Dixon the last laugh—the last two laughs in fact—on his Tourist Trophy jinx. With full factory backing and

*Dixon Nine (below): the car in which Freddy astounded the crowd in the 1932 Tourist Trophy.*

*Sprite: One of the prettiest of all Rileys, the Sprite was a comely two-seater which made its debut at the London Motor Show late in 19[*]

using engines of this type, he won two T.T.'s in a row, driving *à seul* in 1935 and paired with another former racing motorcyclist, Cyril Dodson, in '36. The former was taken at 76.9 mph, the latter at 78.01.

Although it needed the genius of a Dixon or the talent of a Hector Dobbs to whip up the unblown editions of the six engine to competitive racing performance, it proved prodigiously responsive to supercharging. Among the first, if not *the* first, to discover this fact of life was Peter Berthon, *boffinissimo* behind the formidably potent hill climb and circuit racing cars of Raymond Mays. The outcome was the White Riley-cum-E.R.A., which is another story, albeit one that underscores the great scope for development that Percy Riley built into his sixes.

If Victor Riley doubted this, and he did, Dixon didn't. After the unblown sixes had performed dismally in the 1933 T.T. (only one of the factory entries finished within time limit), Fred took opportunity by the handlebars and announced his willingness to accept two of these cars, plus a large inventory of related parts, as a gift. Given a free hand with them, he undertook to get them off their crutches fast.

These unsuccessful 1933 T.T. engines were only underbored versions of the touring-car sixes; but Dixon, who had gained his car-racing experience with Nine-sized cylinders (60.3 by 95.2 mm) and didn't want to waste it, opted for the makings of a pair of the stock-dimensioned powerplants—displacement 1633 cc. Their bottom ends, however, were T.T. pattern, special in respect of their very robust roller-type center crank bearings (these were plain on the production engines).

Broadly speaking, the Dixonization of Fred's track racing sixes followed the lines he'd adopted earlier with the little fours. The T.T. bodies were junked in favor of lower, longer tailed ones, and these, in conjunction with

"structural" undertrays, were attached to the chassis at multiple points and bore their share of stresses. Simply by piercing the hood deck and allowing the Scintilla Vertex magneto to protrude, he was able to effect a one-and-a-half-inch lowering of the car's whole skyline. (The mag was concealed under a little rubber raincoat, to the mystification of guess-happy paddock prowlers. Ah, power bulge!)

As with the Nines, so with the sixes, Dixon jettisoned almost as much as he retained in the engine department. Notably, on the gasworks side, he used the dashpots and float chambers from six SU's but harnessed them to a one-piece aluminum casting enclosing a single sliding-plate throttle serving all ports. (Shades of Lucas fuel-injection, circa 1956!) To ensure cent-percent accurate register, this plate and the carburetor chokes were bored simultaneously, in one operation. To prevent the side jamming when subjected to the intense suction produced by a slammed-shut throttle against a 13:1 c.r., Fred seated it top and bottom in roller bearings.

To take maximum advantage of the varying class demarcations adopted by different race-organizing bodies, Dixon upped and downed his bore measurements as the spirit moved him; starting at 1633 cc, the sixes' displacement later became 1458 cc, then 1808 cc, then 1750 cc, intermittently a mite under two liters. These fabled Rileys of his were colorless only in the sense that he never painted them, thereby, he claimed, adding fourteen pounds of lightness. Elsewhere, weight was saved wholesale by substituting Elektron for cheaper metals.

Standouts among the many successes scored by Dixon's incredible sixes were two outright wins in the punishing Brooklands Five-Hundred, and another in the British Empire Trophy, also at Brooklands. In his first Five-Hundred, the 1934 event run in nonstop pelting rain, he was one of

*standard power came via a specially tuned 1½-liter four-cylinder engine, fitted with twin SU carburetors and a special inlet camshaft.*

only two finishers to drive single-handedly. His average was 7½ mph better than his sole all-wet rival's. Fred's two-liter Riley was the only un-blown car of its size ever to lap Brooklands at over 130 mph.

In 1934 he lent the same car to Elsie Wisdom for an attack on the women's lap record, which she forthwith broke at 126.73 mph. To rebreak it—by less than two seconds—the tough and experienced Kay Petre needed 10½ liters under her toe (the ex-Land Speed Record Delage).

The sports cars and racing cars of the marque's golden age, like their touring counterparts, tended to conservatism in the suspension depart-ment, though Riley did once go "all independent of the leafy spring," in Keats' phrase. This brief exercise in i.f.s. appeared on a batch of racers built originally for the 1936 British Empire Trophy. The system used was a product of Andre, the shock absorber firm, and married very fat coil springs to equal-length wishbones and long radius arms pivoting two feet back against the frame members. This setup became particularly iden-tified with a car raced consistently and with success (including winning the 1938 International Trophy at Brooklands) by the late Percy Maclure. On his own account, Fred Dixon too dabbled awhile in i.f.s., but *his* design was frowned upon by scrutineers and he wasn't allowed to race it.

When Lord Nuffield, who'd previously put a stop to M.G. competition activity, bought Riley in 1938, *l'état* naturally ceased to be *nous;* the deal also wrote finis to the Coventry firm's direct involvement in motor sport. It did not, however, discourage privateer Riley exponents from pursuing their cherished racing and records projects. Memorable among these was the phenomenal Appleton Special, property of Londoner John Appleton. Foundation of this rumbustious little bolide had been an already much-raced 1100 cc Maserati that Appleton bought in 1934 from W. Widengren,

the speedy Swede. Appleton rebuilt it, installing a supercharged Riley Nine engine along the way and, stage by stage, it progressed to the astonishing point of generating 183 bhp at 7400 rpm by 1939.

A turnover of this order would of course have been impossible with the two-bearing crank that was the Achilles' Heel of all other high revving, high output Nines. There was only one way to beat the problem and the technical *maestri* expensively hired by Appleton took it: They reworked the whole bottom end from scratch, introducing a two-piece Nitralloy crank and supporting it amidships in a third bearing no less than five and a half inches in diameter. Once or twice, on the bench, the engine ran up to 8500 without exploding. In youth and middle age, the Appleton was Zoller blown, though the last version used an eccentric-vane Arnott which pumped a maximum boost of 22 p.s.i. The car, qua car, was, to quote an erudite authority of its day, of "optimum ichthyoid form," or as you or I might say, fishlike. It started breaking the International Class G records for the standing mile and kilometer in 1936 and kept it up, on and off, until the outbreak of World War II. It was then doing the s.s. mile at 91.3, the s.s. kilometer at 82.1 mph.

After surviving the passover from independent, family proprietorship into the Nuffield Organization in 1938, then another into the BMC fold fourteen years later, then a third into British Leyland Motor Corporation when Britain's biggest motor group engorged BMC, Riley joined the ever-lengthening list of expendables in July of '69 and permanently and irrevocably folded. With its demise, one more fragment of the romance of the automobile that had buoyed old V.R. departed, and was lost forever. As long as old Victor had to die sometime, maybe it was merciful that his own demise predated the era of the internal-combustion sausage. ✾    47

# PROMOTING THE PIERCE-ARROW

## *The Art and Artists of Automobile Advertising's Most Glorious Era*

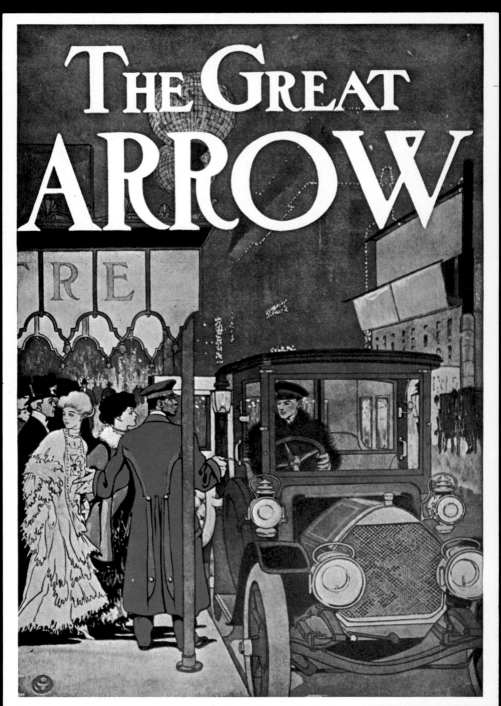

Does advertising pay? Edward E. Goff, editor of *The Motocycle* asked himself that question in his issue of May 1897, and answered that it would "require volumes to produce arguments in its favor"—for after all—"the manufacturer of the motocycle is in a position to take advantage of more free advertising than any other industry." He—and certainly his publisher L.B. McGrath—rather hoped prospective purveyors of the horseless carriage might consider doing so . . . and of course they would, and did, and shall forever more.

Whatever one thinks of automobile advertising today, and the lengths to which it's been driven since it was concluded that a car could not merely be bought but instead had to be sold, there can be no doubt that historically the first was the worst. By far.

What distinguished early automobile advertising art was its utter disregard for being either distinguished or art. Simplicity, Strength, Service, Speed, Silence, such were the copy points stressed, frequently in that order —and tag lines, scarcely as catchy as a cold, ran the gamut from the negative, "the car that has no valves," to the positive, "the car that does things." And an occasional pleasant directional, "nothing to watch but the road." Or "ask the man who owns one." Type styles were chosen—at random, one suspects—by fellows whose *arbiter elegantiarum* credentials were tenuous at best. Illustrations were largely pen and ink sketch, ink drawing, or airbrush with line, or madly retouched photograph—almost invariably monochromatic and inescapably unaesthetic.

The novel idea of applying artistic standards to the business of advertising generally was first thought of by Ernest Elmo Calkins, about 1903. And about a half decade later his Calkins & Holden ad agency was doing same for the redoubtable Pierce-Arrow, that grand motorcar from Buffalo. Though an occasional advertisement during this era from another manufacturer in the luxury arena might betray a touch of class, there was nothing to compare with the formidable series produced by Calkins & Holden for the mighty Pierce-Arrow.

All rules were broken. Why, heavens to a Grout Steamer ad, the car frequently was not even shown in toto; its hill climbing prowess, its high gear performance unalluded to, copy indeed virtually nonexistent sometimes save for marque mention and maybe, just maybe, a discreet address. And the art—it was splendid. Many a fine artist or accomplished illustrator found gainful employment in wielding a brush for Pierce-Arrow. Calkins & Holden secured the best.

There was Edward Borein (1872-1945), a Remington-esque etcher of western life, a literal painter whose work, it's been said, was "true to the last strap and buckle." Louis Fancher (1884-1944), a pupil of Mowbray, Henri, Walter Appleton Clark and Kenyon Cox, with his brilliant use of

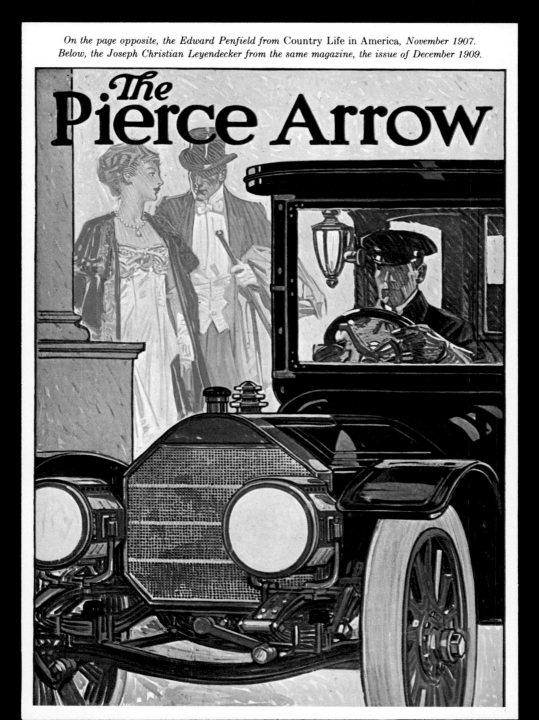

*On the page opposite, the Edward Penfield from* Country Life in America, *November 1907. Below, the Joseph Christian Leyendecker from the same magazine, the issue of December 1909.*

# PIERCE ARROW

color, his boldness of delineation, sometimes Penfield-like, other times derivative of the German Poster School and Ludwig Hohlwein. Hohlwein himself (1874-1949), the most famous of German poster painters with a style of sharp contrasts and simple geometric lettering. Newell Convers Wyeth (1882-1945), dramatic in picture concept and lush in his use of decorative color, a mural painter and charmer of youngsters for generations with his evocative illustrations for such children's books as *Robin Hood* and the novels of Robert Louis Stevenson. Joseph Christian Leyendecker (1874-1951), of the free and dashing technique which, it was said at the time, "possessed all the abandon but none of the disregard for detail that characterizes the impressionist," renowned for his *Saturday Evening Post* covers—the first in 1899, with over three hundred to follow during the next forty years, among them the annual New Year baby series—and for the Arrow Collar man who set feminine hearts aflutter for a period of almost two and a half decades. And his younger brother Frank X. Leyendecker (1877-1924), with a charm of subject and a clean delicacy of rendering which was exquisite, whose hand was more sensitive, if not as dramatic as his brother's, and who put same to the design of stained glass windows as well as magazine covers. Edward Penfield (1866-1925), the Brooklyn-born avant-gardist whose *Harper's* window bills in the wee years of the Nineties were the earliest examples of the American artistic poster and who, art historian Charles Matlack Price commented in 1913, "com-

bined a certain Parisian chic with a London poise of aristocracy and refinement, and blended the two by some curious psychological sleight of hand into an expression of the best that is in America"—this exemplified most effectively by his Great Arrow ad, "an extraordinary example of suggestive 'stage setting,' the light, intangible, indefinable, but all-pervasive of the million lights of Times Square . . . a crush of hurried after-theatre street traffic" suggested by two hansom cabs and one motorcar from Buffalo. Myron Perley (1883-1939), with his fine decorative sense, his art director expertise, and his work also for Stevens-Duryea and later Hupmobile. John E. Sheridan (1880-1948), possessor of a free, spontaneous quality, noted for *Saturday Evening Post, Ladies' Home Journal, American* and *Collier's* covers, later men's fashions for Hart, Schaffner &Marx and magnetos and such for Bosch. Adrian Gil Spear (c. 1885-19—), very Art Nouveau, with the feel of a Gauguin in his vivid juxtaposition of flat panels of color, and who later carried his dramatic flair into work for the theatre. Walter Dorwin Teague (1883-1960), one-time art director of Calkins & Holden, well known as a deviser of decorative borders, as a typographer with several type faces to his credit and ultimately as an independent industrial designer with such divers assignments as the design of the Brownie camera and color schemes for the Marmon Eight of the mid-Twenties. Guernsey Moore (1874-1925), subsequently art editor of the *Saturday Evening Post* whose Art Nouveau style embraced a quaint

# WORTH

The value of a Pierce-Arrow Car has been fixed as the price for which it is sold, but can that price measure its worth? It is easily possible for the fortunate owner to get more out of it than is represented by what he paid for it, just as it is easily possible for the man whose life has been insured to live longer than the years set down in the actuary's table.

The cost of a Pierce-Arrow represents merely the least that one can get out of it; in other words, its value. Its worth is the sum of all its desirable qualities multiplied by the years over which it continues to give the full quota of these qualities. Divide that by the cost of the car, and the quotient is insignificant.

THE PIERCE-ARROW MOTOR CAR COMPANY · BUFFALO N Y

## PIERCE-ARROW

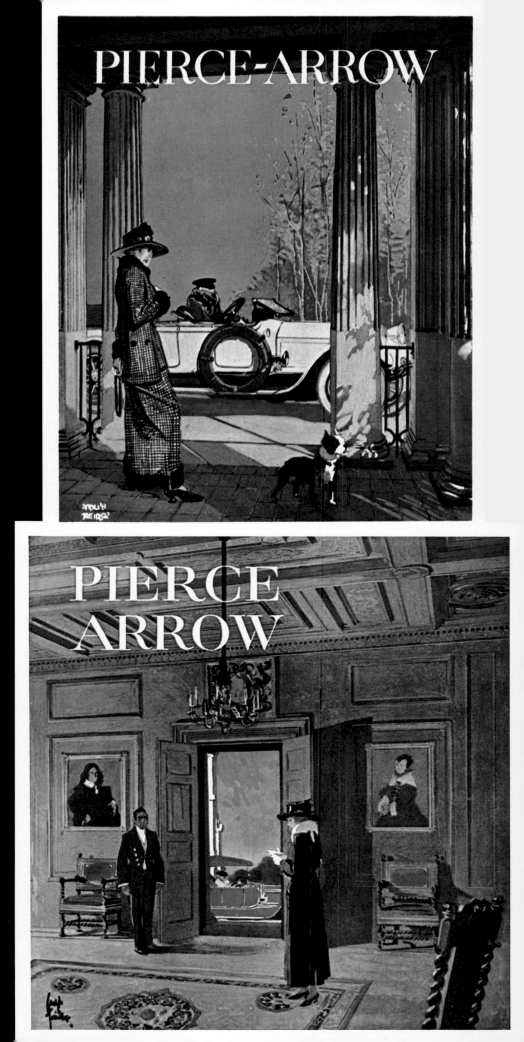

On these pages, clockwise from top left: two varied approaches in advertising from 1917, the Pierce-Arrow reflected in a looking glass by Edward A. Wilson and the blacksmith symbolizing "Worth" depicted by Newell Convers Wyeth; Adolph Treidler presenting the marque in two settings of grandeur, the Pierce-Arrow awaiting decorously without, circa 1919. On the two pages following, clockwise from top left: the Robert J. Wildhack wrap-around of 1910, presenting a dazzling array of strong sunlight-and-shadow values, with the motorcar itself suggested rather than delineated, the beach setting effectively introduced with a mere toy pail and shovel in the foreground; the Adolph Treidler wrap-around, also 1910, demonstrating, as historian Charles Matlack Price noted, the artist's "vigor and dexterity, depending for . . . effects upon strong illusions brought out simply by the skilled handling of broad masses of light and dark, [the] delineation by means of shadows [showing] how much may be accomplished by a kind of negative presentation of values"; the advertisement entitled "The Pierce-Arrow in the Great West" by Edward Borein from 1910; and also from 1910, the Pierce-Arrow in a German setting as painted by Ludwig Hohlwein.

THE PIERCE-ARROW AT NÜRNBERG

THE PIERCE-ARROW MOTOR CAR COMPANY, BUFFALO, N. Y.  Licensed under Selden Patent

humor and who was given to gentle parodies of the styles of Maxfield Parrish, Albrecht Dürer and Howard Pyle, one time including their initials along with his own to indicate credit where credit was due. Robert J. Wildhack (1881-19—), a master of flat tint, whose keynote—and strength—was absolute simplicity. Edward A. Wilson (1886-1970), who worked predominantly in line with washes of color, a nautical enthusiast who illustrated a collection of sea shantys with wood cuts and returned to dry land for a memorable series of advertisements for LaSalle, Coral Gables Corporation and Victrola. And the man who produced more Pierce-Arrow advertisements than all the others, Adolph Treidler, about whose art Charles Matlack Price noted also in 1913, "It is work of this kind that seems of an excellence out of all proportion to its transient function . . . [it is] poster value so far above most current work that it must not be dismissed after its week upon the newstand."

It would be—for a while. Fortunately, in recent years, poster, advertising and cover art has begun to come into its own, to be collected, to be preserved, to be remembered for just what it is—as both an evocation of its age, and as art. The Pierce-Arrow series of advertisements would have to rank at the top of anyone's list of collectible automobile promotion art. Adolph Treidler certainly thinks so—and it is fortunate too that this talented gentleman is with us still, and still painting, and remembering what it was like to work for Calkins & Holden and Pierce-Arrow during the golden age represented here. His memories indicate as well why the Pierce-Arrow advertising program was so extraordinarily and aesthetically successful.

The Pierce-Arrow

# HARPER'S WEEKLY

EDITED by
GEORGE HARVEY

AUTOMOBILE
NUMBER

January 8 1910    HARPER & BROTHERS, N. Y.    Price 10 Cents

LUXURY in a car is as much a matter of engine building as it is of upholstery. Luxury as expressed in a Pierce-Arrow means efficiency first, attractive design second, a perfectly appointed car, built around a thoroughly tried-out machine.

The Pierce-Arrow

# The Pierce Arrow

The Pierce Arrow

*Above, the Adolph Treidler from the "Speed and Sport Number" of* Life, *September 2nd, 1909. Center, the John E. Sheridan, from* Life *magazine, 1910. Below right, the Walter Dorwin Teague, circa 1910.*

It might not have been thus. Initially, some of the better known illustrators of the period felt producing work for advertising purposes was demeaning. "Being unknown tends to lessen one's scruples," Adolph Treidler remembers—he leapt at the chance to work for Pierce-Arrow. He was fresh from a job as paste-up boy in the art department of an advertising agency in San Francisco—he left there soon after the storied earthquake—and a sojourn in the Windy City as back-up artist to staff photographers on the *Chicago Tribune*. Not quite twenty-one, he had arrived in New York, rented a studio on West 23rd Street, and soon thereafter took himself to Madison Square Garden to paint. Parked in front of the Garden were a couple of horse-drawn carriages—and one Pierce-Arrow. "I painted them right in, and then I stood the result in a corner of my studio. The week following, Walter Whitehead—who had become sort of my patron—stopped by with a job for me to do, and he saw it. 'Hmmm, when did you do that?' he asked—and I told him. 'Well, I think I can sell it,' he replied, but he didn't tell me about the very fortunate and convenient change of jobs he had just made. He was now art director of the Calkins & Holden advertising agency, and he sold my painting right

Not only has the Pierce-Arrow turned the tide of imported cars so that there are today far less in proportion than some years ago—not only that, but the Pierce-Arrow in American hands has invaded Europe, giving greater satisfaction to its owners than a native car on its native heath.

The Pierce-Arrow Motor Car Company, Buffalo, New York

*Art Nouveau and the Pierce-Arrow. Above, the playful Guernsey Moore's idea for the marque appearing in* Life *magazine's October 9th, 1913 issue. Below left, the Gil Spear from* Life's *issue of September 1st, 1910.*

away—to Pierce-Arrow.''

That was the beginning. Thereafter Adolph Treidler painted extensively for Pierce-Arrow, and became famous—and illustrators already famous joined the campaign. The reason was simple. "I don't think anyone anywhere ever had the freedom that the artists for Pierce-Arrow had," Adolph Treidler recalls. "They laid down no rules whatsoever, never told me to do this or that. Every year, about the time the new cars were to be introduced, the company sales manager—I remember his name as Hawley—would drive down from Buffalo in one of the new cars and we'd take off for a pleasure trip—up to New England usually—and simply have a good time. I'd get to know the car and get some ideas, take some pictures on a cheap little box camera I'd take along. Then I'd be dropped off back in New York. And I was on my own—completely.

"Pierce-Arrow never knew exactly what I was doing until after I had done it, not the colors I would use, nor the model view, not the setting in which I would place the car, nor how much of the car I would place in the setting. Never once during my long association with the company did Pierce-Arrow return one of my paintings for changes or corrections. They

55

The PIERCE=ARROW differs from other cars in three ways—in its engine, in its body and in the way the two are combined to make the most thoroughly artistic, comfortable, and dependable car ever built.—The Pierce-Arrow Motor Car Co. Buffalo

·LIFE·

The Pierce-Arrow

[Returning in comfort in the Pierce-Arrow]
THE PIERCE-ARROW MOTOR CAR COMPANY, BUFFALO, N. Y.  Licensed under Selden Patent

*Above, from the left: the Frank X. Leyendecker from Country*
*snow and church scene settings, from circa 1911 and 1915 respectively,*

were always pleased—and I, of course, was delighted. I visited the factory several times, pleasantly always, meeting with people in the various departments and being shown around. But my nicest memory of Pierce-Arrow came one time after I returned to New York. Waiting for me there was a letter from chief engineer David Fergusson. Pierce-Arrow wheels then were wood spoked, and Mr. Fergusson wrote me to say that in one of my paintings I had drawn the best picture of an automobile wheel that he had ever seen—and the thing that impressed him the most about it was I had left out almost all of the spokes. I had done this by having the lighting on it in such a way that some of missing spokes—or the apparently missing—were just swallowed up in the shadow, with maybe one or two of them catching the light—but still it was accurate, the feeling of it was accurate. It had to be, or I certainly wouldn't have heard from Mr. Fergusson. Well, that was a real compliment, coming from an engineer no less. That was unique."

As was the Pierce-Arrow advertising campaign. Obviously. Adolph Treidler's recollections indicate that. And so do the advertisements on these pages that he and his fellow artists painted. Their sole purpose was selling a motorcar. Seldom has that very practical function been done so gloriously. ✥

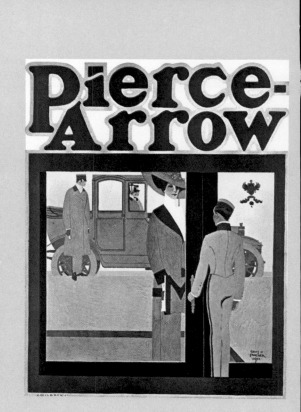

Pierce-Arrow

*Above and right, two very striking advertisements painted*
*for Pierce-Arrow during 1911 by Louis Fancher,*
*both appearing in several prestige periodicals during the year.*

A car that looks equally good from the curbstone,
from the driver's seat or from the tonneau.
*The Pierce-Arrow Motor Car Company Buffalo, N.Y.*

Expectancy of good
service soon ceases to
be expectancy and be~
comes conviction.
The Pierce~Arrow Motor
Car Company *Buffalo, N.Y.*

e in America, *December 1912; two Adolph Treidlers, in*
*Myron Perley, appearing in* Vanity Fair *magazine during 1917.*

# IT'S WILD, IT'S SAFE, IT'S A CONTRADICTION, IT'S THE BMW TURBO

## The Classy Münchener of Which Even the Government Might Approve

For anyone with eyes to see, it's pretty obvious that Bayerische Motoren Werke AG has been coming on very strongly in recent years, not only in the U.S.A., but throughout the world. The company has a youthful, crack management team now, a seasoned, extremely talented engineering force and a future of almost unlimited promise. They are already building some of the most admirable cars in the world, and in the coming years one might fully expect BMW's to be even better still—or at least more desirable.

In Germany, even having fun is taken seriously. So when the directive came down from management early in 1972 that BMW should proceed with the development of an experimental safety car, the idea was not approached or executed in the usual safety car fashion with which we have all become so bored of late—and on which so much American taxpayer money has been thrown away. The purpose was not, as BMW sniffed, to produce a test vehicle "to meet the United States 'safe vehicle' standards long recognized as overstated." Rather, the aim was to come up with something practical and feasible, both technically and economically, using contemporary passive safety know-how realistically. And next came a question.

Why shouldn't a safety car be a high performance car too? If anything, the safety features would have even more meaning, and be more severely tested, in such a car. Moreover, of course, there's a lot more publicity value in a high performance car than there is in a stolid sedan, so BMW's considerable technical expertise would become more widely circulated. And then there's the often overlooked factor of the effect of such a car on employee morale.

Yes, this was obviously the right way to go. And what a fascinating car the BMW Turbo turned out to be.

It looks good certainly, which is what one notices first; its styling was executed under the direction of Paul Bracq, a Frenchman who joined BMW a number of years ago, after having spent ten years during the Fifties and Sixties in the design studios of Mercedes. But since the BMW Turbo is a safety car, it is upon that, perforce, which we should focus.

As is evident in the photographs—the car set, incidentally, against the backdrop of the structures built for the Olympics in Munich—the front and rear ends of the vehicle are separate entities, each with its own impact absorbing structure. Initial or smaller knocks are absorbed by a compressible plastic foam that restores itself to its original shape after contact. For more severe bumps, the entire front and rear are mounted around a U-

beam with a controlled compressibility structure at the rear and hydraulic damping units at the front. All very logical. Another logical idea is the way the windshield posts have been run into the roof, which then becomes a massive roll cage.

The Turbo also sports that most Germanic of all automotive devices, the gullwing door, though BMW was openly pleased—for perhaps obvious reasons—to give credit where credit was due, to an English patent of 1938. And visibility through those big windows in each side, forward and to the rear, is truly remarkable for an automobile of this type. Many mid-engined cars give one the feeling of sitting at the bottom of a well. Even the gills behind the door posts were constructed to be, as BMW put it, "obliquely transparent."

And the BMW Turbo's finish was quite purposively chosen as well, a spectroscopic ruby-red with metallic effect, "a safety-color par excellence," BMW said. It is noticeable.

Inside, and throughout, hard edges were avoided and all interior components cushioned with foam. The seats are orthopedic and consequently very comfortable, and they give excellent support at the sides. A long trip in this car could be a pleasure. For a number of reasons.

Part of the fun would be the occasional glances down at the dashboard. The instrumentation and various other systems in the interior of the car are among the BMW Turbo's most outstanding features. The instruments, apart from the usual gauges one would expect to find, include a few fascinating new ones that might be pretty useful to have around. How about a gauge that tells you how far it will take you to stop—from whatever speed you might be doing? Or another that shows what sort of sideways g-loads you are attaining? Or the schematic display of the entire braking system to the driver's left, that tells you the condition of all the brake pads, the pressure in both dual-overriding systems, the level of brake fluid and the anti-lockup system? Or an engine over-rev warning light?

Another nice thing. The BMW Turbo arrived during that period when we—those of us driving new cars anyway—had to live with that irritating buzz informing all and sundry that seat belts were not fastened. The BMW variation on that theme reaches the same objective, but by the simple expedient of not allowing the car to start until the seat belts are hooked up. And with safety belt on, all controls and switches remain within easy reach from the driver's seat.

The basic structure of the BMW Turbo comprises a tube frame with

platform center, the engine and rear suspension carried in a separate, rubber-mounted subframe. Front suspension is via MacPherson type with diagonal torsion bars; rear the fully independent MacPherson with coil springs and parallelogram trailing arm. Steering is rack and pinion, with an overall ratio of 17.5:1. A four-speed, fully synchronized transmission is fitted, the clutch is the dry, single plate variety. Stopping the car is accomplished by four-wheel power-assisted discs with anti-skid system.

Making it go is, essentially, a standard 2000 tii unit set at a ninety degree angle to the axis of the car just behind the seats. A short shaft takes the power to the differential. The big story in the engine department of this car, of course, is the turbocharger. And, as with engines boosted this way, the amount of power produced is easily increased/decreased by the simple matter of tightening up or opening up the wastegate of the exhaust turbine. Power ranges from 200 DIN to 280 DIN—that would be over 300 American type horses, which is a lot of poke to move one long ton.

The Turbo's performance parameters were determined by a computer before the car was built, an easy enough thing to do these days. Here's what it said: zero to a hundred kilometers an hour (62 mph) in 6.6 seconds; zero to one hundred sixty (99 mph), 15.7 seconds. Top speed: 155 mph.

Who's to argue with figures like that?

At whatever the speed, the BMW Turbo has traveled a lot during the past couple of years. It's visited the United States and South Africa, and wherever it's been, people—safety conscious or not—have been impressed. So obviously have been the powers-that-be at BMW, and they've come up with an entirely new idea. The latest directive to emanate from management has authorized the development of a mid-engined sports car based on the BMW Turbo design to be ready for the 1978 World Championship Series for Manufacturers. The car is planned to be sold in Europe as a race or street car, and, if we're lucky, it might come to the States as well. A pleasant thought to conjure.✣

# THE CAR CALLED E.R.A.

## *A Portrait of England's Upright and Proper Champion*

"That ain't the cockpit—that's the crow's nest." This aspersion, which a caustic bystander cast upon the original A-Type E.R.A. when it made its public debut in 1934 at Mannin Beg, hit off the car's fashion defiant and aback-taking loftiness with some nicety. Contrasting strikingly with the low build of both predecessor and contemporary racing machinery, this reversion to the perpendicular, visually accented by the narrowness of the single-seat bodies, provided E.R.A. pilots with a positively nearer-my-God-to-thee mien.

Too, whereas the independent springing of at least the front pair of wheels, and both pairs in the enlightened cases of, for example, Auto Union and Mercedes, was currently regarded as the panacea for all suspension arcana, here was E.R.A. actually starting out in life with a beam front axle and a solid rear one.

The reason why, in these two vital areas, E.R.A. appeared to champion obsolete practice was not that its chassis designer, Reid Railton, hadn't given the matter considered thought but precisely because he had. Let "laughing friends deride," as the lyric would have it, until their buttons blew, but *he* knew that his tall-in-the-saddle configuration gave the driver an uncommon sense of mastery, his downward slanting sightline conducing to millimetric accuracy of front placing in tight corners. And if replicas of the cars were to be built for sale to private owners—and that was planned from the start—economic stringencies ruled out elaborations in the suspension department in any case.

That Railton was right and the laughing friends wrong was triumphantly proved during the racing era 1934 through '39. E.R.A.'s rarely failed to beat the stuffing out of continental competition in voiturette action, hill climbs and straight sprints. Relative to the marque's total build—seventeen cars of Types A, B, C and D—it copped more wins than any other marque ever had or indeed ever has done.

Lest the impression be given that Railton laid claim to, or rated, alone-I-dunnit kudos, one hastens to enfocus some other similarly indispensable figures: Raymond Mays, Peter Berthon, Murray Jamieson, Humphrey Cook, Victor Riley, for instance.

*The third E.R.A. built, R3A, world standing kilometer record holder in 1934, with the Shelsley record and an Eifel win in '35 and an Avus class victory in '37.*

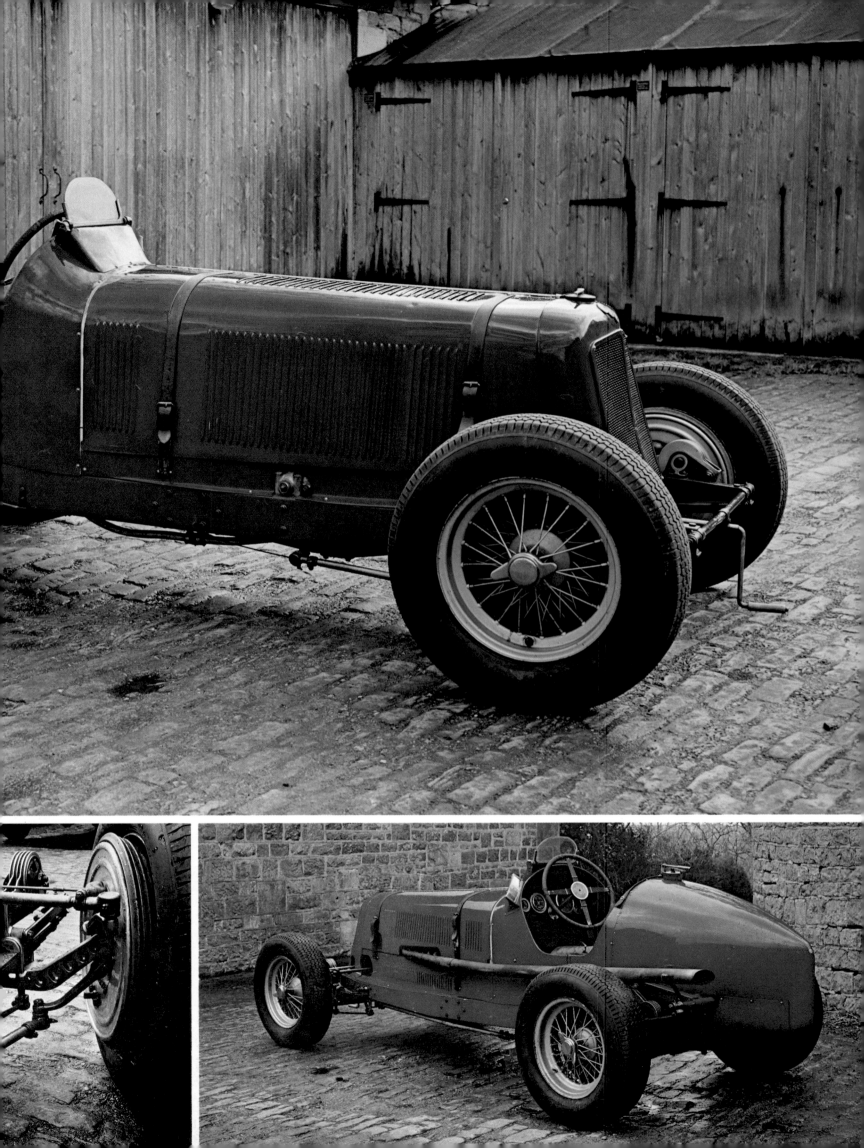

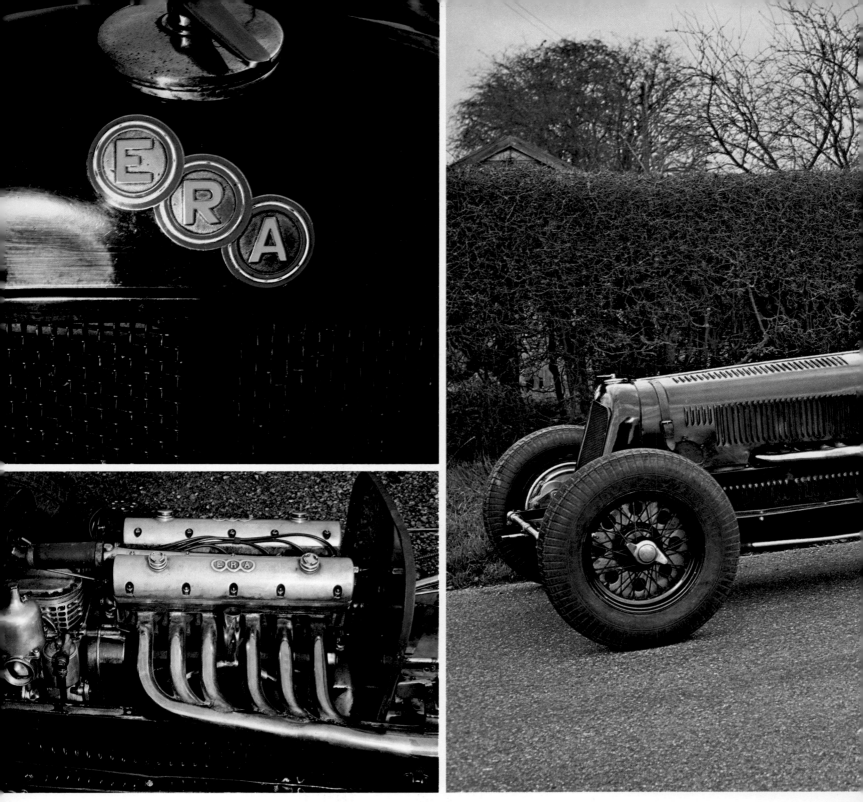

*The E.R.A. R1B, completed in 1935, fitted with a 1500 cc engine and Jamieson supercharger, and raced by G.F.A. Manby-Colegrave and W.E. (Billy) Cotton among othe[rs]*

The E.R.A.'s engine was a derivative of and closely akin to the six-cylinder Riley unit, which first saw the light of day in 1928 and had a checkered career thereafter. In 1932 Berthon and Mays conceived the idea of supercharging and otherwise gainfully molesting the 1½-liter version of said engine and installing it in a chassis of the same make. Victor Riley, perhaps not sorry to see the back of some unfavorite *matériel*, promptly unhanded it and provided a modest financial sweetener for the venture. The resulting car, universally tagged the White Riley on account of being white and a Riley, managed a couple of eye-catching records at Brooklands and Shelsley Walsh.

Among the many whom these performances impressed was Humphrey Cook, a successful and wealthy amateur of speedsport. Fired by the thought of fathering a British voiturette to challenge the pesky Italians at their own game, and convinced that a further developed version of the White Riley could do it, he unbosomed his ambitions to Mays and Berthon. The finance he was willing to commit proving sufficient, a company, English Racing Automobiles Ltd., with workshop facilities on the

grounds of the Mays family home in Bourne, Lincolnshire, was formed, and the project got under way.

From the first, the E.R.A. became a force to be seriously reckoned with. In particular, it excelled in the acceleration Railton and Jamieson had taken pains to design in, the former by his far-back siting of the driver and engine/gearbox masses, to the obvious benefit of traction, the latter by his use of a blower giving an uncommonly flat power curve. Straightaway, Cook, who'd not unreasonably voted himself works driver status, broke two International Class G (1100 cc) records at Brooklands, and Mays did the same with one in Class F (1500 cc). Ray furthermore broke his own White Riley lap record for the Brooklands Mountain circuit and turned fastest time at Shelsley Walsh in opposition to the talented Whitney Willard Straight whose full GP Maserati had a thirty-three percent advantage in cubes over Mays' triumphant E.R.A.

The Railton-designed chassis was to say the least ordinary: far-in and on-beat, as one might say. Shallowly upswept front and back to surmount the axles, the side members were of unboxed channel section, interspaced

*"others" including Dick Seaman who drove this car to the fabulous hat trick of wins at Pescara, Berne and Masaryk during the halcyon sporting days of '35.*

by four tubular crossties, and a network of other supports. The laminated leaf springs were frictionally damped and located north/south by radius arms that, up front, also resisted braking torque. Attachment of the worm and nut steering gearbox and its droparm to the right-side chassis member, conjunctive with the central placement of the driving seat, involved a pronounced offsetting of the steering post and a resultingly different "reach" to the laterally opposite arcs of the spring-spoke wheel. The Wilson preselector gearbox, currently gaining popularity on some costlier British passenger cars, but which hadn't hitherto won racing adherents, won one in the E.R.A. Aft of this cunning box, drive to a straight-tooth bevelled back axle was via a torque-tube encased propshaft.

Main elements of the Riley-derived engine included dual camshafts located high in the block, pushrod-cum-rocker operation for two valves per cylinder in hemi heads, and three bearing crank. The Jamieson blower, geared to run between 1.285 and 2.25 times crank speed, was mounted vertically at the front of the block and bevel driven off the nose of the crank. The Riley's wet-sump lube system was replaced by a dry sump layout, and

the crankshaft, much stouter than any Riley's, ran in plain bearings front and back and on a Hyatt roller in the center. Three displacements, dovetailing with three international classes, were available: 1098 cc, 1488 cc, 1990 cc.

High as the car was, it presented a frontal area of no less than 13.5 square feet. Aside from this dimensional factor, it was, even by the unexacting standards of its day, something of a porcupine pie aerodynamically, so it certainly needed some power to push it through the atmosphere. As long as you spared it excessively bumpy surfaces, an E.R.A. seemed equally at home on circuits of widely different characteristics, lap mileages and speed potentials. Charles Martin, private owner of an A-Type, turned history's fastest-ever race winning speed by a 1½-liter car at Avusrennen in 1937—119.67 mph. Also in '37, in Phoenix Park, Dublin, Raymond Mays and his two-liter E.R.A. dominated the annual 100 miler at the highest speed for any road race in the British Isles, regardless of the winners' engine size—102.9 mph.

Not only with race audiences but drivers as well, E.R.A. was a prophet  67 with honor both within and without its homeland. It's impressive that in relation to Bourne's total output, the unEnglish operators included a Siamese (B. Bira, or more formally Prince Birabongse), a South African (Pat Fairfield), a German (Prince zu Leinigen), a Frenchman (Marcel Lehoux), a Greek (Nicky Embiricos) and a Norwegian (Eugen Björnstadt). Of the lot of E.R.A. drivers, Bira was doubtless the most outrageously colorful, and Englishman Mays the winningest. But it was another Englishman, Dick Seaman, who probably provided the marque its most dramatic success in a single season. Unforgettably, he won the Coppa Acerbo at Pescara, Switzerland's Prix de Berne and the Masaryk Voiturette Grand Prix in the brief period August 15th through September 29th, 1935. Unfortunately, the year following Seaman switched allegiance, bought Lord Howe's 1927 straight-eight Delage, had his friend and mentor Giulio Ramponi rebuild it—and pulled another hat trick of important wins in even less time than taken by his E.R.A.

Although 1936 was by no means a bad season for E.R.A., this slaughter by Seaman must have helped jolt the minds of Cook, Berthon and Mays

into realization that some aspects of the existing E.R.A. design were, as U.S. Ambassador Walter Annenberg was later to say of his embassy in London, "subject to the need for elements of refurbishment." For one thing, the car was too damn slow, didn't have enough power. For another, its front suspension was antiquated. For yet another, it needed a stiffer frame.

All these requirements were met, the first quite dramatically by use of a Zoller vane-type compressor with dual SU carbs, in place of the Roots pattern Jamieson blower and single SU carb, which sent the output rocketing from around 170 at 6500 rpm to 240 bhp at 7500 rpm. The gain in bmep was from 204 to 280 p.s.i.

The contours and crossbracing of the original Railton chassis stayed as they were but the formerly flimsy channel section side members were boxed in at the front. Even more importantly, i.f.s. to a Ferdinand Porsche design, as used on GP Auto Unions, was adopted. The brakes, which had been Girling mechanicals, became Lockheed hydraulic. There being no change in either weight or frontal area, maximum speed in 1500 cc form not

unexpectedly rose by about 15 mph to 140 mph. A loss in acceleration from zero to around the 2300 rpm mark was counterbalanced by a gain from there on upwards.

The result was called the Type-C, though any cars thus designated were really B's converted to these revised specs. The predecessor A's and B's had been labeled such almost solely by fact of manufacture date. And if that confuses, the mind will be set to reeling by mention that the to-come D-Type, of which there was only one and with an all-new fully boxed chassis, had previously borne both B and C designations. E.R.A.'s were an incestuous lot, obviously.

However called, the E.R.A. continued in the forefront of the voiturette battle, interspersed with action in mixed company, right up to the outbreak of World War II. Meanwhile, though, Humphrey Cook boldly embarked on an entirely new project—the creation of what was originally conceived as a full Grand Prix car, the E-Type. It was jinxed from the start. Prewar, it actually started in exactly one race, the Albi GP—and crashed. Postwar, two more E-Types were built, and after the assets and title of E.R.A. Ltd. were acquired by the late Leslie Johnson, were sold into private ownership. Driven by a series of ever-hopefuls, they went from failure to failure and finally dropped from sight.

Latterday glories there were, however, for E.R.A. When he unplighted his troth to Cook in '39, Mays bought the solitary D-Type, overhauled it and mounted a formidable attack on the lap and hill records for almost every British course one could name. When he desisted, he had a nationwide records massacre without parallel in the history of British speed competition. Postwar, he demothballed the car and captured the R.A.C. Hillclimb Championship in 1947, a fulsome twenty-seven points ahead of his closest rival.

E.R.A.'s formal racing story ended then. But E.R.A. competition did not, and has not since. Today, four decades from genesis, every single one of the *pur sang* E.R.A.'s survives, most driven in vintage races by latterday Lochinvars, many of whom weren't born when Railton's laughing friends derided and that jibe about cockpits and crow's nests was heard on the Mannin Beg sidelines. Breeding tells.✦

# THE HUDSON MOTOR CAR COMPANY STORY

## The Spirited Automotive Years of the Car That Was Named for Jackson's Wife's Uncle

The Hudson that started it all, and the one that followed it, left above and below: a Model 20 roadster built in 1910 and a Model 33 torpedo from 1911.

The 1912 "Mile-A-Minute Roadster," a Model 33 standard roadster minus a bit of coachwork and with smaller wheels and the top speed guaranteed by its name.

Most prospective customers in 1908, thin-skinned about their choice of a car, might have been expected to avoid a marque named after the head of a department store. It seemed to be asking for a nickname or a catchphrase—a likely laugh-raiser at the owner's expense: "Pick that up at the five and ten?" But Hudson owners could have been worse off. If the car had been named for its engineer rather than its sponsor, they would have found themselves riding in a Coffin.

However that may be, Hudson owners were probably much the same then as they are today, a hardy, devoted, strongly opinionated group, not easily swayed, fiercely partisan, often highly biased—and possessing keen insight into the merits of automobiles. The marque deserves the loyalty. Hudson offered the good old American formula: value for money. That it failed to get its own money's worth from the American public should not obscure the decades of its very substantial achievement.

As with other cars of pronounced character, the Hudson story began with men of very strong personality: Roy Dikeman Chapin and Howard Earle Coffin by name, sales manager and chief engineer respectively of Olds Motor Works, which in 1905 was the world's largest producer of automobiles. But that fact did not overly impress Chapin and Coffin, and reflecting upon the comparative delight of the big-fish, small-pond principle, they decided their combined engineering and sales talent was a fine basis for yet another automobile company—their own. But there had to be a "meanwhile" stage. First, in 1906, Coffin convinced E.R. Thomas who had a rather successful automobile business in Buffalo to finance yet another car, the Thomas-Detroit, to be built in Michigan but marketed by the powers-that-be in upstate New York. Chapin and Coffin, and ex-Olds associates F.O. Bezner and J.J. Brady, owned one-third of Thomas-Detroit stock and found soon they didn't like that arrangement, so after a year they convinced Thomas to sell his block of shares to Hugh Chalmers, which when done resulted in a reorganization to Chalmers-Detroit.

The Coffin-designed, four-cylinder Thomas-Detroit of 1907 had been an expensive car—$2750—and Chapin was convinced that was about a thousand dollars more than most men could afford, or wanted to spend. So the Chalmers-Detroit was brought in at a cost allowing a $1500 price tag, and it was a sales hit straight off. This success prompted Coffin and Chapin to extend their thinking even further down the price line. A still cheaper car would, their experience showed, bring sales and profits in inverse proportion to its price tag. Already they were beginning to think along big-fish, big-pond lines. But they couldn't do it alone. Enter now another ex-Olds duo: George W. Dunham and Roscoe B. Jackson. The former was an engineer, the latter had a wife who had an uncle by the name of J.L. Hudson, who was, conveniently, the owner of a very prosperous department store in Detroit. The idea was a scaled-down Chalmers-Detroit—and the target was under a thousand dollars. Both Coffin and Dunham got to work right away. And Roscoe Jackson went to see his wife's uncle. Whether Chalmers was enthused about this turn of events is moot, what is definite is that J.L. Hudson put up the cash and in return was made president, though he would take no active part in the business and in fact would remain "somewhat apprehensive" about the entire venture until the company started paying its own way.

The Hudson Motor Car Company was thusly founded on February 24th, 1909, with a capital of $100,000. The stockholders were Chapin, Coffin, Bezner, Hudson, Jackson and Dunham. The first factory was a two-story building of 80,000 square feet. The payroll numbered five hundred workers. And the first Hudson left the factory, on July 3rd, priced at $900—just fifty dollars above a Model T Ford—and carrying the designation "20" and the first of the famous Hudson triangles, symbolizing "performance, service and value."

By the end of 1909, more than a thousand cars had been sold, and in December the Hudson people severed from Chalmers-Detroit, Chapin taking the presidency now, with Hudson moving to chairmanship of the board. Jackson was general manager, Coffin vice-president of engineering, Bezner in charge of purchasing. Brady and Dunham had decided to stay behind with Chalmers.

A new 223,000-square-foot factory, designed by Albert Kahn, was begun at Jefferson and Conner Avenue during 1910, 4556 cars were

*At the top, from the left: a 6-40 lightweight six from 1915, a Super Six touring limousine from 1918 and a Super Six seven-passenger touring car from 1916.*

produced that year, and Coffin came up with a new Hudson. Designated the "33," like its predecessor for developed horsepower, it had a monobloc four-cylinder engine with unit-mounted transmission, die cast bearings and cork insert "wet" clutch running in oil. One wheelbase—114½ inches—served for all models, and the price range was $1000-$1450, spanning a market somewhat above the first Hudson and marking a reversal in trend for the company. Hugh Chalmers had decided to challenge Henry Ford head-on in the three-figure price field. Roy Chapin had meantime decided not to. He had another idea. Hudson sales for 1911 were 6486 cars, another plant extension of 128,000 square feet was begun late in the year. And bigger plans were afoot.

From very small beginnings around 1907, the six-cylinder motorcar had risen to ten percent of the market by 1910, and two years later had almost doubled again. But most of its manufacturers were in the three-thousand-and-up class—the three P's, and others like Stevens-Duryea—double-barreled in name, reputation and price. In a move reminiscent of their initial market-broadening four, Chapin, Coffin and Jackson decided to bring the extra two cylinders down in price. Hudson would build a six. It was a daring move, one that might have wrecked a company with only three years behind it, little cash on hand and sales for 1912 which had slipped to 5708 units. No one was sure a six could be successfully built in quantity—technically it had been a problem only recently mastered by engineers who had the advantage of building such engines in limited numbers, and carefully too—nor whether a market for such a car existed in the medium-price class. The project was the biggest the company had tackled and a team of forty-eight engineers worked on it. They had a prototype under test in July of 1912—in which month, incidentally, J.L. Hudson died—and shortly afterward the six-cylinder Model 54 was announced for the 1913 model year, along with an improved four called the "37." Both cars featured the Delco system of starting, ignition and lighting, and comprehensive touring equipment, all for a base price of $1875 in the 118-inch-wheelbase Model 37 and $2450 for the 127-inch-wheelbase Model 54.

The latter's performance belonged in the high-priced class. Top speed

*Above, from the left: a Super Six four-passenger phaeton from 1921, a Super Six four-door brougham from 1926 and the pace-setting Essex coach from 1922.*

was 65 mph, and it could reach 58 mph in thirty seconds from standstill, figures which Pierce-Arrow and Peerless were hard put to better. The Hudson was no match in standards of finish, luxury or prestige, of course, but its performance per dollar and comprehensiveness of equipment were trend-setting. In the future, American car buyers would demand more and more good cars of moderate price, refuse to put up with nasty cars at cheap prices or mediocre cars at inflated prices, and show less and less interest in super cars at sky-high prices. Ford had already begun the trend at one end, Cadillac would soon do so at the other, and Hudson was equally influential in the middle. Sales went back up to 6401 in 1913.

Next move was a lightweight six, the Model 6-40 introduced at the 1914 New York show, where it was displayed on a set of scales to prove its claim as the lightest six-cylinder car in the United States. At 2772 pounds with a five-passenger body, it was certainly that. More important to the public, at a price of $1550, it cost only slightly over a half-dollar per pound—fifty-five cents to be exact. The company dropped fours altogether, sales for 1914 soared over the 10,000 mark and Hudson began advertising itself as

the "world's largest manufacturer of six-cylinder cars." Profits were at the quarter of a million mark, the company ranked sixth in new car registrations—up from seventeenth in 1910—and Detroit factory facilities now extended over twenty-six acres.

The next forward leap was not long in coming. At the 1916 New York show, the Super Six was announced. It shared the classic 3½ by 5 bore/stroke dimensions the 6-40 had pioneered, but was an altogether new engine with cylinders cast en bloc, enlarged gas passages, an improved cylinder head, refined cam design and carburetion and a new four-bearing crankshaft featuring a special counterbalancing method using eight counterweights of unique design. Thus, without any increase in the 288-cubic-inch displacement, the power output in the new engine went up to seventy-six from the forty-eight of the old, and the output per cubic inch was .27 bhp, well above the industry average and actually better than some sporting vehicles like the Mercer. In many ways, the Super Six was a precursor of the 1924 Chrysler. Both used essentially simple L-head designs which gave efficiency and performance figures equal to that of 73

*Among the loveliest of Hudsons during the Twenties were those with coachwork from the house of Biddle and Smart, as witness this dual cowl phaeton produced during the model year 1929.*

costly and complex contemporaries. The key was patient research pulling out every possible gain from a basically sound design. Like the engine, the chassis was entirely new, and Hotchkiss drive was used with long semi-elliptic springs.

What put the publicity seal on the Super Six, of course, was its competition career, and a lot of the gloss on the seal rubbed off from the driver, Ralph Mulford, one-time star of the glamorous Lozier team. It was he who took a Super Six to Daytona Beach and clocked 102.5 mph over the measured mile, a new stock car record. But that was only the beginning. Less than a month later, he was at Sheepshead Bay for an all-out assault on the twenty-four-hour record, then held by S.F. Edge and Napier at 65.9 mph. Mulford and the Super Six broke it with a vengeance—averaging 75.8 mph for the duration and putting up a fastest lap of 89.4 mph, after 1500 miles had been covered. It was a record which would stand for fifteen years. Then there was Pikes Peak. If any proof be needed that the Hudson was already in a class by itself, one need only quote a Denver newspaper which publicized the event as a contest featuring "Fours-Sixes-Eights-Twelves and Super-Sixes." With a racing body on his otherwise stock Super Six, Mulford took the Peak in the 231-300-cubic-inch class event in 18 minutes 25 seconds, a record which was to stand for eight years. Trailing far behind were a Duesenberg and Barney Oldfield's Delage.

Nineteen sixteen had been quite a year for Hudson. For the one following, the company fielded a factory-sponsored team—with Mulford the star, and Ira Vail and A.H. Patterson on the first string—which acquitted itself admirably, though the company bowed out mid-season, after some misguided individual accused race officials at Omaha of being unfairly pro-Hudson, which they weren't. Hudson, infuriated, turned the cars over to the team—Super Sixes would continue to be raced independently, and successfully—and went back to the business at hand.

Super Six production passed the 50,000 mark by 1918, and on the 19th day of the first month of 1919 came the Essex. It was an F-head four of 55

bhp (nearly three times the Model T), was durable, reliable, economical on fuel and a good value at $1595. It was competition tested as well—with a fifty-hour run at a 60.75 mph average at Cincinnati Speedway performed by a group of top drivers including Tommy Milton, and a four-car transcontinental trek that was quite sensational. The fastest car (4 days 14 hours 43 minutes) broke all existing San Francisco-New York records, but more important was the overall average of all four cars at 4 days 21 hours 32 minutes, truly a testament to performance, reliability and endurance.

Even though 1921 saw the collapse of the postwar boom with sales down to 27,143, Hudson-Essex finances stayed in good shape, and in the winter of 1921-1922, the company actually cut prices by $700 on Hudsons and $500 on Essexes, tagging them at only $1700 and $1100 respectively and making them better buys than ever.

Meantime Chapin and Coffin prepared a masterstroke. A packing crate, the opposition said; actually it was a special Fisher body design, fitted with glass and doors, upholstered, trimmed, painted and installed on the Essex chassis—a closed car for the masses. In late 1921, the Essex coach was offered at $1495, $300 above the touring car. By 1925 Chapin had lowered its price to $895, five dollars *less* than the touring car on the same chassis. "Nothing like that had ever been seen before in the automobile industry," commented GM's Alfred P. Sloan, adding with characteristic understatement, "The Essex coach had considerable vogue."

By the end of 1925, the "vogue" had spread to Sloan's own GM line. And at Ford, among other factors, the reality that the Model T was an open car design unsuited for heavy closed bodies was causing concern. The trend would continue irresistibly. The typical car at the beginning of the Twenties had been a tourer. The standard automobile of the next decade would be the sedan.

Meantime there had been some mechanical changes at Hudson, the most notable the two extra cylinders Essex received in 1924: a new and refined powerplant but one with displacement and output (130 cubic inches, 28 bhp), as well as performance and durability markedly inferior to the bigger (and rougher) four. The following year the Hudson experimental department tested a six-cylinder F-head of 175 cubic inches, capable of 125 bhp and compact enough for installation in the Essex. Since the power output was so massively over that of the Essex, it was never marketed but developments continued on an enlarged and detuned version as a successor to the L-head Super Six. In January of 1928, the F-head Special Six emerged, combining the best features of the previous Essex and Hudson engines. It had the deep breathing efficiency of the Essex four, with the refinement of the Essex Six and the beefy torque curve, durability and effortless high speed cruising of the Hudson Super Six.

Every marque has its all-time great, and this was probably Hudson's. For a price as low as $1095 (and as high as twice that), the buyer got a 92 bhp 289-cubic-inch engine, tough and quiet, capable of "70 miles an hour all day," with top over 80, and acceleration to match, *plus* better gas mileage, hydraulic double acting shocks all around, brakes equal to its speed, remarkable ease of steering and control, and a great many other features ranging from safety glass windshield to adjustable *rear* seats. And with this car, too, came custom bodies for Hudson, from Biddle and Smart.

Business was excellent until 1929. Total Hudson-Essex sales peaked at 298,832 that year, with Essex third in national sales. The company's specific earning rate on unit sales was the highest in the industry. But the Wall Street crash forced a drastic rethink in Hudson engineering. All of what went before was fine when there was money—but suddenly there was none at all. Hudson's new car, in essence, would be powered by the Essex engine, with the addition of a couple of cylinders and a few more bearings. It was called the Great Eight, and it was a straight eight of relatively small displacement (214 cubic inches), with an integral cast block and crankcase and integral counterweighted crankshaft, the first time the latter feature had appeared in a straight eight. Power and torque were naturally less (80 bhp at 3600 rpm) than the big six, but so was the car weight and size. The power-weight ratio was maintained at about 40 lb/hp, although the higher revving eight soon became known as the less gutsy engine.

The new factory bodies, restyled, were lighter and lower. Meanwhile Biddle and Smart had decided to cease production, not in bankruptcy, but preferring to quit while ahead and before the effects of Wall Street's crash forced the company out anyway. Hudson had to turn elsewhere for its custom work, and Briggs and Murray were selected.

The eights were offered in two lines in 1930-1931, and the Essex Six,

which had grown in stages from 1924, was now up to 60 bhp at 3000 rpm from 175 cubic inches. Not many Essexes, or Hudsons, were being sold now. Sales fell off at an incredible rate: 113,898 in 1930 (one-third of 1929) to 57,825 in 1931. So Hudson decided to try something dramatic in the low-priced line, following the lead of Ford who in March 1932 had introduced a V-8 with high-priced performance at a figure of $500. Hudson would match Ford's performance-price ratio, the only one to do it. The Essex six-cylinder engine was taken to 193 cubic inches and 70 bhp at 3200 rpm, and marketed in a short 106-inch wheelbase chassis with semi-unitized all-steel body at $425-$590 price tags and under the name Essex Terraplane Six. On July 21st, 1932, Amelia Earhart christened the new line, and Orville Wright took delivery of the first car built. Detractors called it the "Terrorplane," but fly it could. The claim that the sedan "could amble at 80 mph all day and still do 20-25 mpg," although exaggerated, gives a good

mind's eye picture. It *could* do 80 mph, although probably not all day, and it *would* return up to 25 mpg, but not at 80 mph; 30 mph more likely. The dry weight was a mere 2010 pounds for the roadster, and even the sedan was only 2250 which, with axle ratios between 4.1 and 4.54, gave performance factors at or near the top for any production car, regardless of price, and a claimed "airplane ratio of power to weight." (Actually about 30 lb/hp.) Despite the light weight, the designers had provided a box-type diagonal truss frame for high speed stability. A nice package, all around. The Terraplane shared headlines with the Ford V-8 as the low-priced sensation for 1932.

The model name "Terraplane" soon overshadowed "Essex," so the latter was dropped, and the 1934 line was known simply as Terraplane—and added was a model with the Hudson Eight engine for 94 bhp at 3600 rpm from 244 cubic inches—and hotter performance still,

*Above left and right, two Hudsons from 1929, a two-passenger coupe and the Greater Special sport sedan; at the left, center and below, two cars by Biddle and Smart, a roadster on the 1927 Essex Six chassis and a sport phaeton on a 1929 Greater Special chassis; below, a Great Eight boattail speedster from 1931 with coachwork by Murray.*

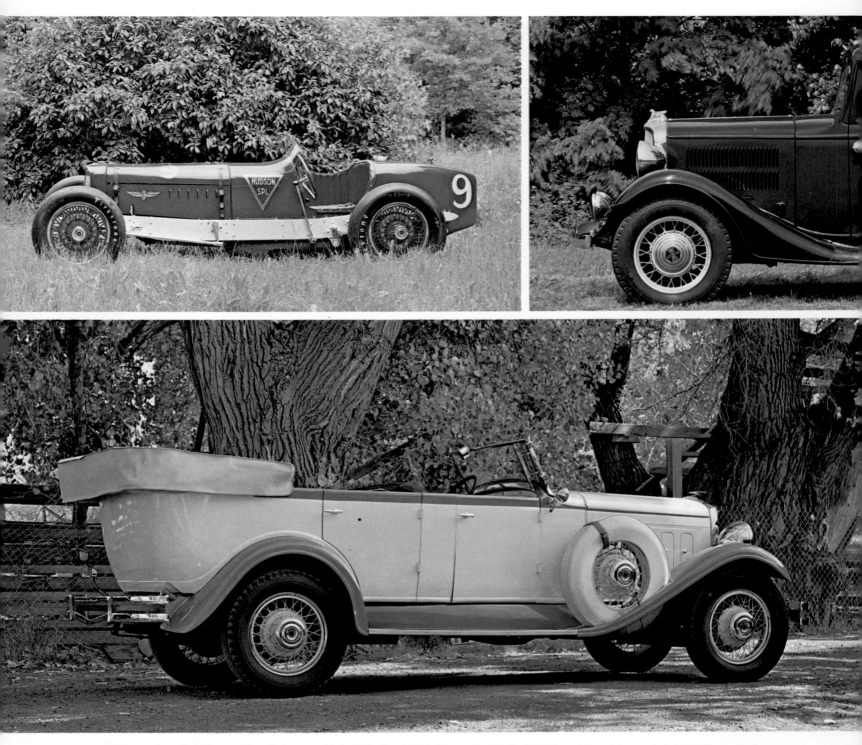

*At the top, from the left: one of two Hudson specials built for the 1932 Indianapolis 500, the 1933 Essex Terraplane coach, the 1930 Greater Eight roadster.*

upon which Hudson quickly capitalized. Between 1932 and 1933 the company sent a number of certified stock models to hill climbs across the country. They swept the boards. Pikes Peak was typical. In 1932 Chet Miller and a Terraplane six took the Penrose Trophy, shattering all existing stock car records in the process. In 1933 it was the Terraplane eight and Chet's brother Al who took the honors—and a new record. Three more Terraplanes finished second, third and fourth in the stock car class. By the end of the 1933 season, every AAA hill climb record for stock cars was in Hudson hands, and many of these records—there were fifty in all—would still be in the book as much as seventeen years later. On the flat, at Daytona, the Terraplane took a bunch of records as well.

The Hudson Eight had been broadened to three lines by 1932, the Standard, Sterling and Major and in 1933 the Super Six reappeared, with Essex engine and chassis, and Hudson returned to two lines, Standard and Major. Mechanically, things had been happening too. The Hudson rotary brake equalizer, for example, was an ingenious attempt to build inherent brake equalizing into a cable system and thus compete with hydraulics. And 1933 models had *power* braking—with a vacuum reservoir for added

safety. Fresh styling and "Axle-Flex" came in 1934, the latter a cross between true independent front suspension and a beam axle, designed by Baker and used also by Nash. It gave some of the advantages of i.f.s. without costly redesign of the entire front end of the car, making it attractive to independents whose smaller engineering budgets suffered much more in the Great Depression than did those of General Motors or Chrysler. Nineteen thirty-five brought the Bendix "Electric Hand" which shifted gears by vacuum power. By now the big Hudson Eight was developing 113 bhp at 3800 rpm.

Although Hudson lost three million dollars in 1934, factory sales at 85,-835 were double that of 1933, and in 1935 the company shipped 101,080 cars and showed a profit of $584,749. That year also saw a Hudson Eight set thirty-five AAA records at Muroc Dry Lake. Business continued to improve, and in 1936 the company's sales were up twenty-five percent over 1935 with a profit figure that surpassed the loss of 1934. This impressive recovery, made at a time when independents were dropping off like flies and even the giants were worried, was the last major achievement of Roy Chapin. In July 1932 the great man had been appointed Secretary of

*Above, from the left: the phaeton model of the 1931 Greater Eight, the brougham from the 1932 Major Series, with style, equipment and finish approaching the Packard class.*

Commerce in the Hoover Administration, not only because of his administrative talents, but also because the Republicans hoped that his oratory would help to keep Hoover in power. But Hudson had lost five and a half million in 1932, and Hoover lost the election, so in May of 1933 Chapin returned to his company. In a sense, he was on his own. The brilliant team that had created Hudson had disappeared, for Roscoe Jackson had died suddenly in 1929, and Coffin had retired in 1930. Bezner had retired even earlier.

So, alone of the old guard, Roy Chapin saw Hudson through its most serious crisis thus far. That the name still had magic, or that he still possessed his business acumen and persuasive eloquence—or all three—is clear from Chapin's record. By 1935 he had raised the six million dollars that Hudson needed to keep solvent. During the same period he had worked equally hard to save the Guardian Trust Company of which he was a director. Regrettably, the worry, strain and overwork affected his health, and he contracted pneumonia. He died February 16th, 1936, aged only fifty-six.

But Hudson had to go on. Succeeding Chapin as president was shy,

reserved A.E. Barit, who had been with the company since 1910, rising from stenographer to treasurer to vice-president to general manager. He had worked closely with Chapin, and from 1933 the two men had been jointly responsible for management and policy, so Chapin's death saw little change in company strategy. Heading engineering since 1928 was Stuart G. Baits. Styling director since 1931 was Frank S. Spring, formerly of Murphy Body.

The 1936 models were as completely restyled as the 1934 line had been. The crispness was gone; in its place was a not entirely happy bulbous shape, characterized by a new radiator grille that looked like the head of a praying mantis. With few changes, the theme continued up to 1940. Mechanically, the '36's introduced "Duo-Automatic" brakes, hydraulic Bendix duo-servo, with both pedal and hand lever mechanically linked as a safety feature in case of hydraulic failure. And Hudson's directorate began considering a problem, the fact that the Terraplane designation was becoming even more popular than Hudson now. It was decided to phase out that name and introduce a new low-priced car. In 1938 the Terraplane became the Hudson Terraplane, and the Hudson 112 made its debut. Its

*Above left and center, the 1936 five-passenger Six sedan and '39 three-passenger Six coupe.*

designation came from its 112-inch wheelbase, which was five inches shorter than the 1937 Terraplane. (Like other smallish cars, the Terraplane had grown and grown from its original 106 inches.) The 112 used a destroked version of the H-T six-cylinder engine, for 175 cubic inches and 86 bhp—and one of the lowest performance factors of any American car of the day. In seeming defiance of calculated performance figures, however, the 112 set a string of AAA stock car records at Bonneville in 1939. A standard five-passenger sedan took every mark in Class D from the standing kilometer to 30,000 kilometers, and from one hour to twelve days. Its average for the hour was 80.54 mph, and at the end of twelve days (20,327 miles), it was still averaging 70.58 mph.

Hudson celebrated its thirtieth anniversary in 1939 with a line consisting of the 112, the larger six and the eight. Since 1937 the former boasted 101 bhp at 4000 rpm, the latter 122 at 4200. The 1940 models had a completely new look. Hudson called it "symphonic styling," and it was very clean and attractive, a combination of the best features of earlier Lincoln Zephyr and Studebaker models. The eight now produced 128 bhp. Fully independent front suspension was used with wishbones, coil spring and telescopic shock absorber inside the coil spring, a feature which has since become universal. John Cobb drove a completely stock sedan to an AAA Class C record of 93.9 mph for the mile in August of 1939 at Bonneville, and at the same time the Hudson Eight took virtually every Class C closed car record from the standing mile to 3000 kilometers, and from one hour to twelve, its average speed for the half-day being 91.29 mph. The company by now held 121 AAA records!

While making records, Hudson had lost money, a million and a half dollars in 1940. But in 1941 the company showed a $3,756,000 profit, and by 1942 was heavily into war production, whence it would remain until August of 1945. When peace came, Hudson went back to what it did best, managing to get nearly a hundred thousand cars to a public clamoring for them by the end of 1946. And in 1947 the company produced its three-millionth automobile. Profits had risen from $672,000 in 1945 to $2,382,000 in 1946 and $5,763,000 in 1947.

The models for these postwar years were similar except for their engines—which remained the durable duo of big six and eight. Respective prices were $1574 and $1686 for four-door sedan. Meanwhile, in the wings, Baits, assisted by Sam Frahm in engineering and Frank Spring in styling, was readying a memorable new model.

Since the mid-1920's, Hudson had been a leading exponent of all-steel bodies and unit construction. The company did not build the first unit body-chassis, but its designs evolved into a very practical one-piece "unit" in which weighty sills were eliminated and the frame and body riveted, not bolted, together to give great strength with low weight. All these bodies were trademarked "Monobilt." Others, of course, made similar

*Below, the sedan in the Traveler series from 1941; above, the 1947 Commodore Six sedan.*

developments during the same period, Chrysler with its Airflow, Lincoln with its Zephyr, for example. Nash in 1941 put its "unitized" 600 in full production. And that same year, Hudson had built a prototype to Frank Spring's designs and patents for a "step-down" semi-unit construction. Spring showed it to Barit, but A.E. had baroque tastes and complained that it was "too low." The car was shelved—almost literally. For the duration of the war, it rusted on the roof of the Hudson plant.

After the war Barit was still not interested—at first. Hudson, in common with every other manufacturer, had no trouble selling existing designs to a car-hungry public. But when this market started to run dry, Spring took his pet design down from the roof, cleaned it up a bit and, hopefully, re-presented it to Barit. Still muttering about the styling, Barit drove it home from work one evening, and changed his mind overnight upon finding what an excellent road machine it was. He ordered it into production for the 1948 model year—at a reputed tooling cost of $18 million.

When it was announced, even the conservative, phrase-careful *Motor* in England called it "something of a sensation . . . a daringly original innovation." The body and frame were welded together, with the floor dropped between them until it was the lowest part of the structure. The drive line was lowered by using a hypoid axle and two-piece driveshaft, thus minimizing the floor hump. Cramped footwells were eliminated by passing the box section frame longerons outside the rear wheels, with subsidiary branch members inside. Adequate headroom was maintained with exceptionally low car height. Interior space was vast, and elbow room aided by "tumblehome" windows sliding at an angle into the doors which were recessed inside.

The car's center of gravity was the lowest in the U.S. industry; it was only sixty inches high, although seventy-five inches wide. The sleek, squat appearance suggested outstanding roadability and speed which the car had no trouble at all proving in practice.

Beneath the modern shape? Still the faithful sworn at and sworn by straight-eight engine. Why not? It put out as much honest horsepower as some engines with seventy cubic inches greater displacement, gave an easy 90 mph and would accelerate the car from standstill to 80 in thirty-six seconds. Using the Warner overdrive, average gas mileage was 16 mpg. Backing up the elderly eight was a new Super Six, still an L-head but with 270 cubic inches giving 123 bhp at 4000 rpm. The Hudson line comprised three series, Super Six, Commodore Six and Commodore Eight.

For 1950 the company added the Pacemaker Six, a smaller car using a short-stroke version of the Super Six engine for 221 cubic inches and 112 bhp. Production figures that year were mid-way between 1948 and 1949, at 143,586 units, and profits rose to $12 million.

Next came the Hornet—in 1951—with a new 308-cubic-inch L-head six developing 145 bhp at 3800 rpm and 257 lb/ft of torque at 1800 rpm—the

latter a thirty percent increase over the eight's 198 lb/ft at 1600 rpm. It gave a ten percent increase in top speed, reduced the standing quarter-mile by about a second, and considerably improved passing acceleration. Ample in its displacement, working well within its capacity, with a chrome alloy block, it was also very tough and durable—similar in concept and function to the famous Super and Special Sixes of the Teens and Twenties.

This reversion to type carried a penalty. Superior performance was undeniable, but whether the eight's level of refinement had been maintained, let alone surpassed, was something else. Although the engines were all statically balanced before assembly, then dynamically balanced electronically, there were complaints from owners and road testers that the new engine was neither as quiet nor as smooth running as the old—hardly surprising in view of the increase in displacement and the loss of two cylinders.

It was the last big six ever to be built in America—and an L-head at that. To offer this as a new engine in 1951 clearly implied that, in contrast to the advanced design of the car, the Hudson engine department was failing to move with the times—or was hamstrung by management allocating research funds elsewhere.

But the implication was overshadowed in the public mind by Hudson's decision to go racing in 1951. The company was an old hand at this game, and it showed. There were six other makes that year with models more powerful than the Hornet, but by the end of the 1951 NASCAR racing season, Hudson already stood third in the list, behind Oldsmobile and Plymouth. In 1952, although the Hornet stood eighth in horsepower ratings, it ran first in twenty-seven out of thirty-four NASCAR Grand Nationals—driving Olds and Plymouth down to a shared second place with but three wins apiece. In AAA stock car events, the situation was much the same. For instance, the 1954 season's results were, for the sixteen races: Hudson eight wins (and forty-three cars in the first five places);

Chrysler three, Packard three, Oldsmobile one, Nash one.

Hudson gained enormous free publicity and intensified the loyalty of its followers. Somebody in 1952 queried the value of Hudson's racing program in the columns of *Speed Age*. In the next few months, an avalanche of 3000 letters followed, three to one in Hudson's favor.

Nineteen fifty-two was the Hornet's peak year. In 1953 it remained champion but with twenty-two NASCAR victories, a decline of five. It was still champion in 1954, but there was again a drop of five, down to seventeen victories. Noting the decline, the press ran articles titled, "Is Hudson Slipping?" and "Has the Hornet Lost Its Sting?" Prophetic headlines, those. Meanwhile Hudson's track competitors had tackled their problems and improved their suspensions. The net result was that Hudson went from top to virtually the bottom in handling qualities among stock car entrants, with the inevitable eclipse of the name in racing results. From the time when a well-tuned Hornet struck fear into its foes, the tide had turned to the point where one Hudson fan commented bitterly, "NASCAR and AAA drivers ran out of the Hudson camp like rats out of a burning barn." During the good years, Hornet drivers had included Marshall Teague, Herb Thomas, Tim Flock, Frank Mundy and Lee Petty.

Hudson had been in trouble at home. The company had a bad year in 1951, when sales fell to 92,859 and a loss of $1,125,000 was recorded. In 1952, however, although sales dropped further to 79,117, there was a profit of $8,307,000. The company could actually make money on an annual production of 70,000 units; the 1951 losses were blamed on strikes and steel shortages and such. And Hudson had a new idea, which would turn out to be an expensive one.

After watching the early success of the Nash Rambler and Henry J for a couple of years, Barit announced in May 1952 that Hudson would build a "light" (2800-pound) car. It arrived in February of 1953 and was called the Jet. It used the step-down unit body frame on a 105-inch wheelbase and

*The figures tell the tale. The Hudson step-down carried production handsomely over the 140,000 mark both in 1948 and in 1949 when the Commodore Six, left, was produced. Then in 1951 came a car fantastic in the sport, but not quite so in the marketplace, and by 1953 when the Hornet, above, was built, production was down to the 70,000's, to plummet to the 30,000's by 1954 when the Jet Liner, center right, was trickling out of the factory. The last Hudson to be built in Detroit rolled off the assembly line on October 31st, 1954, and production transferred to Kenosha for a while longer, with the Hornet from 1957, below, built around the basic Nash body, with a "Hudson" grille which seemed strangely anything but that, Hudson's safety brake system and a hydramatic transmission. Few more than 4000 Hudsons were built that year before the end came on June 25th.*

had a scaled-down Hornet engine of up to 114 bhp, which gave it near-Hornet performance far superior to its compact competition. Like its bigger brothers, it offered overdrive or hydramatic transmission and Twin H Power—Hudson's dual carburetion answer to four-barrel V-8's using a manifold originally designed in 1944 for the first postwar six and which provided the Hornet with up to 170 bhp at 4000 rpm, a top speed of more than 100 mph and 0-60 in fourteen seconds. The Jet was almost as quick, and was possessed as well of good quality trim and workmanship—although that distinctive Hudson relic, the wet cork clutch, had been abandoned in favor of a dry plate. Unfortunately, the Jet had also abandoned the sleek, low line. It was boxy and chunky. This was a management decision, for the styling division had originally shown a prototype two inches lower—but were ordered to change it.

This, and Barit's procrastination in getting it on the market three years after the Rambler and Henry J, have been blamed for the commercial failure of the Jet, though it is questionable whether a volume "compact" market existed at the time anyway. Sales were dismal, and the last Jet came off the line on August 23rd, 1954—the shortest-lived production car in Hudson's history.

In 1953 Hudson had sold 78,183 cars and lost ten million dollars. An alarmed Barit asked George Mason, president of Nash-Kelvinator for an appointment. It would reopen discussions the two men had had seven years before, when Mason had suggested that a merger would have advantages of common tooling, pooled purchasing power and increased market penetration. Barit was not interested at the time. Hudson was making plenty of money. Now the shoe was on the other foot.

On June 16th, 1953, the two men worked out a merger plan over a two-hour lunch in the Book-Cadillac Hotel. Barit was not another Chapin, nor did he hold any aces, so it was hardly surprising that the agreement, as it developed, was nothing less than a death warrant for Hudson. Negotiation

*The Italia, below, on a Jet chassis, announced in late 1953 and priced at $4350.     The X-161, above, on a Hornet chassis,*

*designed in 1954 and slated for production in '57.*

and preparation continued through the winter of 1953-1954, with Packard and Studebaker being discussed as possible third parties. Those two companies, however, would decide to go it alone, together—as would Nash and Hudson.

On January 14th, 1954, both companies' directors approved the transaction, in which Hudson was absorbed into Nash-Kelvinator, and the latter's name was changed to American Motors. This was the largest merger—up to that time—in the entire history of the automobile industry, involving 30,000 employees and 100,000 dealers and distributors in a hundred countries. The two companies had built more than six million cars between them. The book value of the new enterprise was just under two hundred million dollars.

Breakeven point for the Hudson plant on the 1953 dollar was thiry-three cars an hour for a forty-hour week. This worked out to 65,000 cars a year. But new car registration for the first five months of 1954, at 13,373 units, found Hudson sixteenth in sales and ahead only of Willys, Kaiser and Henry J—all of which were headed for the cemetery. So was Hudson. During most of 1954, the factory worked no more than a two- or three-day week, and on October 31st, the last Hudson left the line at Jefferson Avenue. The last "real" Hudson, that is. Frank Spring had an advanced prototype ready that year for introduction as a 1957 model. It was the X-161, successor to the Hudson Italia, designed also by Spring and built in Italy by Carrozzeria Touring. Carrying a price tag of $4350, twenty-six Italias were built—the original idea had been limited production and a car that would win the Mexican Road Race—before the Nash merger ended that project. The X-161 fared even worse, not proceeding beyond the prototype stage.

Production did continue for another two seasons, however, with cars bearing the Hudson name and model designation and built on the Nash basic body at Kenosha, Wisconsin. They featured a grotesque grille, Hudson Jet and Hornet engines and Hudson's safety brake system. Hudson had switched to Borg-Warner transmissions, but in these models a return was made to hydramatic. In the largest model the new Packard V-8 was used. By now Hudson dealers were being badge-engineered back into the compact business with "Hudson Ramblers"—identical to the Nash Rambler but bearing Hudson's distinctive white triangle. The last Kenosha Hudson was built June 25th, 1957. American Motors had lost money from the start, even Nash becoming unprofitable, so it was decided to do away with both names—Hudson first—and stake all on Rambler, which became a marque in its own right for 1958.

Of Hudson's seven thousand employees, several hundred transferred to Kenosha, as well as four executives, including Barit, though he would depart in December 1956, angered at the decision to drop the Hudson name. Appointed head of the automotive division was Roy D. Chapin, Jr., son of the man who had started it all so many decades before. Ironically, the brilliant Frank Spring was killed in a Nash Metropolitan.

One reason for concentrating American Motors production in Wisconsin on Nash designs was the elaborate and costly multi-million dollar jig and fixture installations for step-down body production at Jefferson Avenue. Too massive to move, the whole setup was junked. In 1958 the building itself was demolished.

The long line of performance greats—Super Six, Essex Four, Special Six, Terraplane, Hornet—had come to an end. Success begun by the two C's—Chapin and Coffin—continued under the two B's—Barit and Baits—and terminated under the one A—American Motors.

There is a business saying: "All successes are the result of management, all failures are the result of mismanagement." For decades Hudson had survived under the wise management of the elder Chapin. Subsequent management was satisfactory in that it kept the company going and making profits for many more years, but the impression remains that it lacked the same sure touch, shrewdness and vision in crisis. And crisis came in the Fifties. Had the engineering department been authorized to produce a V-8 instead of just another six, had the body been restyled earlier, and had the Jet been introduced sooner or its original styling left alone by management, the story could conceivably have been different.

Hudson's loss was a particularly bitter one. Gone was the sense of spirited rakehell independence, the stamina and style, the personality of a marque that was quite individual. Above all else, Hudsons were interesting cars. Memorable cars. The tragedy is that they are only this, and no more, today.

A memory. ✠

# AND NOW ...FOR MY NEXT NUMBER

*When Tin Pan and Gasoline Alley Converged and the Air Was Filled With Motor Music*

The rolls of Tin Pan Alley's favorite sons do not include the name of Valentine J. Bonk. Yet seventy years ago, Mr. Bonk composed a tune which marked him as one of a special breed among American popular music composers. For, in the copyright registrations for 190_ it is duly recorded t_ Valentine J. Bonk wrote the "Automobile Ride March Two Step," one of the more than six hundred songs known to have been written about the automobile.

It is not recorded that Mr. Bonk reaped handsome profits for his efforts. Yet he had every reason to harbor high hopes. For in 1907, America had already fallen in love with the automobile and Tin Pan Alley was going along for the ride. Today it is difficult to realize how completely motoring had hypnotized turn-of-the-century America. Still, some measure of the nation's automobile obsession is revealed in the sheer volume and variety of motor music that was published. There were short songs and long songs. ("Hurrah for Henry That Builds the Famous Ford" had twenty-one verses!) There were comic songs and symphonic pieces. There were songs that warned of the dangers of motoring. There were tunes without words, such as "The Low Backed Car," whose authors tried to reproduce in music the rhythmic bounce and bump of an automobile ride. The greatest of all was, and still is, "In My Merry Oldsmobile," published by Vincent Bryan and Gus Edwards in 1905.

None of the romantic possibilities of the automobile escaped the lyric writers. Some were serious: "Down the road of life we'll fly, auto-mobubbling you and I." Some, like "Ray and His Little Chevrolet," told about "guys" who couldn't attract "dolls." Naturally, the Chevrolet proved the answer to all Ray's problems. Some songs gave good advice: "Beware of the Man in the Automobile." Some were inclined to be a bit too clinical: "On the Old Back Seat of the Henry Ford." Others extolled the automobile's powers as an aphrodisiac: In "Love in an Automobile," some sort of all-time record for fast work was set when a heartsick young swain's proposal was refused in the first verse only to be accepted eight bars later on the promise of an "automobile honeymoon."

The most bizarre group of motor-bred love songs put romance on a decidedly nuts-and-bolts level. In these ditties—"The Love Song of the Packard and the Ford" being a perfect example—a large car, male, inevitably fell in love with a lonely smaller car, female. Blushing from grease cups to tonneau, the romantic lead would begin his courtship by honking sweet nothings to his beloved. Usually, along about the second or third verse, the two would retire to some secluded garage. Shortly thereafter, their union would be blessed with a litter of sputtering coupes. In the case of the Packard-Ford, it was "twenty little Buicks . . . drinking gasoline."

The minstrels sang of incredible feats. An entire automobile race was recreated in "I Love My Horse and Wagon But Oh You Buick Car." Still, Byron Gay and C.R. Foster reached the pinnacle of puffery in "The Little Ford Rambled Right Along." Imagine a car that "don't need gasoline!" A car that one could "patch . . . up with a piece of string, spearmint gum or any old thing." And think of the convenience! "When she blows out a tire, just wrap it up with wire."

There were songs about the passing of the horse ("Whoa Dobbin"), the passing of the Flivver ("Poor Lizzie, What'll Become of You Now"), and the coming of the Model A ("Henry's Made a Lady Out of Lizzie"). Not surprisingly, the cars of Mr. Ford proved the most prolific subjects for wordsmiths. One of the best of comic songs was Bobby North's "He'd Have to Get Under, Get Out and Get Under." Picture the unhappy predicament of one Johnny O'Connor, young dandy about town who bought an automobile only to find that while "he was just dying to cuddle his queen . . . every minute, when he'd begin it, he'd have to get under, get out and get under . . ."

When the automobile became a bit more predictable, when it in effect became commonplace, the automobile song largely died. Tin Pan Alley and Gasoline Alley went their separate ways. True, an automobile song turns up every so often. "There's Nothing Like a Model T" was written for *High Button Shoes* just after World War II. During the war, a rash of "jeep" songs appeared. A souped-up Rambler broke into song a decade or so back, and a Cadillac crops up every once in a while now. But these tunes never capture the rollicking good humor of toe-tappers like "Mack's Swell Car Was a Maxwell" or "Rolls-Royce Papa." Perhaps the motorcar is too much with us now to serve as an inspiration for today's young songwriters. Too many seem to prefer a far cruder form of rocking and rolling than even the old Tin Lizzie so proudly provided. ✥

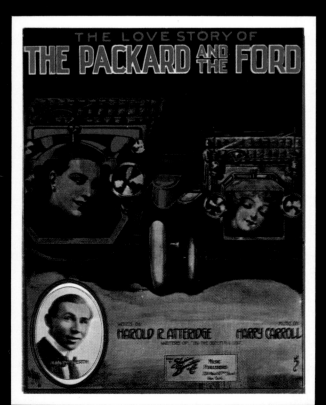

THE LOVE STORY OF THE PACKARD AND THE FORD

WORDS BY HAROLD R. ATTERIDGE    MUSIC BY HARRY CARROLL

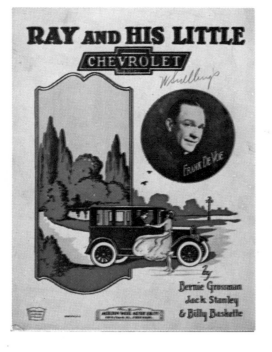

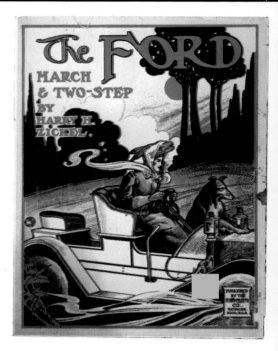

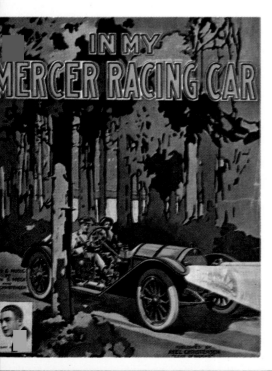

# TALES OF THE 300 SL

## *The Timeless Two-Seater With Doors That Raised or a Top That Neatly Furled*

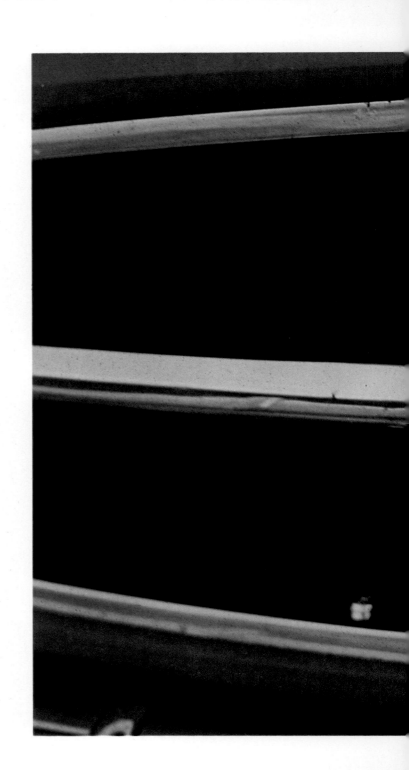

He didn't, alas, live to witness the fact, but the late Laurence Pomeroy, the automotive world's greatest technical writer of his day, and arguably of any day, committed an understatement with his 1961 assessment of the Mercedes-Benz 300 SL: "It is easy to imagine driving one with pleasure ten years hence, and is one of the few cars which is worthwhile owning as an end in itself." Today, some fifteen years later, possession of one of the many surviving 300 SL's represents heaven above seventh to owners. It will doubtlessly continue to do so for as long as their aging faculties and muscles remain a match for a car which, notwithstanding its all-around brilliance as a parcel of engineering, shows its least *sympatique* side to the meek and the weak.

Rob Walker, who will be well known to AQ readers as a long-time sponsor/manager of Grand Prix enterprises, and also as a reporter of the Formula One scene, doesn't have a meek or a weak fiber in his being. And he nutshells his opinion of this Mercedes-Benz in these thirteen words: "I think it must be the greatest road car that was ever built." Rob has personally owned four 300 SL's and isn't relying on anything as delusive as memory in passing this verdict. He still has one of the most potent examples at large in his native England. "I get great enjoyment from driving it and was using it only yesterday"—a yesterday late in 1974. (On a more

somber note, when Mike Hawthorn, Britain's first world champion, crashed to his untimely death in 1959, he was demonstrating that Walker and his current 300 SL couldn't stay in the slipstream of his, Mike's, Jaguar. They weren't racing each other—just having some fasting fun on a country road.)

This story's English authorship, and the fact that much of its constituent material comes from handpicked U.K. sources, inevitably gives it a British slant. But it's nonetheless widely acknowledged on this side of the Atlantic that the world is in a sense as much indebted to America as to Germany for the emergence of the 300 SL as a production entity. Daimler-Benz AG, after a sensationally successful 1952 season in international sports car racing with a team of factory-entered three-liter coupes bearing no visible resemblance to anything it then catalogued, didn't intend or want to market replicas or even close derivatives of these machines. It was an Austrian in America, Max Hoffman—he'd already founded a fortune of some considerable substance with the importation of foreign sports cars into the eastern United States—who assailed and finally overbore the Germans' include-us-out resolve.

The saleable, streetable, even comfortable result of the translation of the competition car into a stock line was, of course, the original Gullwing

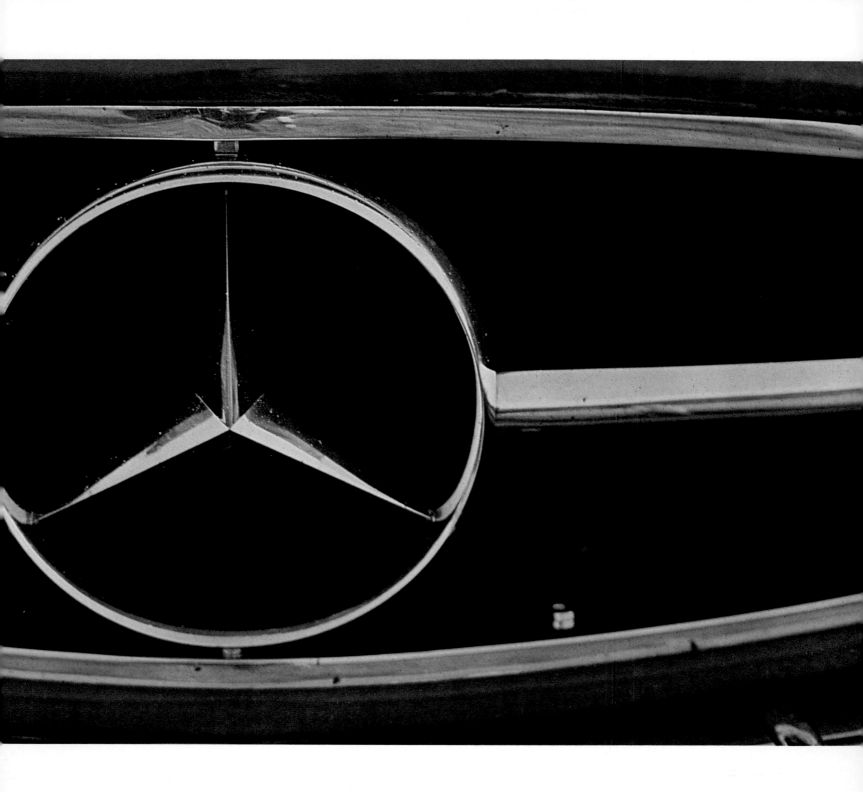

coupe, launched in 1954 and distinguished from its racing forebear (W.194) by the factory symbol W.198.

Again, it was pressures from American distributors and dealers which prompted the introduction of a roadster 300 SL in 1957. In California and other Stateside regions with a surfeit of sunshine and high year-round temperatures, a demand existed, these traders perceived, for a version of the SL with a roof that would furl. Many of their customers and prospects felt a bit enwombed in an unopenable two-seat body that, with its lowish ceiling and fairly marked tumblehome, admittedly was no loosebox.

So the Stuttgart firm obliged with what was variously called a convertible, a cabriolet, a roadster or a drophead in different parts of the world. At that, as we'll see later, the operation involved an ingenuity-taxing rethink of the chassis engineering, apart from the body metamorphosis.

But the joke was that when it was too late and the bell had irrevocably tolled for the Gullwing, a chorus of let-'er-live pleas broke from the selfsame Americans who'd figured they could sell fresh air and an unhindered skyview easier than the GW's non-optional encapsulement.

All cars, good and bad alike, have their detractors, and often it's those of the greatest all-around excellence and striking individuality that occasion the most dishing of dirt. This, in some quarters, was the way it went and

still goes with the 300 SL, and paeans of disparagement, much of it uninformed, have been spoken and written about, for instance, the Gullwing's behavior at or fringing its cornering limits. Most of this debative nonsense, one might think, is prompted less by actual experience and power of analysis than a desire to attract and impress an audience, as one analogously might by claiming that Da Vinci had a one-track mind or Raquel Welch is mammarily deficient.

For a start, competition statistics alone proved that if there'd been anything dangerously wrong with the Gullwing's handling, it could never have gone straight from the drawing board to the circuits, as it did in its W.194 form in 1952, and hit a four-out-of-five victory score in contention with the best of the international rest. ("Look on my works ye mighty, and despair," as Ozymandias diffidently put it.) Belittling a car that, in earliest infancy, placed one-two at Le Mans, same in the Carrera Panamericana; one-two-three in the Prix de Berne and the GT class of the Nürburgring's major sports car event; and second, only a mite over four and a half minutes behind the fiery Bracco's Ferrari, in the Mille Miglia, is unworthy even of lamebrains.

True, the heroes of these conquests, men of the caliber of Lang, Kling, Reiss, Helfrich and Niedermayer, and later such noted *Ausländerers* as 89

Britain's Moss, America's John Fitch and Paul O'Shea, and Belgium's Gendebien and Mairesse, weren't exactly timid tyros. But the fact remains that a "lethal" car—this was the standard adjective—doesn't consistently excel, even in expert hands, when facing opposition, human and mechanical, of the kind the Gullwing repeatedly met and downed.

This isn't to say, though, that it couldn't be faulted in point of handling; rather that, with its combination of 220 bhp (or 240 when later equipped with a sport camshaft, or more with the aid of other optional *objets de vertu*), 2600 pounds dry weight (or less, for cars with the extra-cost aluminum body) and swing axles at the back, it behooved you to get your discretion/valor ratio right in fast turns. You didn't need to be balsa footed, but indiscriminate booting of the throttle while under the influence of higher lateral $g$ admittedly could lead to trouble.

This sensitivity, proneness to power oversteer, was on the one hand abated to an extent that no one can exactly assess by the ZF limited slip differential the transmission package included; and on the other hand aggravated by what would nowadays be considered the poor tractive qualities of some of the tires on which Daimler-Benz rang changes. Dunlop Racing rubber was good insofar as it allowed the Gullwing's maximum speed—140 mph or upwards, depending on such variables as compression ratio, the cam specified, and overall gearing—to be used with confidence in a straight line on dry roads, but left much to be desired during power-on cornering in the wet.

Other available tires included cross-ply Continentals and Michelin X radials. The latter, which didn't become original equipment until the roadster's day, were excellent in all respects except the element of doubt about their vulnerability at the top of the mph scale; significantly, one would think, 300 SL's on X's carried a don't-exceed-120 warning on their speedometers.

But the Gullwing's safety and general roadability, or the lack of it, is very much a *quot homines tot sententiae* subject. Even among authorities of the best standing and most experience, there is some want of unanimity. Here is a paraphrase of evidence winkled out of the secretary of the British-based Mercedes-Benz Club, Gerald Coward, who owns two Gullwings, one

*The 300 SL, this Gullwing from 1955, one of 867 such cars produced during that year.*

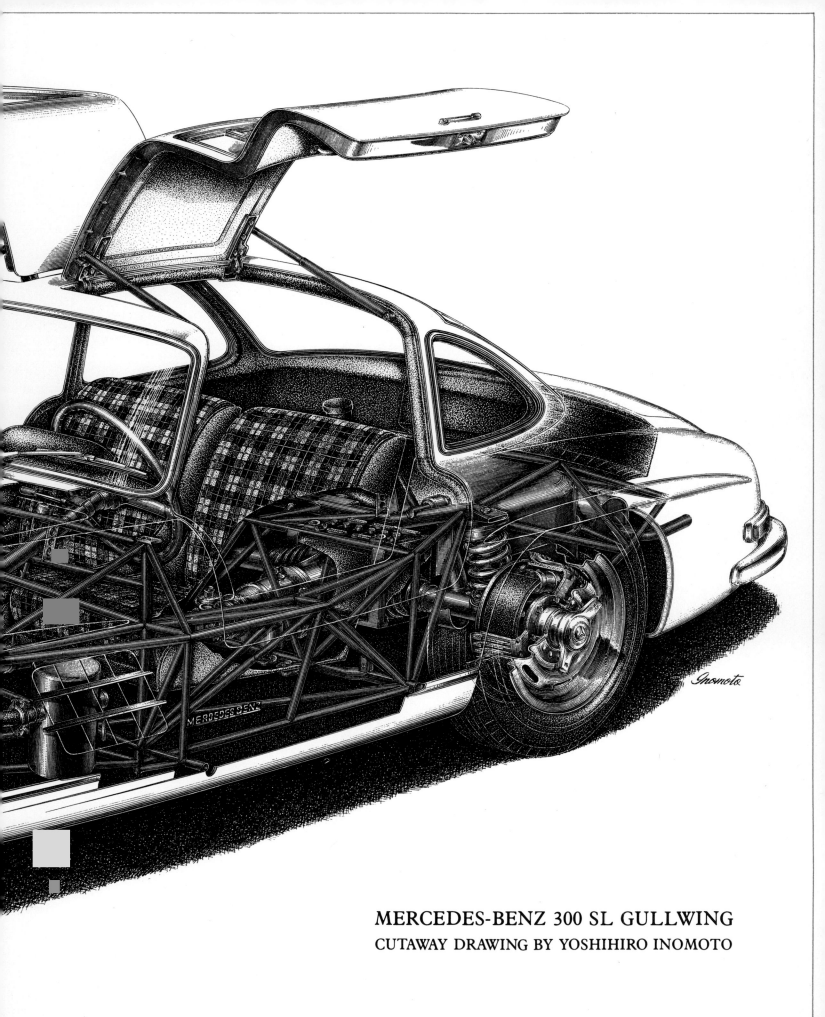

**MERCEDES-BENZ 300 SL GULLWING**
CUTAWAY DRAWING BY YOSHIHIRO INOMOTO

*Some 1400 Gullwings were sold in the four years before discontinuation of the model in 1957, its successor, above, being one of 554 roadsters produced that year.*

of them the relatively rare lightweight species with aluminum body, hot cam, centerlock wheels, et cetera: The GW, contrary to an oft quoted press opinion that the car is "somewhat lethal" is not. It doesn't suffer fools gladly but the exercise of reasonable respect for limitations that were a long way short of heinous when the design was laid down in '51, leaves little ground for gripes.

Recalling a wreck resulting from an attempt by some sort of lunatic to drive a rebuilt second-hand Gullwing from Stuttgart to his port of embarkation for England and home in two hours—the distance was 300 miles—Coward says: "This was the only documented crash I know about"—evidently he's excluding racing dramas—"and so far as I can tell it wasn't oversteer but a peculiarly located back axle that caused it. Fierce oversteer is, I think, only encountered in on-the-limit cornering." He too cites the number and diversity of the GW's successes in racing and other forms of competition (it won the horrendous Liège-Rome-Liège twice in a row, and other top ranking European rallies galore) as further disproof of that old "lethal" canard. Rudi Uhlenhaut, the great Daimler-Benz engineer who'd been mostly responsible for the 300 SL's design and development, is appropriately resolute. "The 300 SL did not have an abnormal accident record," he said recently and matter-of-factly.

It's never been denied, however, that the redesigned swing axle arrangement that came in on the roadster was a major improvement on the original; this, unlike the Gullwing's simple and classic dual-pivot sternworks, gave the half shafts a single and common articulation point,

located well below a line drawn through the two hub centers. The reworked layout, resurrected from the pre-World War II 540K—with its two-pivot swing axle and transverse spring—reduced roll stiffness and helped minimize oversteer. The staple suspension media, viz, dual coil springs, slightly inclined inwards at the top, were supplemented by a horizontal compensation spring, also a coil and set east/west, above the final drive unit, which did not compress under cornering forces but only when both road wheels took "bound" shocks at the same time.

There is a story that Stirling Moss once asked Rudi Uhlenhaut if it would be possible to splice the roadster-type back axle and suspension into a Gullwing. Certainly, replied Uhlenhaut, all you need do is take two chassis, one ex-GW, the other ex-roadster, cut them in half and join up the unakin bits in the middle. "Moss didn't bother," Coward says, but he has an idea that Paul O'Shea at one time campaigned a GW with a roadster pattern rear end.

O'Shea and his 300 SL's spread havoc of course in the relevant branch of American speedwork during the mid to latish Fifties, winning the U.S. Sports Car Championship three seasons in a row, 1955 through '57.

But internationally rather than just nationally, another American, John Fitch, has the more secure and honored place in the memories of students of motor sport. Co-driving with Hans Gessel in the Mille Miglia of 1955, the year of the legendary Moss/Jenkinson victory with the 300 SLR, Fitch achieved his finest hour, or to be absolutely precise, his finest 11 hours 29 minutes 21 seconds, by homing his privately owned Gullwing in fifth place,

*Among the 250 roadsters produced during 1961 is the car pictured on the pages following. Production ended in 1963, with a total of 1858 roadsters built in seven years.*

first in the GT category.

In everyday street service, you could expect high standards of reliability and durability from a car that differed in few pertinent respects from the W.194, with its Homeric record in races of the length, duration and rigor of the Carrera Panamericana and the Mille Miglia, and you wouldn't be disappointed. These qualities, plus ease of maintenance that was and still is unmatched by most cars of greatly inferior performance, are among the 300 SL's chiefest charms; and go far to explain why, in Britain and in the U.S. too, a man once bitten by the 300 SL bug will often expose himself to further bites anon buying a second or even a third copy.

Rightly credited with knowing more about 300 SL's, in practical terms, than any other Englishman, is Tom Johnson, longtime foreman of the sub-department of the service department of Mercedes-Benz (Great Britain) Ltd., London, which always has and still does look after these cars. Contrary to expectation, Tom is candid about any faults of the SL and doesn't bore you with unrelieved encomia. But it somehow symbolizes his love of the species, notwithstanding its one or two weaknesses, that the one pinup adorning his workshop walls portrays a Gullwing with its wings rampant, rather than the traditional dollybird *in puris naturalibus*.

On the debit side, he reminds you that, particularly when new, the engine was prone to progressive lacing of its oil by gasoline supplied by the Bosch direct fuel injection system. This, unless you changed the oil at higher than average frequencies, resulted in fast bore wear, piston slap and ring breakups. On the other hand, he's known cases—where the lube was

replaced regularly and often—of engines remaining in the frame undisturbed for 130,000 miles. Out of those which his department maintains, and this includes the great majority of the surviving imports, few have less than 80,000 miles on the meter, many a lot more.

The fuel dilution problem naturally has been aggravated by the low speed limits latterly enforced in most countries, Britain among them; seldom subjected to the rpm and loadings for which they were designed, engines don't get hot enough to burn infiltrating fuel out of their oil. For this, Johnson's antidote is to blank off the oil coolers fitted by the factory and make a one-third cutback on the amount of lube in circulation. (Unlike the racing W.194, the W.198 has a dry sump and a huge oil tank standing on its own grounds.)

Daimler-Benz was a bit slow off the mark in adopting disc brakes on the 300 SL (they didn't appear until 1961), and the GW's drum system, contrary to appearances, was in some respects disappointing—"the car's real weakness," as Tom Johnson says without scruple. "If you used the brakes once, hard, at 120, you had to remember to let them cool off." Also, their water exclusion qualities were poor. On the other hand, as you'd expect considering the total rubbing area was a colossal 285 square inches, the rate of lining wear was truly glacial; Coward speaks of one helping of Ferodo lasting around 200,000 miles, in spite of the high pressures exertable through dual leading shoes at the front.

How quiet, or how noisy if you like, is a 300 SL? In terms of decibel output from the pipe at the back, it's creditably quiet up to around 120 mph 95 and corresponding speeds in the indirect gears, but from there on up you assuredly don't have to be audiovoyant to catch its throaty, exuberant bellow . . . "accidents terrible of dire combustion," as Shakespeare puts it. The engine itself, either with or without the hot cam, is remarkably quiet mechanically as long as it isn't suffering from piston slap induced by fuel contaminated oil; but standard Gullwing gearboxes emit a loudish whine resulting from the coarse cut of their gear teeth. The roadster's were finer pitched and Johnson has carried out some roadster-to-GW gearbox conversions to remedy this defect.

He's only ever known three cases of actual gearbox crackup and all these were caused by the owners' habit of engaging reverse while rolling forward at say 10 mph. The sole instance known to Tom of a 300 SL breaking a back axle half shaft occurred while a car was undergoing a road test by a technical magazine writer of international renown; Lang couldn't do it, or Moss, or Mairesse, or Fitch, or any other of those lead-footed Jehus, but this scribbler could, and afterwards neither donned sackcloth nor showered himself in ashes.

In the W.198's infancy, quite a proportion of the cars sold in Britain became the playthings of a rich, plethoric and mostly middle-aged incognoscenti, typically inhabiting the environs of London's Berkeley Square and concerned more with wowing the female populace than getting its boots into the Boschware. Because its members wouldn't have recognized a spark plug if they saw one, it isn't surprising that they were often in trouble with flameouts, due to using hard plugs for soft duty. The Mercedes engine was and is, indeed, sensitive to nuances in this department, but it seldom wets, soots or burns plugs that are wisely chosen from the wide range the makers and concessionaires offer and advise upon. Now that 300 SL's are, with the passing of time, advancing towards the dread day when they'll be rarer than Bugatti pushrods, appreciative connoisseurs predominate heavily among owners, and the consumption of plugs is low.

Soup-to-nuts descriptions of the 300 SL, nit-picking listings and analyses of what it won and where and when, add up to an oft-told tale that we've no intention of retelling here. The broad outline of the story is, however, indispensable to a proper understanding of the car's unique charm. And that we'll provide.

The W.194 sports-racing cars, which won their spurs in 1952, were designed by and under the guidance of Dipl. Ing. Rudolf Uhlenhaut and his staff. There had been no intention—as we've seen—of going into production with anything even remotely resembling the W.194, which was an all-new concept with the exception of its triple Solex carbureted six-cylinder engine, measuring 85 by 88 mm for 2996 cc. This had first seen the light of day in 1951, set vertically in the chassis of the then new Type 300, which had been given birth by Fritz Nallinger; a full passenger body of relatively mild character, it had 115 bhp on tap at 4600 rpm. The following year, the same powerplant, upped to 150 hp at 5100 rpm, was adopted for another Stuttgart deb, the 300 S, a sports tourer notable more for refinement than ferocity of performance.

Corporate intentions notwithstanding, a cabal headed by Rudi Uhlenhaut did contrive to have a single car, recognizably based on the racing W.194 but extensively restyled, modified in important engineering respects and fully equipped for street use, built and exhibited at the New

York automobile show early in 1954. There it created an overnight sensation, which inspired the earlier mentioned Max Hoffman to pressure the makers into listing it for sale. This, with some misgivings, they did, and the Gullwing 300 SL was born.

In production form, the SL used a version of the 300 engine with power and torque factors that not only surpassed the 300 S's by miles but also those of the Le Mans, Carrera Panamericana and Prix de Berne winners. (Horsepower rose from the carbureted W.194's 185 bhp at 5200 to, eventually, no less than 240 at 6100, with a torque rating of 217 lb/ft on the lower of the optional compression ratios: 8.55 to one. The higher was 9.1 to one, which hoisted the power to 250 bhp.) Main sources of the extra soup were the Bosch fuel injection, a raise in compression ratio, a new cam and improvements to porting, combustion chamber space, etc. The sohc unit, which in the W.194 application had been sloped 40 degrees to the left, took a further 10 degrees of tilt in the W.198 blueprint. On both cars, it was bodily offset two inches to the right to maintain east/west equilibrium and allow for a low hood line. Features common to all generations of this powerplant were seven main bearings and drive by single-stage chain to the camshaft.

Cylinder block and head material was iron. Largely accounting for an unvarying smoothness throughout an rpm range for which the engine had never been designed was a massive vibration damper mounted on the nose of the crankshaft.

The chassis, almost wickerlike in the multiplicity of its slender chrome-molybdenum tubes, all of them straight, was a complete breakaway from previous Daimler-Benz practice. The front half was pyramidlike, and the

beam formed by the two-level flanking members unprecedentedly deep. This fact rationed styling overlord Karl Wilfert on side panel area available for door apertures, and Uhlenhaut came up with the gullwing inspiration. Conventional doors would necessarily have been so shallow that if you'd succeeded in toothpasting a driver and/or passenger in, he/they would have had to be winched out. The Gullwing frame, bare, weighed 181 pounds—lighter than it looked.

The front wheels were sprung on coils in conjunction with double wishbones, telescopic shocks and an antisway bar. Steering was of recirculating ball type, provedly efficient inasmuch as, although requiring less than two turns of the wheel for lock to lock sweeps, it never reminded you of its high gearing except maybe when inching into a tight parking slot. Transmission essentials were a single dry plate clutch, an all-synchro four-speed gearbox in unit with the engine and with rather wider ratios (it incidentally had its own oil pump), an open propshaft and the limited slip diff and swinging half shafts already mentioned.

Although the high sills somehow had the effect of making the body interior as cozy as a nesting box, it wasn't short on *Lebensraum* for two well knit occupants. How much lighter than standard the lightweight Gullwings were (some say as much as 315 pounds) has never been exactly established. Other features of this coveted subspecies were the high compression head, more brutal cam, special competition rear springs and centerlock wheels. The highest speed ever authoritatively clocked by either type of 300 SL was, one suspects, 153-odd mph for a two-way mile by Don Ricardo, a Californian, at Bonneville, where the thin atmosphere resulting from the Flats' high altitude would have purloined a few bhp. Acceleration figures naturally varied according to which of three optional overall gearings was specified, but a steel Gullwinger in good shape could be expected to do the standing quarter mile in around sixteen seconds.

The roadster, whose ragtop body was of course incompatible with gullwing treatment, had to have lower sills, which in turn dictated a redesign of the chassis frame. The reduction made in this structure's depth amidships diminished its stiffness to some degree—despite the use of stronger frame tubes—though, in driving, one was never conscious of, or heard complaints about, any jello effects. It must still have been a lot more rigid than most sports car chassis.

The fiercer of the two cams was regular on the roadster, late examples also had aluminum engine blocks and heads. The term Grand Touring in its original and rightful sense was never more aptly applied than to the 300 SL, whose big gas tank (34 U.S. gallons) gave it a between-fillups range of better than 600 miles.

Quests for performance bonuses, on the part of the makers and sundry owners both, were fairly numerous. For a start, Daimler-Benz had experimented with a blower on one of the 1952 racers, distinguishing it with a type number of its own, W.197. Tryouts *mit kompressor* during Le Mans practice proved the thing abortive and it was dropped. Some years later, at least one British Gullwing fancier tried a supercharger setup (more "agricultural" than the factory's camshaft driven installation) but came to the same conclusion. In the Panamericana dice, the W.194's were run with engines overbored to 3.6 liters, and the cylinder head of Rob Walker's current GW has received porting and combustion chamber treatment by Westlake.

If you take comfort to include freedom from fatigue over long distances at very high average speeds, then the Gullwing is a comfortable car even by modern criteria. You don't stay comfortable long if, as the GW's detractors claim, you are all the time fighting the bedclothes on turns. Complimentarily, the 300 SL in both its forms is a labor saving device by virtue of its outstanding flexibility. This, on paper, would seem to be contradicted by the fact that the standard engine develops maximum torque at a turnover as high as 4800 rpm; but nonetheless you can floor the throttle in top gear at a mere 10 mph, whereon the power peters in, plenteously and instanter . . . not a gulp or a hesitation, just a smooth clean zoom to something likely between 130 and 140.

Inconsequentially, the 300 SL always brings to mind a remark by the late Mike Todd to his wife, Elizabeth Taylor, when for some reason they were taking refreshment in a very unpretentious London teahouse: "Why, it's just like we was ordinary people." Driving an SL, or savoring bystanders' envy as with studied deliberation you darken its doors, gullwing or otherwise, you're never in any danger of feeling like you was ordinary people. ✿

# A LITTLE ON THE BIDDLE FROM PHILADELPHIA

It's really a shame about the Biddle. It couldn't do much of anything impressively well, except get you where you were going—and look awfully nice doing it. It was simply an ordinary car with, for its age, often extraordinary good looks—and it died, as one might expect was inevitable. Melancholia about such an automobile, whose death certificate was signed more than a half century ago, might seem silly to some, but it's not really. For anyone who has spent any time reliving the rise and fall of the myriad marques that exited the automotive scene soon after the close of World War I, there is a bittersweet feeling not easily masked. There were a lot of cars like the Biddle, cars whose virtues were not overwhelming, whose commercial pretensions were modest—none of them made it . . . for very long. And it's obvious why. One is left only with the wish that they be remembered.

The Biddle was good idea—a medium-sized car, "individually made and thoroughly refined," for those discriminating drivers who cared not for the larger, more imposing varieties dominating the market. And then there was the name. Though it had appeared before on an automobile (in 1902, on a vehicle built in Knoxville, Tennessee) and a truck (the Biddle-Murray, produced from 1906 to 1908 in Oak Park, Illinois), and graced a prominent coachbuilding concern (the legendary Biddle & Smart, which coursed its elegant way in Amesbury, Massachusetts from 1870 to 1930), the Biddle we're talking about was produced in Philadelphia, where the name carried as much clout as Cabot in Boston.

Conceivably, the name alone might have seemed sufficient authority to introduce the company, for one is hard put to discover contemporary references to such details as the officers behind it. There *was* a Biddle, of course, though not one who made *Who's Who* as an explorer, lecturer, diplomat, major general, or for devoting himself to "business, literature and philanthropic pursuits." Our Biddle was R. Ralston Biddle. And, if not as luminary a member as some of his brethren, he could indeed claim ties to the family begun by William and Sarah Kempe Biddle with their arrival on these shores in 1681, R. Ralston being listed (Owen Biddle branch) among the approximately five hundred descendants in a booklet privately published in 1931 in celebration of the family's first two hundred and fifty years in America. If other Biddles were involved in the enterprise, their names do not survive in the records of the company. Its president, so said *MoToR* magazine in 1917, was one A. Mc. I. Maris, whose background remains as curiously obscure as his name. The Biddle designer, Charles Fry, made news in 1917, though peripherally because of his handicap; he had but one arm and was the first man so disabled to be allowed to enlist in the Naval Reserve. His duties were as an automobile instructor, his qualifications must have been high.

At Biddle, Mr. Fry lorded over the components, built to company specs, which found their way to the factory. The Biddle was an assembled car, with scarcely a part it could call its own. (Automobiles so put together are frequently looked down upon, then as now, unfairly.) Its engine was a Buda four (with 3 3/4 by 5 1/8 bore/stroke dimensions, for 226.4 cubic inches, an SAE horsepower rating of 22.5, horsepower developed being 48 at 1700 rpm on brake test); ignition by Dixie high tension magneto, starting and lighting by Westinghouse; carburetion by Zenith (replacing the bothersome Biddle-built "atomizer" on the earliest models); dry plate disc clutch and four-speed transmission by Warner; Hotchkiss drive; three-quarter floating Salisbury rear axle, inverted Elliott front; semi-elliptic front and three-quarter rear "W. and H. Rowland" springs; Warner worm and gear steering; gasoline feed via Stewart Vacuum; wire wheels by Rudge-Whitworth, safety tires by Goodrich; Mercedes-type internal expanding brakes and a *very* Mercedes-type vee radiator by English and Mersick. All this was solidly put together in a chassis frame of pressed steel channel, with a wheelbase measuring 120 inches in early production, 121 by 1917.

Interestingly, the Biddle Motor Car Company, Inc. did not at first envision the "carriage trade" idea of its enterprise—or didn't say so in any case. The announcement of the firm's entrance into the automotive field—this arriving in mid-October of 1915—noted only the two types of cars then available, a tourer at eighteen hundred dollars and a roadster at seventeen, as well as a town car and "another fashioned with foreign lines, with a Duesenberg motor" said to be in the works and slated to sell at an even three thousand dollars. By March of the following year, however, after the Philadelphia automobile show, the Biddle's model designation changed from C to D, prices rose to $1800 for roadster, $1850 for the close-coupled and $1865 for the standard touring—and $1650 for the chassis, upon which Biddle was more than willing to provide just about any type body a client might desire.

Even the standard Biddles were strikingly individual, so the press duly noted, "as compared with the average run of bodies offered . . . a marked departure from anything even approaching conventionality." (One departure, the curious angle fenders of 1915, were thankfully discarded after 1916.) By 1917 Biddle declared that only the aluminum-bodied open tourer was a "stock" design, and it offered "large latitude for choice in top, fender design and color." Amusingly, Biddle also said that when this car had been introduced two years previous, its use of a dual cowl was unusual, but wide adoption of the style since had "robbed it of distinction." So they summarily took it off the car!

In 1918 Biddle admitted that one of its roadsters and also the collapsible town car were also pretty much standard designs, though with agreeable custom touches available. Any other car ordered from Biddle was a special, expressing "exceptional taste and novelty." And so they were. Built for Biddle to Biddle designs by such diverse firms as the Keystone Body Company and the French Motor Body Company, with Biddle even willing to make "certain changes in the chassis if need requires it," these coachbuilt cars were certainly eyecatching: a Park Phaeton with canework sides, patent leather fenders and *two* folding tops, a special victoria tourer with out-

*Being a Narrative on the Hazards
of Venturing into
Business With a Good Idea
and a Good Name
But Not Much Good Sense*

side exhausts of polished brass, a brougham with a disappearing windshield for tonneau passengers which, when raised completely, commodiously enclosed the rear section (chauffeurs did have a tough time of it in those days).

And when the people at Biddle said they'd build a car for anyone, they meant it. One day a young Maryland lass with a penchant for sporting cars (and a banker father who could indulge it) visited the Biddle offices. Mercers and Stutzes were always going wrong, she said; she wanted a Biddle, and set forth her ideas for a racy raceabout, with pointed headlamps to match the pointed radiator, "crab's eye" sidelamps, separate fenders and running boards, absolutely no top (she was a true believer) and a canary yellow color that would outshame the bird. Miss Miriam Warren Hubbard may have been the first woman to style a motorcar. Biddle built it for her.

The no-top dictate of Miss Hubbard's, incidentally, was no mere feminine caprice. If anything, it was an open rebellion. "In our family car [and these had included a Chalmers, a Lozier and one of the early Packard Twin Sixes]," she would later write, "my father always wanted the top up, and I always wanted it down, so in my own car that question was to be forever settled." But no foolish young thing, she. She ordered rainwear, in matching yellow of course—a slicker and a hat the brim of which fell to her shoulders in the back, so whatever fell from the skies slid out of harm's way. It is not on record that Biddle cottoned to the idea of providing car and raiment to match—happy to oblige Miss Hubbard as the company was—but Biddle did adopt another of the young lady's ideas in its production line. She had specified wire wheels—"still fairly new in America"—and these forthwith appeared on most open cars built by the company, the wooden-spoked variety remaining an alternate for the traditionalists among the Biddle clientele.

The company was trying hard. In its instruction manual, it took pains to point out that "Many excellent motor cars are to be found today, but the Biddle can scarcely be found to compete or compare directly with any other make. If the Biddle conception were but to add another car to an already overcrowded market, neither the purchaser nor the maker would benefit to an unusual degree." The Biddle people were sure they were different—and therein was the key to success.

It seemed likely to be thus, for a while. The company had in a short time gathered unto itself an image of snap and trim in sporting cars, of long sweeps of line and elegance in the more formal variations. Meanwhile, of course, prices were going up: from $2200 to $3900 in 1917, $2600 to $4100 in 1918. And higher still for the very special custom jobs—the Biddle chassis alone cost $2095 in 1918. (Doubtless the price increases were due to the exigencies of production expense and operation as the company became more familiar with the wherefore and wherewithal of the automobile business, though perhaps the desire for a little added exclusivity might have been a factor as well.)

It was 1918, too, during which the Biddle Model K joined the newly designated Model H in the company lineup. The Model H differed from its predecessor only in the substitution of Gray & Davis starting and lighting equipment and Eisemann magneto ignition for the previous Westinghouse and Dixie units. But the Model K boasted the 350.5-cubic-inch walking-beam Duesenberg four-cylinder engine (the rights to which the brothers Duesenberg would forthwith sell to the Rochester Motor Company while they turned their attention to a straight-eight). The Duesenberg engine—which, as we've seen, had been announced for the Biddle in 1915—delivered around a hundred horsepower in race tune. Though it was sedated somewhat for Biddle use, it had to help the car's performance, which had never previously been much to talk about.

Not that there would be much boasting now. The suppliers to the Biddle Motor Car Company frequently used the car in their own advertisements, predicating this on the fact that the Biddle was, as Gray & Davis put it for example, "distinctly a class car." Duesenberg Motors did show a Biddle tourer in one of its ads, photographed perkily parked at the Mineola (Long

Island) air field with jaunty aviator types checking out the skies above, but again the performance angle was decidedly low key. And when the Biddle people tried a similar approach themselves, the result was just a bit amiss. "AUTOMOBILES • BIDDLE • SPEED" read the headline, but the caligraphy belied the intention. And the copy was anything but racy, with an embarrassing faux pas that might cause one to wonder if Biddle was absolutely sure of just what it was offering. "The thrills of speed with perfect control are his who drives the Biddle car," it said, "equipped with Deusenberg (sic) Motor. Security and comfort are also his—for the character of construction assures them." The illustration was distinctly country club, complete with caddie.

No, Biddles were not performance automobiles. Though a Rochester-Duesenberg-engined Roamer would establish the passenger-car land speed record of 105 mph in 1921, a Biddle's nose would have bled with but the thought of a speed so high. There is no evidence that a Biddle ever won anything, or even tried. Racing was perhaps deemed a bit too vulgar. Indeed, from advertisements, it was difficult to discern that Biddles moved at all; they were generally shown standing, beautifully, still.

For the real sports, of course, there was always the Mercer or Stutz, and most, unlike Miss Hubbard, found one of them entirely suited to their purposes—and at a price that compared favorably with the sporting bodied Biddle. The Biddle couldn't keep up with either, on the road or in the marketplace. And the more formal Biddles had by now crept up in price

toward the rarefied realms of the Packard, the Pierce-Arrow, the Peerless. And the motorcar from Philadelphia was, in no way, to be measured against the vaunted Three P's.

Not that all this bothered the Biddle people terribly, they were quite satisfied with a comparatively small production, and in fact developed a rather cavalier attitude toward the entire matter. The Biddle company wasn't listed in the handbook prepared by the industry's National Automobile Chamber of Commerce, nor did it ever make *The Horseless Age*'s "Leading Cars for the Past Six Years" (whose likes included the Detroiter, the Elcar, the Glide, the Inter State, the Pilot, the Ross and the Westcott). The company never bothered notifying most of the leading automotive journals of the availability of the Model K, and the serial number request sheet the promotion department returned to *Motor Age* in 1919 indicated that the firm found such minutiae as keeping records of engine and chassis numbers somewhat a bore and most of the time simply didn't bother. From what figures are available, it would appear that Biddle production hovered around the hundred mark in 1915 and 1916, and rose to not more than five hundred cars each—if that—in the three succeeding years.

Biddle brochures noted New York, Providence, Boston, Pittsburgh, Detroit, Chicago and Cleveland as sites of company agencies, and 44 Whitehall Street in Manhattan as the "Foreign Trade Department"—the latter looked impressive on paper, but it must have been the slowest office

in Gotham; if any Biddles went overseas, no one, it would appear, knew about it.

The Biddle company did make a move itself, however, in 1919—from Germantown, Sedgley and Allegheny Avenues in Philadelphia to Fifth Avenue and 142nd Street in New York City. Exactly why the move was made seems to have eluded history, although it was apparent by this time that the Biddle idea of low key survival in the automobile industry wasn't working in the reality of postwar America. Conceivably the change of factory location might have been step number one to a brighter future. But the Biddle people ran out of working capital. Unfortunately, step number two was selling the company.

This happened May 18th, 1920. The syndicate formed for the purchase was headed by Stephen N. Bourne, formerly secretary of the United States Shipping Board, Emergency Fleet Corporation, and included Walter H. Lippincott, Myers Fitler, hat manufacturer G.H. Stetson, Wilson Potter, Van Horne Ely and H.C. Maibohm. Of the lot, Mr. Maibohm was the most important. As president of Maibohm Motors Company, he had experience in the automobile industry, envisioned for Biddle a plant expansion to provide for an annual production of 1200 cars, and in mid-June sent a letter to his own company's stockholders giving them the glorious opportunity of subscribing to some of the Biddle stock.

The Maibohm automobile company was an outgrowth of the Maibohm Wagon Company of Racine, Wisconsin, which had been plying its trade for

*It looked faster than it actually was, that was certain, though to devotees of the marque, appearances perhaps were as important as reality in their automotive purchases.*

thirty years previous to 1916, during which year H.C. Maibohm—who had put an automotive foot in first at Locomobile—announced a $595 Maibohm roadster and a 2000-car-per-year production schedule. Early in 1917, he offered Maibohm stock to the public, by summer incorporated the company in Maine with a capital stock of $500,000, and by fall had added a six-cylinder model in four body styles to the line. Despite a factory fire resulting in heavy losses in 1918 and the subsequent hubbub in searching for a new plant site, Maibohm was able to declare a six-percent annual dividend and a surplus of some $32,811 on March 29th, 1919, and less than a month later proudly proclaim that the company was already beginning to occupy its new and commodious $175,000 plant on seventeen acres in sunny Sandusky, Ohio.

It appeared that Biddle might be in good company. But there had been a monkey wrench thrown somewhere, and it seems that Mr. Maibohm tossed it. On July 21st, 1920, two months after the syndicate took over, three of its members—Messrs. Lippincott, Fitler and Ely—filed an involuntary petition in bankruptcy against Biddle. Mr. Maibohm, you see, had taken upon himself the task of providing the Biddle company with $189,000 in cash and three thousand shares of the Maibohm company stock—although, as *Automotive Industries* pointed out, "it was not the understanding that the cash was to be his own." Parting with the shares of Maibohm stock had been no problem, of course, but coming up with the

cash obviously had. Therewith was the making of a problem.

Meanwhile, forty Biddle cars languished, for which orders were already on hand, but alas two parts were missing for final assembly—and there was no money to do anything about it. Maibohm's associates-*cum*-creditors now wanted their loans back, subscriptions from Maibohm stockholders were returned, and by January of 1921 it was announced that Biddle assets were $172,063, liabilities $333,563, with a host of new creditors at the company door, including the United States Government for sales taxes on automobiles and parts.

That the Biddle motorcar enjoyed an excellent reputation, despite its commercial duress, is best attested to by the fact that the car didn't die right then. The company did, to be sure, but defunct as it was, there was another group ready to give the Biddle another try. The plant equipment, the two score unassembled cars and whatever other assets remained were purchased in April by F.L. Crane, Ralph R. Owen and R.W. Stanley, who would serve as president, vice-president and general manager respectively of the firm, now renamed Biddle-Crane Motor Car Company. Mr. Stanley had been with Biddle since the old days, and he together with his new associates decided the original Biddle philosophy had been right after all. As *Automotive Industries* reported, "Operations will be continued with practically the same models as those previously built by the Biddle company and it is the purpose of the new owners to turn out a small, high class

*The four-cylinder Rochester-Duesenberg engine powered this Model B1 Roadster which was produced by the Biddle Motor Car Company during 1920.*

job which will sell at around $3,400. No attempt will be made to reach quantity production and if 200 cars are built this year the new owners will be well satisfied."

The new Biddle brochure reflected all this, with its conservative approach to engineering and performance (a carefully worded rationale for the continuation of the four-cylinder engine as preferable to the "cumbersome multi-cylinder" variations with their added weight and maintenance problems), an emphasis on appearance and workmanship ("A distinctive charm invests Biddle Motor Cars. Beneath graceful lines and pleasing proportions, they clearly show evidence of intrinsic worth"), the appeal to the discriminating, if snobbish, buyer ("To have a list of Biddle owners would be like having a Blue Book of the whole country.") Even the mistakes were in the old Biddle tradition: The raciest Biddle of 1921 was named after America's birthplace of speed—it was called the "Ormonde Speedway Special."

Biddles by now bore the B model designation, as they had since late 1919; bodies came from Rauch and Lang in Cleveland; prices ranged from $3475 to $4350; and the company was already in trouble. In February of 1922, Biddle-Crane tried slashing prices—a common ploy—to the $2950 to $3950 range. Biddle-Crane didn't last out the year.

As for the Maibohm outfit, 1922 was the year of its undoing as well, the moribund company being taken over in July by the newly incorporated Arrow Motors (headed by A.C. Burch, formerly of the Signal and Clydesdale truck manufacturing companies). By August, Arrow Motors changed its name to Courier Motors—and a new line of six-cylinder Courier motorcars was presented at automobile shows for 1923. They lasted a year.

The demise of an automobile in those days, of course, was hardly noteworthy—it happened so frequently that it often went unreported, unless the bankruptcy proceedings held some particular interest. From the heady optimism of its beginnings, when the good news flowed forth in torrents, a company was only of interest so long as it survived. And so many died. Some were sadder than others. The Biddle is one of those. In one of the rare obituaries published on the car, a prominent trade magazine of the period said only, and rather offhandedly, "The Biddle car enjoyed an excellent reputation and the failure of the company was considered unfortunate."

Unfortunate? Yes, to say the least. In an age when pleasing proportions, grace of line, restraint and good taste were scarcely attributes one could apply to many automobiles on the road, the Biddle was an aesthetic oasis, and built in quantities sufficiently small to lend to it a distinction peculiarly its own. But that wasn't enough. It didn't survive then. It certainly wouldn't now. Perhaps it should be remembered as a car that deserved to live . . . but couldn't.✥

# THE HEROIC AGE

*Six Days From Those Raucous Years
When America First Went Racing,
Painted by Peter Helck*

*Saturday, October 6th, 1906: The Vanderbilt Cup*

*Saturday, October 24th, 1908: The Vanderbilt Cup*

"Chain your dogs and lock up your fowls."

Road racing had come to America—courtesy of a young man who was, as one unctuous reporter explained, "a bully good democratic fellow" not "to blame for being a society swell and a millionaire." He was William K. Vanderbilt, Jr. Whether his aim was to prod American manufacturers to engineering and trade advances through motor sport, as was the European experience, or simply to indulge his sportsman's love of motoring competition—whatever his motivation, it mattered little. What resulted was wild, reckless, charged with excitement, rife with pathos, studded with farce—what resulted were the classic Vanderbilt Cup contests.

The first was in 1904. It was the beginning of an era like no other in American speed sport. The monstrous beauty of those giant racers, machines of heroic proportion bearing with strain the enormous burden of their huge engines, set in chassis frequently riddled to conform to weight requirements, riding on wheels that were wooden, tires that were troublesome and with brakes that were at best haphazard. The men who dared to drive them—intrepid young paladins comprised of equal parts bravery and bravura, aware always, as one of the greatest, Ralph Mulford, reminisced years later, "that there would be little more between us and an accident than the clothes we wore."

And the roads. The first was a 30.24-mile stretch winding through Long Island's Nassau County, with one short leg in the Queens borough of New York City. Its condition was, as driver Wilhelm Werner reported, "mauvais," translated by the *Motor Age* correspondent as "French for rotten." The new course for 1905 was shaped something like a butcher's cleaver and was just about as potentially lethal—one section along the Glen Cove road being termed a "snare and a delusion." Things improved by 1906—"annoying, but not dangerous" was the conclusion of young Albert Clément, on leave from the French army to contest that year's running of the Vanderbilt.

Whatever the course, whatever the roads, crowds in the hundreds of thousands came to watch. "A race mad army," *The New York Herald* said, in comparing the night-before revelling to a Roman circus. The Waldorf offered elegant champagne breakfasts—and canny promoters around the course were fetching Waldorf prices for Coney Island frankfurters. Even more enterprising were the fellows who merely built a fire and rented out spots on a log for a quarter apiece to warm the bones of the chilly who chose not to sleep as they awaited the early morning start of a Vanderbilt. There

*Friday, April 24th, 1908: The Briarcliff Trophy*

were housing and transportation problems galore. The accommodations for William C. Carnegie, nephew of old Andrew, and his party were cots in the billiard room of a Garden City hotel. An unidentified befurred gentleman offered ten dollars to spend the night on a barber chair in the same hotel; he was referred to the barber. *The New York Times* delighted in reporting that the Long Island Railroad and its 12 mph specials were breaking no records in getting spectators to the scene.

What the crowds saw when they got there, in the initial Vanderbilts, was a lamentable parade of European car victories: 1904, a French Panhard driven by the American George Heath, "six feet two of magnificent manhood," one adoring reporter noted; 1905, the Frenchman Victor

Hémery driving a French Darracq. Nineteen six would prove no different. The battle royal during the early going was between the No. 3 Mercedes of Camille Jenatzy—whose beard, piercing eyes, funny Spanish-monk-like driving cap and sinister mien had earned him the nickname Mephistopheles—and the No. 4 Fiat driven by Vincenzo Lancia—who bore, as always, a "heavy look as if he was thinking too much for an Italian" and who became curiously deaf whenever megaphoned by his team manager to slow down. But ultimate victory went to the less flamboyant Louis Wagner—and the car again was a Darracq. It had been a finely contested race among the Europeans—the best American finish was eighth, a Thomas—and Wagner himself admitted it was the finest he had ever

to build the nine-mile Long Island Motor Parkway and see to the procure ment of fourteen miles of easily-patrolled public roads to complete a circuit for a run for the cup in October of '08. Six months previous, in New York's Westchester County, another race idea was tried, after Walter W. Law, founder of Briarcliff Manor, was induced to put up an impressive trophy. Unlike the Vanderbilt, the Briarcliff was to be contested by stock cars, meaning as the rules stated, "that the maker shall have actually manufactured and delivered, or have ready for immediate delivery, at least ten similar cars . . ."—though with entries lagging, this was ultimately revised to "had been, or would be, built." Eleven American and eleven European cars managed to qualify thusly, their makers undeterred apparently by the serpentine course chosen, bearing such doom-portending sections as "Dead Man's Gorge" and "Breakneck Hill." As one of the drivers sagely put it, "It's so dangerous that any recklessness would be fatal. It's a safe circuit." He was Lewis Strang, an American and he won the event—alas, again, on a European car, an Isotta—though Guy Vaughan and his 60 hp Stearns No. 8 put up a gallant struggle and finished a creditable third.

Still, the result was to nay-sayers among the press simply further proof of the futility of racing. Chief among these opponents was *The Horseless Age,* who viewed speed sport as satisfying "a depraved taste for excitement . . . classed with such public spectacles as bull fights and prize fights, which are suppressed by all advanced civilizations." The only object racing served was advertising—and, *Horseless Age* editors pooh-poohed, the events run so far "[have] certainly been a very poor advertisement for the American industry."

They should have seen the '08 Vanderbilt. They didn't; they refused to attend, officially. Had they, they would have witnessed—it is true—the pre-race hosing down of spectators to persuade them to leave the course for a safe viewing distance on the sidelines. But they would also have seen an American car triumph at last in a major international road race. As firebrand George Robertson hurled his Locomobile Old 16 round the course, in the stands a spectator named Henry Ford shouted, "I'd give five hundred dollars to see that American car win." There is no record that he ever did, or to whom if he did, but George Robertson did capture the Vanderbilt, and at a record-breaking speed of 64.3 mph.

There were but a few mishaps. Hordes of intensely nationalistic enthusiasts rushed to throw themselves on the winning car and driver, of course. In the confusion, a Mercedes racer bumped into a spectator's touring car, damaging its radiator and breaking the leg of a bystander. That—and the singed moustache suffered by Foxhall Keene when his Mercedes momentarily caught fire during the race—were the only calamities of the day. After receiving the congratulations and adulation of the crowd, Robertson drove his own car into New York City to have dinner with a friend, parked, stepped out and onto a corrugated manhole cover—and fractured his ankle.

*The Horseless Age,* betimes, ignored the Vanderbilt altogether, turning its editorial venom instead upon the newest wrinkle in motor sport: the automobile race track. Brooklands had just opened in England, and as the editors commented, its "comparative failure [as viewed then] . . . should prove a lesson to others who may be tempted to invest in any similar schemes."

Meanwhile, in Indiana, Carl Fisher had exactly that sort of scheme in mind. The Indianapolis Motor Speedway was finished in 1909—or so Carl Fisher thought. Ever impatient to get things moving, Fisher overlooked the obvious imperfections in his gritty, hastily-prepared, two-and-a-half mile oval as the August date for its inaugural meet approached. Any lessons he might have—and *should* have—learned from the hard-topped and steeply-banked surface of the vast motordrome at Brooklands were strangely ignored. However, as an ex-dirt track specialist himself, Fisher was fully aware of the added drama offered by high-flinging dirt from skidding wheels and the blinding dust blending with the smoke of open exhausts. These spectacular bonuses for the crowds during the inaugural meet were had, but at the expense of fatalities to both participants and spectators. The woeful drama began on Thursday the 19th when Knox driver William A. Bourque and his mechanic Harry Holcolm were killed after their car overturned three hundred yards north of the grandstand during the 250-mile stripped-chassis contest. It was the fifth event held that day, and already the track was treacherous. There was talk of cancelling Friday's program, but ultimately Fisher and company decided a patching up here and there and a coat of oil along the straightaway was

driven. But, he added, the miracle was "that hundreds were not killed in my doing so." And he was right.

Vanderbilt had largely trusted in what he called the "inherent good sense of the American people" insofar as crowd control was concerned. It wasn't enough. There were, to be sure, the humorous erratics. The bewhiskered gentleman in a faded Grand Army uniform, for one, who would step into the road after a car had passed, shake his fist down the course at it and dare another to come along. But the average spectator was the real problem—the average spectator en masse, watching the race from the middle of the road. One was killed in the '06 Vanderbilt.

There wasn't a Vanderbilt in '07, as Willie K. and his associates hurried

On the left, below:
Tuesday, May 30th, 1911
Indianapolis Motor Speedway
Indianapolis 500, Inaugural

*Saturday, October 5th, 1912: The Grand Prize*

all that was needed. And they prevailed. Eight events were staged Friday, and since the day produced no losses of life, or limb, there was no question but that Saturday's program would go on as scheduled. The track surface was, however, by now thoroughly butchered. The third event—the twenty-five-mile run for the Remy Grand Brassard—was a free-for-all among three stellar combatants: Barney Oldfield with his 1908 Grand Prix Benz No. 27, Len Zengle with his giant Chadwick No. 50 and Ralph DePalma aboard the stripped stock Fiat No. 24. The latter was a last-minute substitution for DePalma's fleet track special, the Fiat Cyclone, a lightweight speedster that the driver was not about to risk on such a deteriorated track. For Barney's structurally sound Benz, a veteran of some gruelling Grand Prix racing in Europe, the wretched circuit was taken in stride. He won the Brassard with ease, smashing records for five, ten, fifteen, twenty and twenty-five miles in the process. Had the day ended there, the Indianapolis inaugural probably wouldn't have received an unfavorable press, save from the fellows at *The Horseless Age*. But Event No. 5, a 300-mile stripped-chassis race, was doomed, resulting as *The Automobile Trade Journal* stated, "in the sacrificing of three more lives." Within hours it was rumored that AAA officials would refuse sanction for future speed events at the track. But Carl Fisher took matters into

hand—and quickly declared that Indy would be resurfaced into "the world's finest and safest road course." He didn't at this point mention how.

Then he got together with the National Paving Brick Manufacturers Association. Four months and some three-million-odd bricks later, the Indianapolis Motor Speedway had been transformed from a treacherous dust bowl into The Brickyard. Racing resumed, but the attendance figures were scarcely to Mr. Fisher's liking—and he concluded that Indianapolis was possibly giving racing enthusiasts too much of a good thing. There was, after all, only one Vanderbilt Cup a year. "Something they can't see any place except at Indianapolis" was what Carl Fisher wanted for his Brickyard. Discussion centered awhile around a race of either twenty-four hours or a thousand miles, both meeting with approval by manufacturers who looked upon such endurance encounters as proving matches and thus good advertising for their automobiles. But from the spectator point of view, they were deemed too lengthy. The final decision: a race of 500 miles duration to be run on Memorial Day. It was a brilliant idea—and to sweeten the pot, the organizers did exactly that, guaranteeing a $25,000 purse, with accessory firms adding to the largesse. Never before had so much money been offered racing drivers for an afternoon's work. The Indianapolis 500 would obviously not want for entries.

And so the day came, with forty starters lining up in eight rows—Ray Harroun aboard the single-seater Marmon No. 32, a racing special headline writers would later dub The Wasp, and Ralph Mulford behind the wheel of the stripped stock Lozier No. 33. Ray had added a rear-view mirror to his car, deleted his mechanic—and won the first Indy 500. So well attended, so well received and so exciting was the race that no one doubted it was but the first of many 500-mile treks of the track to be held for many years to come.

But the big premier road races were by now fading. There had been no '09 Briarcliff; indeed the donater of the trophy had not been heard from since his donation. The Vanderbilts moved from Long Island to Savannah, and henceforth would go to Milwaukee and California, and Willie K. would pretty much lose interest in them. The Grand Prize contests, begun in Savannah in 1908 and rivalling the Vanderbilt in prestige, were ebbing by now too. For 1912 the Grand Prize promoters would try to take a successful leaf from the Indianapolis 500 book. Their race at Milwaukee was billed as "the richest road event ever held"—and that it was, though its $10,000 prize money hardly approached the 500's dole. And Milwaukee shared the problem Indianapolis had solved with brick—its 7.88-mile course was utterly deplorable, so pocked in fact that the contest had to be

postponed from its original September date. Of the fifteen cars that started the race—the smallest field ever in the Grand Prize series—all but three were European. It was to be Fiat's day, Caleb Bragg's No. 41 racer triumphing over Erwin Bergdoll's huge 928-cubic-inch Benz No. 40, the ultimate second-place finisher. In second place on the last lap, however, had been Ralph DePalma, but his belated effort to pass Bragg brought the right front wheel of his Mercedes in contact with the rear left wheel of the leading Fiat. DePalma left the road in a near fatal crash. Aware of the accident to his comrade, Bragg took the checkered flag at a modest crawl and made a full report. It was a somber victory for him. His teammate and friend, David Bruce-Brown, had been killed in practice only days before when a blown tire had sent his Fiat off the road.

The death knell would soon be sounding too for the big-engined racer—and for road racing in America. What ended all the glorious—and sometimes tragic—madness was progress. Sophisticated engineering would replace the massive brute strength of the giant racers—and the circuit or track would just as irrevocably displace public roads for sporting contests on this side of the Atlantic. The Heroic Age was over. There's been nothing like it since. But every Memorial Day there is a reminder of that raucous era when America first went racing. We still have the 500.

# THE HOUSE VINCENZO LANCIA BUILT SO WELL

Nowadays, engineering is one of the respectable professions. Status, security and salaries to compare with the best add up to the kind of job description which can fall trippingly off the tongue at cocktail parties. Thanks to the enormous wealth, prestige and economic importance of giant industrial combines like General Motors and Ford, backed up by the still unbelievable success of the space program, engineering comes close to outranking the traditional standbys of medicine and the law in the neighborhood pecking order.

But it wasn't always so. Nineteenth Century fathers thought they knew best, and viewed signs of mechanical enthusiasm in their sons in the same light as an interest in piracy or the white-slave trade. Sound, safe, well-established roles were planned for their offspring: Ferdinand Porsche had a seat booked in the family plumbing business, Henry Ford was to be a farmer's boy, and Vincenzo Lancia was aimed at a career in accountancy. Yet, fortunately for the automotive world, the generation gap isn't merely an invention of the 1960's and '70's, and these particular young men were rebels from the cradle, in a society where youthful dropping-out from parental schemes was a whole lot harder than it is today. Had they not been so determined, the world might have gained a cheap and reliable flushing toilet, a robust fertilizer spreader or a revolutionary new method of double-entry bookkeeping, instead of being lucky enough to get the VW, the Model T and the Aprilia.

Jumping the rails of patriarchal society could be a long, tough and costly business. In Vincenzo Lancia's case, his weapons were stubborn determination and cunning in equal proportions. When he was only twelve, his future was already being mapped out; papa Lancia ran a thriving soup-canning business in the mountain village of Fobello in Northwest Italy, and a son who could look after accounts for the family firm would be a distinct asset. Young Vincenzo was enrolled in a school to study same in the graceful old princely capital of Turin, where the family owned an elegant town house in which to enjoy the winter social season. But papa Lancia was far too shrewd a businessman to allow the house to remain completely idle the rest of the year, and he rented out part of the courtyard to one Giovanni Ceirano whose trade was the repair of the newly fashionable bicycles. His son would also quarter there while pursuing his studies. Vincenzo Lancia didn't realize it yet, but already his future was taking shape. It was 1898. He was seventeen years old. He saw the Ceirano business grow, from repair of bicycles to manufacture of the firm's own—called Welleyes—and finally a light car bearing the same name. Dull columns of figures could never compare with realities like these. Before the year was out, Vincenzo left his studies and joined the Ceirano outfit. His father still thought he was working to become an accountant. In that case, an accountant he had to be—and it was as a bookkeeper that the Ceirano-Welleyes concern took him on.

From the beginning it was apparent that the young figure-totter had a rare genius in matters mechanical. With no experience or knowledge, Vincenzo showed a sixth sense for fault-tracing and repairing which was almost frightening. He could look at a car which he had never seen before, isolate the weak points, and put things right with a speed which amazed his more experienced colleagues.

Ceirano's backyard workshop was an ideal training ground, but it soon became obvious Lancia needed wider fields to expand his new gifts to the full. His astonishing luck held. The rapidly growing local automobile firm of Fiat was looking around for fresh talent and equipment to feed its

# What the Soup Canner's Son Began...
# A Tradition That Has
# Endured in Turin for Seven Decades

growth. Giovanni Agnelli noticed the thriving Ceirano business, and made a handsome bid for it—and the services of Vincenzo Lancia. Just nineteen now, Vincenzo was offered a post as chief inspector at Fiat's new factory.

Nor was that all. Like many another young man at the dawn of motoring history, Vincenzo discovered the excitement of motor racing. First time out—a speed-trial meeting at Padua in 1900—he won, whetting his appetite for more. Racing seemed to change him—although a big burly extrovert with a lively sense of humor, Lancia was an essentially modest man as far as his own achievements were concerned. But seated behind the wheel of a racing car, he became a different person altogether; in place of his acute sensitivity to every vibration from the car he was driving, he showed a dedicated ruthlessness, a determination to win or drive the car into the ground. A racing car was not a delicate piece of machinery to be tested, analyzed and tuned to persuade to give of its best; it was a willful thoroughbred which must be hammered into submission and driven as hard as humanly possible. In the years that followed, Lancia amassed a total of nineteen outright and class victories, but more often he retired with a broken car. After 1908 he began to lose interest in competition, and in 1910 gave it up altogether, doing so without apparent soul searching.

By now he had discovered another field to conquer in any case, that of a full-fledged manufacturer, in union with a commercially minded friend from Fiat named Claudio Fogolin. In 1906 the pair had taken the fateful plunge, each contributing 50,000 lire to finance the partnership and renting a little space in the Itala factory when that old established Turin car company moved to more spacious quarters. With the new company's future heavily dependent on his first design, Vincenzo decided to play for safety and produce a fairly conventional model with which to start the Lancia line. He drew up plans for a prototype four-cylinder engine, with cylinders cast in pairs, and side valves. The designed output was to be 24 bhp at 1450 rpm, then considered a dangerously high speed, as most engines were flat-out at 1000 rpm. This unit was to be fitted into a low, lightweight chassis using a shaft drive instead of the more common chains.

After only two months, disaster struck—a leaking oil stove, a fire, the destruction of all drawings and patterns, damaged tools, machinery and spare parts. The cost of putting things right swallowed up the rest of the capital; the company coffers were empty. It was now that Lancia showed his mettle. Moustachio bristling, he vowed to start again; nothing would stop him. At the same time, he determined not to let the mishap interfere

114

*Vincenzo's first Lancia, the Alfa, was available in varieties for luxurious motoring (pages preceding) or sporting pleasure (above left). Early American enthusiasts of the marque preferred the latter. Within a few weeks after the Lancia set its wheels on these shores in 1908, it had already "proven itself a little wonder"—these the words of its importer, The Hol-Tan Company. And it wasn't idle publicity. In mid-September the Alfa finished both the Mechanical Efficiency Test round Long Island and the Bay State Automobile Association Endurance Race through the White Mountains with perfect scores. In October in the Long Island Motor Parkway races preceding the Vanderbilt Cup, it finished third in the Meadowbrook Sweepstakes ahead of twenty-four cars, "although it was in size of cylinder" the smallest car in the race. William Hilliard, who had driven the Alfa on Long Island, next took it to Savannah and the International Light Car Race in late November. There he drove an impeccable race, averaging 52.6 mph for the 196 miles, winning handily and proclaiming afterwards that he had never extended the car fully and could have managed another 200 miles at the same speed. His victory was a popular one, despite the defeat it administered to the field of domestic Buicks, Maxwells and Chalmers. Especially enthusiastic, however, were European drivers who had gathered in Savannah for the Grand Prize to be run the next day.*
*Fiat ace Felice Nazzaro wrote up a telegram of congratulations, had Louis Wagner, Victor Hémery and others sign it and sent it off to Vincenzo in Italy.*
*Lancia advertisements in the United States would carry a caption, "Built by the Man Who Knows." Two years later, when racing returned to Savannah, a Lancia would again triumph in the light car event, with Billy Knipper running away from the field, capturing the Tiedeman Cup and, like his predecessor, beaming afterwards that "my car was never let out."*
*The new Beta (above right) carried forward the Lancia prowess, with a third-place in the 1909 Targa Florio —and the Theta which followed (right) returned the Lancia to a more cushy motoring theme.*

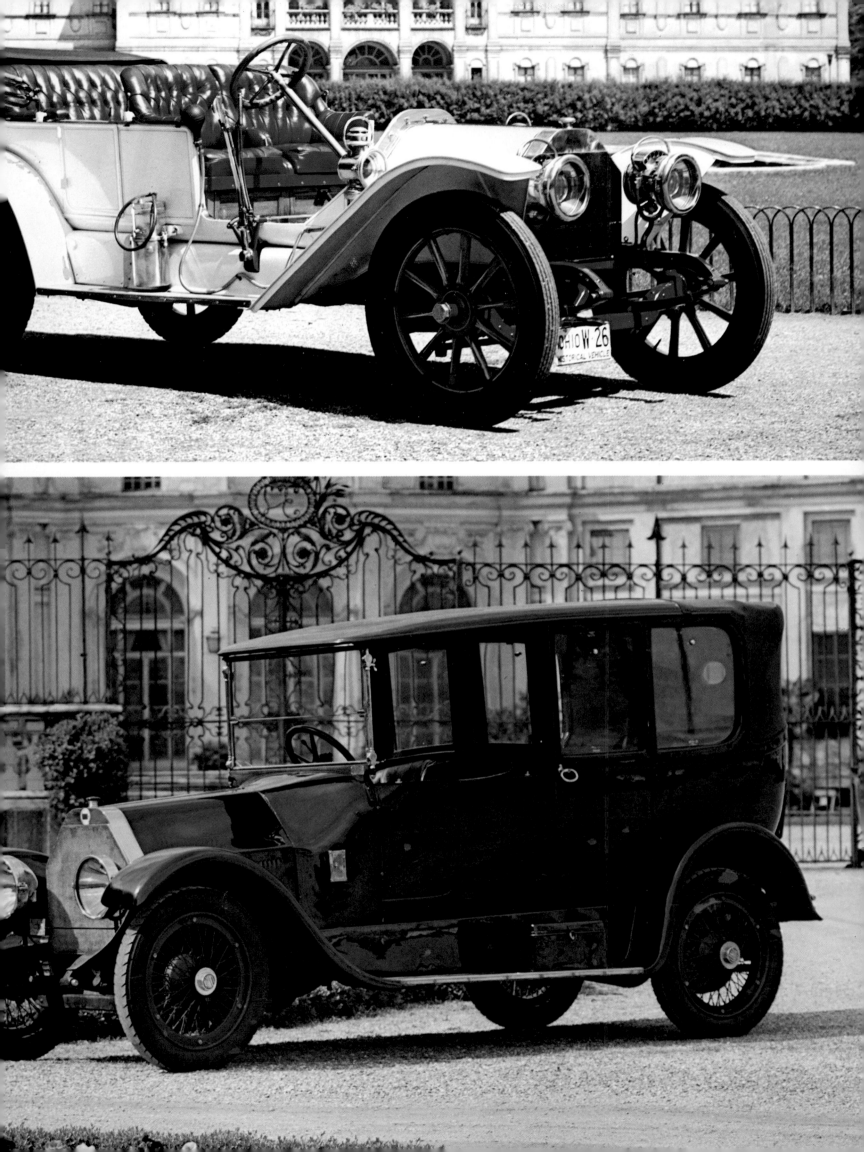

The Lambda—it was Vincenzo Lancia's masterwork, the result of his rare genius as an inspired designer whose powers had reached full maturity. The mind of any man is an impossibly complex organ, and that of an artist or designer even more so than most, so that isolating the influences which shape a particular creation or theory is almost impossible. One thing, however, is certain; the Lambda inspiration had been burning in Vincenzo's mind on a slow fuse for a long time. He had changed a great deal over the years, putting behind him his early fanaticism for racing. One particular experience began him thinking more about safety than speed. During a drive with his mother along one of the treacherous mountain roads near the family home at Fobello in an early Kappa, the constant pounding over rough surfaces broke a front-spring leaf. Lancia managed to keep the car on the road only by the narrowest of margins, and according to his friend Baron Mazzonis, the accident affected him greatly. From then on, safety and strength were placed high on his list of priorities. Both requirements

strongly influenced the Lancia Lambda design. Lancia had yet another experience which directly influenced the Lambda. At about the same time as the accident, he took time off for a short sea voyage—and his keen engineer's eye could hardly help noticing the toughness required of the ship's hull to withstand the enormous forces of the sea. What a contrast, thought Vincenzo, with the fragile frame of a motorcar, still being constructed on the same lines as the venerable stagecoach. From that point onwards, he was determined that one day he would adapt naval design principles in order to produce a prodigiously strong yet light car chassis. The chassis he envisioned would possess the same general lines as a ship's hull, but would still serve as the basis for a series of alternative bodies. Introduced at the Paris and London motor shows in November of 1922, the Lambda surprised press and spectators with both its technical specifications and the long, slender line of its bodies, quite the contrast to the more typical squat coachwork of the day—as these Lancia Lambdas attest. The limousine (above) and the sporting two-seater with coachwork by Casaro (below) are Second Series cars introduced during 1925 and virtually identical to the introductory First Series, which made the name Lancia famous wherever in the world men talked about cars.

with his established personal routine in the slightest and continued to keep his regular weekly appointment with some card-playing friends as if nothing out of the ordinary had happened.

By mid-September of 1907, the chassis was ready to be tested on the road. Two crude seats were bolted in place for driver and mechanic—and proud Lancia workers rolled the car to the factory door, which proved a bit too narrow. Roaring with laughter, Vincenzo Lancia bellowed for the pickaxes and cut his way out. Once outside, he took the wheel and slithered away over the cobbles. It was clear that Lancia's thinking was right; the combination of a light chassis and fast-revving engine produced exhilarating performance. The years spent in the Fiat test department had not been wasted on Lancia. Modifications were made, engine power uprated to 28 bhp at a staggering 1800 rpm—and in January 1908 there appeared at the Turin show three examples of the new car, now christened the Lancia Alfa (after the first letter of the Greek alphabet, which the Italians spelled phonetically). In addition, a longer-wheelbase chassis with a six-cylinder version of the same engine also appeared on the stand, named, logically enough, the Dialfa.

The cars had a mixed reception. The technical pundits said they were too light and too fast to be safe and reliable, but the first customers loved them. By the summer of 1909, 108 Alfas had been sold.

The Alfa's success meant big changes for Lancia. The tiny workshop was now hopelessly crowded, and the company began to take over more and more of both the old Itala works and other adjoining buildings, very soon occupying the whole block. And the enthusiastic Vincenzo realized that pride in one's work could be carried too far. No longer would he personally test drive every car produced. After the sixteenth Alfa, he changed his routine and spent more time in the office, less on the road. Prototype testing, however, he kept firmly under his control.

For 1909, the well-proven Alfa was replaced by the Beta, with a slightly larger (3120 cc versus 2544) en bloc version of the Alfa's engine, and in 1910 with the still larger 3460 cc Gamma model, which proved a runaway success—and created more space problems at the works. So, at the beginning of 1911, the firm packed its bags, left its tiny, cramped birthplace and moved to another empty car factory, this time the premises of the Fides-Brasier company on the via Monginevro.

With room to breathe at last, Lancia quickly produced another new model, the Delta, at 4080 cc, then the Didelta with a hotter version of the same engine, then in 1912 the Epsilon and the Zeta, in 1913 the 5030 cc Eta in a shorter and lighter body. By now, the motoring press had begun believing in Vincenzo Lancia's unorthodox thinking. And, increasingly, more customers were noticing these fast and agile cars; 1145 of the various models were sold in just two years.

Nineteen thirteen also saw the appearance of one of the most successful Lancias of all, the Theta, based on a tough military vehicle called the 1Z which the company had been building under government contract. The 1Z used a 70 hp version of the four-cylinder Lancia engine in a truck chassis, and without expensive redesigning and retooling and only a few chassis refinements, he turned it into a grand limousine. Seventeen hundred of them were built. But even in 1913, Lancia had come to realize the old Alfa formula had had its day. Even at this stage, he was convinced of the value of high-efficiency multi-cylinder engines instead of the large, solid, slow-revving power units of motoring's early days, and his thoughts were turning to mounting twin cylinder banks in V-formation to save space and provide extra strength and smoothness.

But other minds had other ideas, and the result was World War I. The Italian government designated the Lancia works an Auxiliary War Factory, and production of automobiles was stopped. Instead of a new V-12 powered car, the 1Z went into mass production, followed by a long wheelbase version called the Iota, and a shorter one called the Diota.

By the time the war had ended, Lancia had expanded beyond all recognition. Vincenzo Lancia was now head of a firm which had grown fat on big war contracts, and which occupied twice the space taken up by its factories in 1913. But his prewar plans for a V configuration internal combustion engine, using an ingenious system of twin connecting rods which allowed opposing cylinders in each bank to be joined to the same crankshaft, had had to be abandoned, though the idea had been patented in 1915. Still, by the fall of 1918, with war production tailing off, Vincenzo took out a further patent for a V-8, with cylinder banks at 45 degrees—and in October 1919 a patent for a V-12 with cylinder banks at 30 degrees.

117

The war had changed the automobile business. Vincenzo Lancia recognized that, knew the old leisurely production methods would no longer be good enough in an era of frenzied competition. He knew also that producing prototypes of the new engine would take a lot of time and money. What he needed in the meantime was an interim design which would use as much of the well-proven earlier cars as possible, yet which would be not only more up-to-date but also offer a chance to develop some of the systems and components intended for the new generation of cars. First of these postwar compromises was the Kappa, derived from the Theta and fitted with a light, semi-streamlined open touring body which allowed it to exceed 75 mph flat-out. Like earlier Epsilon and Eta models, it had a novel single dry-plate clutch, but it also featured electric starting controlled by a floor pedal, a floor-mounted gearshift, and a variable-rake steering column, a highly unusual detail for 1919.

But Vincenzo was never more than half-hearted about the Kappa or its 81 mph sports version successor called the Dikappa. Lancia was concentrating all his enormous energy on perfecting a V-engine, with nothing spared to ensure that this would be his best design yet. In a year of furious activity, he tried one configuration and then another, at last settling for a long, narrow V-12 with the banks inclined at 20 degrees. As a piece of engineering beauty, it was a masterpiece. It was fitted into a completely new chassis and was ready for the 1919 Paris show, where it appeared alongside the Kappa. The press went wild with enthusiasm. Vincenzo Lancia was showing the way with a vengeance.

But the new Lancia's strength was engineering, not economics. Such a large and expensive engine, powerful enough to pull the biggest and most luxurious of limousines, was a magnificent piece of work, and would have been ideal for the market which existed when Vincenzo first sat down to work on his new engine ideas. But since the war, demand had changed so much that trying to produce the design in quantity would have ended in commercial suicide, and the plans were dropped after a great deal of heart searching. Back to the drawing board went Vincenzo, to produce a smaller and less costly alternative.

Three years later, his work was rewarded. He had modified the V-12 design to produce a V-8 with the banks set at the same angle, but with narrower cylinder bores and a slightly longer stroke to produce a capacity of 4595 (the V-12's was 7837), and a peak power output of 98 bhp at 2500 rpm. This was fitted into a Kappa chassis—the earlier model was selling encouragingly well—and the result was the Trikappa, last in the progression of first-generation Lancias and, with its new and sophisticated engine, a forerunner of one of the most original and sophisticated creations in all motoring history, the brilliant Lancia Lambda.

With the Lambda, Vincenzo Lancia was setting out to write an entirely new chapter in car design, virtually single-handed. Every morning he held a conference with the others in his small team, expounding his ideas, listing targets, arguing through all the thousands of problems inseparable from the birth of any car, let alone one as radical as the Lambda. He carried a sketch pad and notebook everywhere he went. When he was at home, tired out, at night, the pad stayed beside his bed—often he would wake, still thinking about a problem which had been plaguing him all day, and sketch a solution or a line of inquiry before dropping off to sleep again.

Slowly, the new engine design took shape. A 2121 cc V-4 that employed much the same thinking as the successful V-8, the new engine produced 49 bhp at 3000 rpm, though this figure would later be upped to nearly seventy. With a cylinder angle of just 13 degrees, the new engine was one of the strongest and most compact V-type powerplants ever built. Its square cylinder block and head allowed room for well-shaped combustion chambers and efficient circulation of cooling water. The short, rigid crankshaft was well supported in three main bearings and the valves on all cylinders were operated by rocker arms from a single overhead camshaft driven by an offset vertical shaft and skew gears. Both the aluminum cylinder block—poured around the four iron cylinder liners—and the crankcase were made of beautiful one-piece castings.

Another of Lancia's priorities was the best possible roadholding and this, it seemed to Vincenzo, dictated the use of independent front suspension in place of the old rigid-axle arrangement. He finally selected a system using sliding pillars with coil springs enclosed in cylinders and hydraulic dampers. The Lambda became the first large car with independent front suspension.

This type of suspension, Lancia realized, would mean heavier stresses on

The Lambda proved a sensation at its introduction. The long and low body, the absence of a separate frame, the compact engine, sophisticated suspension and four wheel brakes which The Autocar called "extremely powerful," better "than any of the cars we have tested . . ." created a turmoil in the motoring world. Engineers argued a bit, but customers didn't. Oddly enough, in view of Lancia's reputation over the years, just about the only thing the Lambda quite definitely wasn't was a sports car. It handled well, and it was light enough for its two-liter engine to move it along at a respectable 71 mph, but thanks to the original three-speed gearbox, it took some time to get there. Its roadholding was superb, but its long, ten-foot wheelbase body lacked the close-coupled compactness of a true sports car. And for all the efficiency of its narrow V engine, there was little that private owners could do to raise the performance level significantly. As a mechanical illustration of the views of Vincenzo Lancia, the Lambda was remarkably accurate: safe, comfortable, solid and predictably efficient on the road and in performance, with no potential at all for competition development. And yet the Lambda could still give true sports cars a run for their money. Year by year, improvements were made without any basic changes to the design: wider cylinder bores, taking the capacity up to 2370 cc and later 2570 cc, with concomitant power increases to fifty-nine and finally sixty-nine horsepower and a top speed up to eighty miles an hour. Larger brake drums were fitted, the track was widened by three inches, detail changes were made to the body frame, and a four-speed gearbox fitted. The Lambda's chief attraction remained its supreme roadability, a combination of adequate performance, faultless handling and top class reliability. And in 1928, Vigin Gismondi —Vincenzo's old friend and mechanic at the works since Alfa days—showed just what the car could do by narrowly missing a win in the storied Mille Miglia. With 180 miles to go, only Campari in a powerful blown Alfa Romeo lay ahead of him, and Campari had an extra refuelling stop to make —but an unlucky accident put Gismondi out of the race before the end, and Alfa Romeo won after all. That scarcely cast a pall on Lancia fortunes. The customers knew exactly what they wanted from a car, and trifling detail modifications were quite sufficient to keep more than thirteen thousand of them perfectly happy during the ten years that the Lambda was in production from 1922 to 1932. Two such customers bought the Lambdas pictured here, the Casaro roadster (above) in 1925 and the Pininfarina variation (center) in 1927. If anything, the enormous publicity about the Lambda proved something of a two-edged weapon. After it, anything Vincenzo did would attract the attention of the automotive world, but if it failed to measure up to the Lambda's high standard, it could come in for global-scale criticism by the motoring press. The Dilambda (below) was not greeted with that, but it was not the revolutionary motorcar its predecessor was either. With a four-liter V-8 developing 100 bhp at 3800 rpm, it managed a respectable 80 mph.

There was much to admire about the Dilambda, but performance-hungry buyers found that the extra power provided by the larger engine was often wasted in hauling a separate chassis frame and body which weighed the best part of two tons in full trim. Nevertheless, it was a quite handsome car providing a splendid basis upon which noted coachbuilders could display their talents with line and form, as the house of Castagna did in 1931 in an appealing convertible victoria (above). Castagna also provided striking dual cowl sport phaeton coachwork in 1933 on an Astura chassis, this Lancia (center) having been special ordered by Doris Duke. The Astura, using a shorter wheelbase version of the Dilambda chassis, was fitted with a smaller version of the Dilambda V-8, with banks set at 19 degrees, a capacity of 2604 cc, a 73 bhp power peak and a top speed of 75 mph. Introduced in 1931, the Astura was later fitted with a 17½ degree V-8 of 2972 cc, was produced for another five years and built up an impressive competition record in the hands of private owners. Pintacuda and Nardilli won the 1934 Coppo d'Oro, a 3534-mile road race around Italy, beating the new Alfa Romeo 2300 six-cylinders of the Scuderia Ferrari team. In third place was Farina, driving another Astura. The Augusta was another sort of Lancia altogether, arriving on the scene in 1933. It was powered by a V-4, with the cylinders set at an angle of 18¼ degrees, the capacity reduced to 1196 cc with a power peak of 35 bhp, giving a useful top speed, thanks to the very light body, of 65 mph. In 1936 Magistri, di Pietro, "Gladio" and Cammarata captured the first four places in the Targa Florio with Augustas—and the car was a particular favorite as personal transport for a number of top-flight drivers of that era as well. In itself, that speaks volumes, but the memories of one of those drivers add some delightful sidelights. French champion René Dreyfus, in 1935 a member of the aforementioned Scuderia Ferrari racing team of Alfa Romeos, remembers the Augusta well: "Most of us on the team had Augustas," he has reminisced. "We loved them. Of course, as part of our contract, we had provided to us at a special price a 2.3 Alfa, but as it turned out most of us left that car in the garage and motored to races in our Augustas. Of all the little cars I encountered in my racing career, it left the greatest impression. It was so marvelous in its simplicity, that tiny high little engine that was so responsive, the terrific suspension, the hydraulic brakes—and it was put together so well. We called it 'the little box.' Never did we have any trouble with it, and it gave us more pleasure than words can tell. The seating position was unlike any other car I've ever been in, straight up, no inclination; it was rather like being seated at a piano—and enormously comfortable. Visibility was perfect. And could that little car ever handle. The roadholding was fantastic. I remember that we were always very happy to find ourselves in the mountains en route to one race or another, because then its agility could really be exercised to the fullest." But the very same reasons the car appealed to a driver like René Dreyfus were perhaps the same ones which saw the Augusta less than a smashing market success. For a utility car it might have been a bit too nimble. Other buyers, too, insisted on a body other than the sedan which was the only style initially offered, and Lancia eventually produced another version on a separate chassis, enabling carrozzerias to body it with their own designs—or potential owners for that matter, as the Earl of March did with his special touring Augusta in 1934 (below).

the chassis. So the Lambda body frame was built on the lines of a flat-bottomed boat, from steel pressings with deeply flanged sides for extra rigidity, and riveted cross members which carried fore-and-aft supports for the engine, gearbox, seats and transmission. The compact V-4 engine squatted in the extreme nose of the car; behind it the unusually long body trailed back to a rounded stern providing extra stiffness and valuable luggage space. It was a vital milestone in motoring development. With the possible exception of the 11 hp Lagonda, the Lambda had the first monocoque body of all, setting the style for passenger and racing car design for the next half century.

The first prototype was ready on September 1st, 1921, and Vincenzo Lancia took it out for a test drive. He knew at once he had a winner on his hands. At last he could relax. That night he took ten of his men to a restaurant in the Susa valley above Turin. Afterwards they played bowls. Lancia lost, and so far had he forgotten his worries and his success that he took his defeat badly.

The car's official unveiling came at the motor shows in the fall of 1922, after post-prototype refinements made it, in addition to being years ahead of its time, a thoroughly practical and reliable proposition as well. Customers hurried to form a line, wallets at the ready.

The Lambda's successor, introduced while the Lambda was still in production, and called the Dilambda, was something of a throwback. It reverted to a separate body-frame type construction and used a 24 degree V-8 derived from the one used in the earlier Trikappa of 1922. Its 80 mph top speed, four-speed gearbox, precise steering and fine brakes made the Dilambda a better car than many of its critics suggested. Introduced in 1928, it stayed in production for five years; a total of 1685 were made.

If the Lambda had one true successor, it really had two. The chief criticism of Lancia's classic was that it fell fairly and squarely between two schools of thought: The comfort and roadholding would provide an ideal combination for a bigger and more powerful car, while the neat little V-4 engine was an ideal power unit for a lighter and faster car. Never a man to do things by halves, Vincenzo Lancia decided to replace the Lambda, when at last it became obvious that something new was needed, by two completely different new models.

The smaller of these was the Artena—Greek letters having given way to Latin placenames in designating the cars. This had a shorter wheelbase version of the Dilambda chassis and an engine developed from the Lambda unit. The Artena appeared in 1931 and alongside it was a more powerful version called the Astura. Not surprisingly, sporting drivers picked the Astura, and the smaller car was dropped after only two years.

Lancia himself was busy with other ideas of his own, occasioned by the Wall Street crash and the changing world economy which brought about a completely new market. He knew what the car of the future would be. He knew too that the monocoque construction of the Lambda had been a step in the right direction. What he had to do was take the Lambda theme several stages farther, and give the new customers exactly what they wanted: a small, efficient, economical sedan. It was a problem which was to occupy most manufacturers in Europe through the long, difficult years of the Thirties. But Vincenzo Lancia saw the need earlier than most, and set about solving it in his own inimitable way.

The first result was the little Augusta, a simple four-door four-seat sedan. Soon after it went into production, in 1934, Vincenzo Lancia started work on what was to be his final, and some still say his greatest, creation. At long last, the traditionally four-square functionality of earlier models was to give way to distinct streamlining. All the by-now compulsory features of Vincenzo's ideas were to be used, but the Aprilia, as the new car would be called, would embody a lot of still newer ideas. The engine was an 18 degree V-4 of 1352 cc, with a chain-driven overhead camshaft operating the valves via two sets of rocker arms. The Aprilia's generator was mounted in a decidedly novel manner so that, driven by a pulley at its rear, it ran through the radiator core and had a cast aluminum fan affixed to its front. It was a compact arrangement and, together with the car's thermostatically controlled radiator shutters, made for efficient cooling. In all, the new engine proved both powerful enough and durable, and some examples have run as many as 180,000 miles on their original crankshafts and bearings.

The Aprilia's body carried Lancia's philosophy even further. To put the engine's output to the best possible use, Vincenzo Lancia was determined that the body should be as light as he could make it. The metal paneling

*Lancia Asturas, in variations from 1935 (above left) and 1938 (left), continued doing well in the marketplace while the Aprilia (above) was conceived and being born. In the early summer of 1936, the prototype was ready, and Vincenzo asked his friend Gismondi (by now chief test driver) to drive him to Bologna. The outward journey was dismal. Lancia sat quietly in the front passenger seat, grumbling that Gismondi was driving too fast, and only breaking his grim silence to complain about points he felt needed correcting. His passengers could hardly hide their dismay. Was the new car, which carried all their hopes, really as bad as this? They arrived at last at Bologna, and Lancia vanished into a meeting. After a long and depressing wait, the car started on its return journey. Gismodi stopped to refuel at a gas station near Voghera, seventy miles from Turin. There, Lancia ordered him to change seats, and took the wheel for the first time. He drove faster and faster for the rest of the journey, pouring on the power and testing the car to the utmost, in the way he had learned at Fiat so long ago. Suddenly, as the familiar outskirts of Turin appeared ahead, he broke his silence for the first time. Tossing up his hands, he said with emotion: "What a magnificent little car." It was Vincenzo's last Lancia. He died soon thereafter. His successors carried on memorably, with the Aurelia (the B 20 GT from 1958 and the B 24 with hardtop from 1959, both with coachwork by Pininfarina, shown on the pages following).*

would be thinner than that used on other cars—strength would depend on careful design of the body-chassis unit. So the basis of the body was a flat steel floor, covering the entire underside of the car apart from the exhaust pipe and a gap to allow cooling air to reach the sump. Stiffening this were two Z-section side members; the sides of the engine compartment did double duty as the insides of the front wheel-arches, and the hood was merely a lid on the top of the box which contained the engine. Another box at the rear end of the car held the differential and provided the rear suspension mountings. Fenders were unstressed.

Twelve years earlier, Vincenzo Lancia had staked his reputation on providing safety and stability through a carefully designed independent front suspension. Now he was convinced that this compact lightweight would need independent suspension at the back as well. So he designed a complex arrangement which used two torsion bars housed in a transverse tube and linked by swinging arms to the half-shafts at their splined outboard ends. The splined shafts' inboard ends were fixed to the differential. A transverse leaf-spring pivoted in the center with a flexible mounting to the differential housing. Its outboard ends were connected by cables to the mid-points of the swinging radius arms which carried the wheel hubs. Once the system was perfected, it gave an almost unbeatable standard of roadholding, if at the expense of a harsh ride at low speeds.

Like all post-classic era Lancia sedans, the Aprilia's great technical innovation and sophistication was combined with an unpretentious, starkly functional body. It was the first fastback production car, and apart from the tiny rear windows of the 1930's, it still has the timeless functionality of the VW Beetle in a far more elegant form. The sloping radiator grille and windscreen, the headlamps faired into the fenders, the flattened curve of the roof, all were to produce echoes in endless imitative designs for the next twenty years. Another feature under the skin was equally revolutionary: inboard rear brakes mounted next to the differential to reduce unsprung weight. This feature, later to become almost compulsory on successful racing cars, was here used first on a small, economy-class family sedan, a significant example of Vincenzo Lancia's refusal to compromise over even the smallest detail.

Vincenzo Lancia never saw a finished Aprilia emerge from the assembly line. At the tragically early age of fifty-six, at the height of his creative powers, he died in the early morning of February 15th, 1937. Allied to their natural grief at the loss of their friend, his colleagues worried. How would Lancia fare without Vincenzo?

Commercially, succession was assured, with control firmly in the hands of the family—his son Gianni was to take over the running of the firm. And with the Aprilia, Vincenzo had left his successors good solid foundations on which to build. His farewell present to the company had given it a commanding lead over the opposition. But the time which his genius had bought would one day run out. Therein lay the question of Lancia's future.

Its answer took longer to emerge than anyone could have guessed when Vincenzo died. True, changes were made to the Aprilia in 1939, and a scaled-down version called the Ardea appeared at the same time, but these were still essentially Vincenzo Lancia designs. Then, again, war intervened, and when the Italian economy took its first halting steps back to peacetime conditions in the last months of 1945, the Aprilia and Ardea were still in advance of any possible competitors. Still, the problem of providing a replacement had occupied the Lancia team throughout the war. The technical staff had been evacuated to Padua to escape the heavy air raids on Turin, but when able to return to the factory in 1943, technical director Giuseppe Vaccarino began to revive an old Vincenzo Lancia project for a V-6 engine. He was aided by the inimitable Vittorio Jano who had left Alfa Romeo to become chief of Lancia's research department. Francesco de Virgilio, the young head of the Lancia Patent and Planning Office, drew up the engine with its cylinder banks set at 60 degrees, inclined valves and hemispherical combustion chambers.

The long years of war and the continuing success of the Aprilia and Ardea—a grand total of more than 30,000 Ardeas alone were turned out before production was stopped—allowed Lancia time to experiment with the new design. A 45 degree V-6 was also built and tested in an experimental Aprilia during 1947—but when Gianna Lancia decided the time had come to plan for an Aprilia replacement, the version eventually selected was a 1754 cc 60 degree V-6 developing 56 hp at 4000 rpm. This engine, called the B 10, was fitted into a body strongly reminiscent of its predecessor, but with more modern lines and a longer wheelbase. The complex rear suspension of the Aprilia was replaced by a much simpler but still very effective system of semi-trailing wishbones and coil springs. Although the V-6 was very light for its size—only 320 pounds—the design team was worried about nose heaviness, so that clutch and gearbox were mounted at the rear of the car, next to the differential. Detail design was as painstaking as Vincenzo himself would have expected: The engine had two thermostats, one in the water hose which controlled the coolant circulation, and the other on the radiator, controlling the adjustable shutters. The camshaft was driven by double roller chain, tensioned automatically by increasing oil pressure.

The result of all this careful development was labelled the Lancia Aurelia, and the car was introduced in 1950. Within months it became obvious that this was no poor relation of the splendid Aprilia. Subsequent power increases brought seventy, then seventy-five horses to the Aurelia.

The Aurelia represented the first break in a long Lancia tradition, the first shift of the company under Gianni Lancia's control from the principles laid down by Vincenzo. For years the cars had enjoyed first-class handling and roadholding, because Vincenzo saw these qualities as vital for safety. Now thanks to the new V-6, they had real performance too. The answer to the equation was obvious—Vincenzo Lancia had deliberately turned his back on motor sport, but Gianni, despite some conflict with Lancia directors, felt differently. So differently that he took the unprecedented step of sending Lancia into competition. The Aurelia competed sucessfully in rallies and road racing—and sports-racing versions acquitted themselves admirably too, all of which motivated Gianni Lancia to fix his sights firmly on the last step in a logical progression: Formula One. But that program was ill-starred from the beginning—it cost a fortune and ended tragically with team driving star Alberto Ascari's death (while testing a Ferrari sports car), whereon Lancia turned over its entire équipe to Ferrari in the summer of 1955. The cars were modified by Ferrari who was being backed by large helpings of money from Fiat, and finally proved what they had hinted at from inception. They were world cham-

pionship mounts. Fangio won the Formula One title in 1956 in a Ferrari/Lancia.

At Lancia, emphasis on the competition cars had tended to obscure the very real progress being made in production models. As far back as 1950, Gianni Lancia had set in motion plans for an Ardea replacement, the Appia, a scaled-down development of the Aurelia. Its narrow angle—10 degrees—V-4 engine produced 38 hp compared to the Ardea's 29.5 and was an astonishingly compact powerplant measuring just 13.8 inches from fan to flywheel. The traditional Lancia sliding pillar front suspension, used ever since the Lambda, was improved for the Appia with revised steering joints to reduce road shock. The rear wheels were suspended on asymmetric semi-elliptic springs and a live axle. Introduced in 1953, the Appia remained in production for ten years and broke all Lancia records for small car sales. Steadily and meticulously, the factory turned out the car at a rate of 200 to 250 per week.

And yet it was the Appia which broke Lancia as a family firm. Developing it had taken the last profits from the good years and though its popularity seemingly justified the expense, profits from Appia sales could

*Lancias proliferated as the Sixties dawned. By 1961 the Appia (a GTE by Zagato above left) had forty-eight horsepower, an increase of ten over the original production version. In 1963 Pininfarina showed a special Flaminia at Turin (center left), which he drove thereafter as one of his favorite cars until his death in 1966. The production Flaminia (below left) by Pininfarina proved a solid seller, as did the Flavia (above) from the same coachbuilder. On the pages following, the parade continues. Vignale bodied a convertible (above left) on the Flavia chassis in 1963. The Lancia-designed Fulvia coupe (below left), successor to the Appia, introduced in 1965 and with its rally victories the bearer of Lancia's sporting image, was accompanied by a sleek Zagato-bodied Fulvia Sport variation (above right) capable of 110 mph and featuring a rear window that could be opened slightly via an electric motor to facilitate ventilation. After the takeover of the Lancia fortunes by Fiat as the Sixties came to a close, the first new Lancia was the Beta (below right).*

not recover money lost on the financially ruinous Formula One program. What was desperately needed was capital, and that could only come from the outside. At last, another family firm stepped in—the Pesenti cement combine—with a rescue bid in 1955. Part of the price Lancia had to pay was the handing over of control by Vincenzo's family to a new board of directors. Gianni Lancia resigned in 1956.

On the face of it, this spelled the collapse of everything Vincenzo Lancia had striven to build. But as sometimes happens, the spirit of the company he created was to live on. For the chief result of the new management was the introduction of a completely new series of models with new ideas, new designs, but the same solid reliability, high quality and meticulous attention to detail as had so firmly characterized the name of Lancia for better than a half century.

First of the new-generation Lancias was the Flaminia, with a 2548 cc version of the well-proved V-6. The production version introduced in 1957 had a six-light body with forward-hinged doors and—the first big change in Lancia practice—the sliding-pillar front suspension was swept away and replaced by a coil-spring and wishbone combination created by Professor Antonio Fessia, designer of the Fiat 600, who had just taken over as Lancia's new technical director. Then, in 1960, he introduced a new middle-range model which succeeded in breaking just about every rule in the Lancia book at one move: the Lancia Flavia (later renamed the 2000). Derived from Fessia's own design of 1948 for an 1100 cc front-drive car called the Cemsa-Caproni, the Flavia used a 1500 cc flat-four horizontally opposed engine mounted ahead of the front wheels and driving them through an all-synchro four-speed gearbox. Front suspension was by

double-wishbones with a transverse leaf-spring and anti-roll bar, rear by semi-elliptics with a live axle, and disc brakes were fitted to all four wheels.

For the Appia's successor, Fessia came up with the Fulvia, also boasting front wheel drive, the coupe of which—with steady increases in size from 1.2 to 1.3 and finally a 1.6-liter 115 hp unit—became the basis for a new Lancia competition effort in the fast-paced World Rally Championship where the cars—coded HF—performed remarkably well.

But all was not well at Lancia. The Pesentis, like the Lancias before them, had found the world car market a formidable place for a small firm specializing in careful but expensive development of high quality cars for a limited but discerning market. What Lancia needed, it seemed, was the

security and protection of a brother big enough to take on the First Division teams of Volkswagen, Ford and General Motors on something like equal terms. In 1969, with losses steadily mounting, help came from an unexpected quarter—Vincenzo Lancia's turn-of-the-century employer. Giovanni Agnelli—grandson of the man who had hired Vincenzo nearly seven decades before—wanted a name with the reputation and appeal of Lancia to act as an ally to Fiat in the increasingly tough struggle for the lion's share of the vital two-liter quality car market dominated more and more by Alfa Romeo and BMW. This was a hard-headed business deal, not a sentimental rescue of an old and honored name in the Italian car industry. When Fiat stepped in and took over Italy's fourth largest auto

maker, a crisis in the Po valley—an area already beset by labor troubles—was averted. Lancia's losses by 1969 had become so large that the takeover was accomplished by payment of just 1500 dollars, but the firm's debts amounted to a staggering sixty-seven million English pounds.

The first of the Lancia-designed and built passenger cars intended to improve the marque's financial position after the Fiat takeover appeared in 1972, as did the competition-oriented Stratos. Sixty-four years had elapsed since Vincenzo Lancia's first production car, the Alfa, had left his little factory. The new car was dubbed, appropriately enough, the Beta, utilizing Fiat running gear, an enormously well thought-out vehicle with front wheel drive, independent suspension all-around, four-wheel disc brakes,

five-speed gearbox and perfect use of interior space, doubtless the first of several new Lancias to come.

But whether or not Lancia can retain its old spirit and image under Fiat control—or whether doing so would even be desirable—remains to be seen. Whatever happens though, Vincenzo Lancia can rest easy in the knowledge that his successors will never take his good name in vain. After all, they bought the company for a reason—its great reputation. To aficionados of the marque, this mystique is easy to explain. A case can be made for the argument that Vincenzo Lancia and the factory which bears his name never produced a bad car. How many others would even dare have that suggested of them? ✤

# KELSEY'S MOTORETTE

## Three Wheels, Ten Horsepower, Twenty-Five Miles an Hour— What More Could a Motorist Ask?

His name was Cadwallader Washburn Kelsey—though he early shortened that to C.W., and he asked everybody to call him Carl. He spent his childhood in Chestnut Hill, Pennsylvania, and he built his first car there in 1897—at the age of seventeen. It was, as he reminisced many years later, "a 100 percent flop." It never did run.

His second one did, a three-wheeler with a one-cylinder engine called the Autotri that he produced the year following with a classmate from Haverford College. So did his third; it had one more wheel and one more cylinder than its predecessor—but, like the others, was strictly a schoolboy's whim. Soon after graduation, Carl Kelsey decided he'd better get down to the business of making a living.

If he couldn't do that building his own cars—and he didn't think so, there had been no rush to his workshop door—he could do the next best thing: sell someone else's. He sold the Autocar awhile in Chestnut Hill, opened a garage in Germantown, contracted for and secured the Locomobile sub-agency—and built another car. He gave it no name, but he called it a monster. Its wheelbase was 120 inches, and its engine had four cylinders. He was thoroughly unhappy with the result.

He forgot about tinkering again, for a time. He found the Maxwell instead. Here was a new car that looked like it could go places, and Carl Kelsey wanted to go along. He wrote Maxwell-Briscoe in Tarrytown, New York requesting the Maxwell agency for Philadelphia—and Benjamin Briscoe said he could have it for a $5000 investment. He put up the cash, procured a small showroom /service station on Broad Street—and he was in business. Was he ever! There was a bit of the Barnum in Carl Kelsey. He didn't originate the stunting-for-sales technique, perhaps, but he honed it to a fine art. The steepest steps of the poshest establishments in Philadelphia were his venue—he drove the Maxwell up every one he could find, and he contacted Lubin Film Studios—a pioneer cinematography firm supplying nickelodeons of the day—to capture his ascents on film. The results were headlines, an occasional near arrest—and a lot of publicity. Next was a thousand-mile nonstop Maxwell run up and down Broad Street—and more publicity.

Meanwhile, in Tarrytown, the good people of Maxwell-Briscoe were pondering why more of their cars were being sold in Philadelphia than anywhere else in the country. When they found out, they made Carl Kelsey their sales manager. It was the early fall of 1905. Carl Kelsey was twenty-five years old. He really got to work now. The Maxwell was a good car, mind you, and would have succeeded regardless of how it was sold. But the new sales manager was soon selling them as fast—or faster—than Maxwell-Briscoe could make them. Production practically doubled each year. Carl Kelsey built up the most powerful sales organization in the industry. And he went on making his movies, for nickelodeons and Maxwell agencies, sending Maxwells up steps, back and forth on teeterboards, on endurance runs like a 10,000-miler in the Greater Boston area. He entered the Gliddens, and won the Deming Trophy in 1906. His Maxwell won its class at Mount Washington. He sent a contingent of stripped roadsters to the light car race preceding the Grand Prize of 1908, and early the year next, he sent a willing lady named Alice Huyler Ramsey across the continent in a tourer. In an era when anything more formidable than a frying pan was generally considered too much for the gentle sex to handle, what

could be more headline-attracting than that? Not much, it seemed. No other transcontinental adventurer—not even Cannon Ball Baker in his prime—got the press attention that Alice Ramsey did. Carl Kelsey gave her a new Maxwell for her efforts—and sent the used one on exhibition.

Meanwhile Benjamin Briscoe was having dreams of empire—what Billy Durant was cooking up with General Motors, Briscoe would concoct with his United States Motor. Carl Kelsey thought it was a dreadful idea—and he resigned. Probably he would have left regardless. He was getting the itch to build a car again. It was mid-1909.

The vehicle that ensued had actually been designed as a Maxwell. Carl Kelsey had been among its most ardent proponents, indeed the sketches had been drawn up at his Tarrytown home. It was rather like any other Maxwell except for its feature of full front doors, a decided novelty for an open touring car and one Carl Kelsey thought was a surefire seller. But Maxwell had opted to abandon the project. Now Carl Kelsey took it up again on his own. He called the car the Spartan, it had four cylinders, a 104-inch wheelbase and sold for $1000. Production totaled one.

The prospectus Carl Kelsey had sent out to hoped-for investors glowed with optimism. It was as much a paean to the automobile itself ("the only thing since the beginning of times that has come forward as a true rival of the horse") and to the automotive industry ("the soundest in the country") as to the part he wished to play in it. Very quickly Carl Kelsey concluded the Spartan wasn't the car with which to do it. For one thing, the front door idea had by now been adopted by others, which effectively undercut its novelty; for another, Carl Kelsey heard rumblings that Henry Ford was about to slash a couple hundred dollars off the Model T which sounded ominous indeed, for the Spartan was aimed at the masses as well. He sat back and wondered what he should do now.

One solution suggested itself immediately. If Henry Ford was going to undersell Carl Kelsey's Spartan, Carl Kelsey would undersell Henry's Model T. But how? In a word, the Motorette—a vehicle in a class by itself. Carl Kelsey was thinking three wheels again. Just about everybody else—Bollée, Daimler and Benz in Europe, Knox in America—had given up on the idea, but he reasoned this was because of the "unsurmountable difficulties" they had encountered, which he would forthwith surmount. As, for example, tipping over or leaning in that direction when cornering. This was less likely in any case with the single wheel at the rear than at its more usual position in the front. But like Carl Kelsey said, "We found it essential that the one wheel in the rear must be held at right angles to the road surface at all times." He invented what he called a stabilizer, a cross bar and a system of links and levers so connecting the front axle with the frame that both of the full-elliptic front springs were forced to act together. (There was a truss construction over the rear wheel as well.) It was so simple an idea that Carl Kelsey wondered why no one had thought of it before. (Everybody has used it since, be it called sway bar, anti-sway bar or whatever.) "Like the warping of the wings on a flying machine invented by the Wright Brothers," the advertising would say, the stabilizer made possible the Motorette.

The Motorette had a 74-inch wheelbase, 56 3/4-inch front tread, weighed 900 pounds with steering by tiller, drive by chain. Its engine was a sweet little two-cylinder unit of ten horsepower designed by Carl Kelsey.

Its frame was pressed steel like a Packard's, its front axle an I-beam drop
forging like a Pierce-Arrow's, its seat pressed steel like an Overland's, its
full-elliptic springs vanadium like a Locomobile's, its wheels artillery like a
Stearns', its two-speed transmission planetary like a Buick's, its oiling
system circulating like a Chalmers', its cooling thermosyphon like a
Renault's, its radiator tubular like an Alco's, its bearings adjustable like a
Maxwell's. The foregoing big-name dropping was Carl Kelsey's, aimed at
distinguishing the Motorette from the sleazy, cheap little runabouts which
tended to give economical motoring a bad name. Part for part as well built
as a $6000 car was a popular Kelsey advertising refrain. Not noted in the
ad copy, but equally as significant, was the fact that at $385, the
Motorette was about half the price of the Model T.

The Motorette was introduced at the Grand Central Palace in Manhattan on New Year's Eve, 1910. As Carl Kelsey would proclaim, "critical
New York accepted it with acclaim . . . the seal of approval of the
metropolis was placed on it . . . the occupants of fur coats and $8 Knox
hats, who had just alighted from their big touring cars, found it interesting . . . the man in the slouch hat and last year's overcoat looked at
the Motorette with pleasure . . . the daintily garbed lady in the Worth
gown and Paris hat was also much interested"—and perhaps most telling,
"newspaper men certainly were pleased with it, and they are generally an
indifferent aggregation of men." Some fifty Motorettes were ordered at
the New York show alone.

The C.W. Kelsey Manufacturing Company was incorporated in the
State of New York, the factory was in Hartford, Connecticut, and a spirit
of optimism reigned in Kelsey land. The company's task, of course, was to
make the advantages of the Motorette known and have its unique
character, as readily apparent by the absence of a second rear wheel,
accepted. The three-wheel reality was tackled first, among its factors of
superiority being that the machine was always on three-point suspension

and thus roughness of road surface could never twist or throw out of align-
ment any part of the machinery. Enough publicity photos were taken to
assure all concerned that the Motorette could not tip over, but the Kelsey
organization never lost an opportunity to further nail down the reliability
of Motorette motoring. When the U.S. Government specified three-
wheelers for mail collection, Kelsey advertising was quick to point out that
"Uncle Sam does not jump at conclusions."

But paramount in Kelsey promotion was the factor of savings, which
allied itself nicely with the fact that the only cheap thing about a
Motorette was its price. Allusions to its bigger brothers in the marketplace,
as mentioned earlier, made one point with a minimum of subtlety. And
what the Motorette didn't have that its bigger brothers did made the
other. The lack of a fourth wheel meant that one wouldn't have to buy tires
for it; the Motorette sported heavy motorcycle tires in the front, an
automobile tire for the driving wheel—and the whole set could be
purchased "for $47.50, American gold." Moreover, the Motorette's con-
struction eliminated "a differential with its four gears, six bearings and
housing [and] a rear axle housing with its five bearings, drive shaft and
universal joints." Its little two-cycle water-cooled engine had but five
moving parts, twenty less than the four-stroke variety and meant that
there were "no valves to grind, no springs to get out of order, no push rods,
no cams, no cam shafts, no valve plugs, no cam shaft gearing." The
Motorette did away with the necessity of a body, the frame so serving, and
the seat was attached to it. It was all so simple.

A "healthy girl of ten" could crank it, only the most primitive
automotive skills were required to operate it. And it rode as smoothly as a
four-wheeler under almost all conditions, Carl Kelsey proudly displaying a
letter sent him by the Hillers' Poultry Plant, allowing that in two months
of service over rough rural byways, the company's Motorette, sometimes
transporting over 100 pounds of eggs, did not break one of them.

This was the commercial variety of Motorette, with a package carrier up front. The driver of a standard runabout, alas, would have been hard pressed to carry much more than a dozen eggs along with him. Luggage space there wasn't. It helped too if an owner hadn't many friends. Carl Kelsey envisioned his car strictly as a two-plus-aught. His Motorette, he said, yielded to no car except for passenger capacity and . . .

We come now to the matter of speed. The Motorette's top was 25 mph. Carl Kelsey's rationale: That was the average at which a motorcar was usually run, and the "occasional outburst of [greater] speed" wasn't worth the difference between $385 and the cost of a big car. Neatly said.

But if the Motorette lacked pretense in the miles-per-hour arena, it found other hustings upon which to prove itself. Carl Kelsey went stunting again. The Motorette was one of three cars—a Stanley Steamer and Napier special the two others—that made it to the top of Mount Washington one day. Though the AAA disallowed competition by cars with wheels numbering less than four, the Motorette entered the Glidden Tour as a non-contestant anyway; it had less than half the horsepower of the next smallest car and performed so admirably that the AAA forthwith lifted its ban on three-wheelers. To demonstrate its towing power, a Motorette pulled a 5700-pound Alco truck through the streets of Philadelphia during one busy rush hour.

If there was a snowstorm, Carl Kelsey and the Motorette were out in it, going from here to there, advertising the same in local newspapers the next day. But his greatest publicity-grabber was the Motorette's cross-country trek. This was no run for the speed record, but unlike most transcontinentals of the day, it wasn't announced at its terminus either. "We are going to shout about it now, before [the start]," Kelsey boasted. "We won't pull our stunt off in the dark and then explode when it is all over and we have won out." And the Motorette did win out, after several months on the road—the only untoward incident the entire trip being the three days its

drivers spent in the calaboose of Ludlow, California after it was discovered they had commandeered the tracks of the Atchison, Topeka & Sante Fe for their personal right-of-way.

Meanwhile Carl Kelsey took pen in hand. "Your bank president's opinion of you is valuable," one *Life* ad ran. "When you buy a motor car he will think better of you for buying a Motorette . . . . He knows that it is not for 'joy riding' or speeding, but for sane business and pleasure purposes." And another: "You would not run a big yacht without an auxiliary launch. You should not run a big motor car without an auxiliary Motorette." All of which rather made sense.

But, sadly, so did the reason for the Motorette company's demise three days before Christmas in 1911. With business moving briskly during the early months, Carl Kelsey had elected to concentrate on chassis manufacture, turning over engine production to Lycoming in Pennsylvania. The Lycoming factory was struck. There were no engines. Motorette chassis piled up in Hartford as dealers clamored for their cars. The strike was settled. But not the problems. Motorettes were assembled and delivered, and then the reports began coming in. The engines were freezing up, they were checked, in the crankcase of each—"in every blessed one of them"—about a half teacup of sand was removed. Sabotage. The Motorette was finished. With less than a year behind it, it couldn't weather such a blow to its image of reliability.

In later years Carl Kelsey would try again with another car—the friction drive Kelsey—and thereafter turn to advertising and banking, and more inventions and new ideas for all sorts of things, until death took him away from his tinkering in 1970. To the end, Carl Kelsey regretted the failure of his Motorette. "A more experienced man than I would have succeeded," he would sigh. But how? If anyone could have put over the Motorette, Carl Kelsey could. Just a look at the beguiling car it was, one certainly might wish that he had been able to. ✿

133

# NOW AND FOREVER, THE COBRA STORY

## *Wherein a True Believer Relates the Shameless, Honest-to-Carroll-Shelby Thrill Of Feeling at Home with a Beast*

A friend of mine is crazy about Ferraris, a passion made all the sharper by his lack of enough money to own one. Not long ago he accepted an invitation from a wealthy collector and drove a Ferrari 166 MM, a lovely red roadster with V-12 engine, etc. The car of his dreams turned out to have vague controls, an awkward driving position, indifferent handling, a temperamental clutch, demanding gearbox and the speed and power of, say, a Fiat 124.

This is mentioned for reasons of contrast.

The first time I saw a Cobra was at the SCCA races in Lake Garnett, Kansas in 1963. Ken Miles was team leader. He drubbed all the Corvettes and lesser production sports cars on Saturday. On Sunday they fitted a non-production oil cooler and had the Cobra declared a sports-racer. Miles trounced all the Ferraris, Maseratis, specials and so forth.

No point in giving the details of my career as a Cobra fan, from Ken Miles at Lake Garnett to Elliot Forbes-Robinson in the novice class in San Diego. The thing is, I believed in 1963 and believed better than a decade later that the Cobra had to be the most attractive, most thrilling, all-round great damn roadster in the world.

Then I got to drive one.

I was right.

Why the contrast? I think it has something to do with what might be called the power curve of history. The subject is sports cars, the parameters are speed, power, handling, good looks. The best sports cars will be those lightweight roadsters with superior handling, stunning lines, blazing power and not one item not truly needed for better performance or the numbing requirements of the motor vehicle code.

All these things are, of course, relative. Sports cars got better by steps for generations. When each was new, then, the curve was able to reach a new high. The best of 1949 was the best ever, in 1949. Ferrari was the master and the way to build the best possible sports-roadster was stiff springs, non-synchromesh gearbox and an engine which was no bigger than a bread box and contained as many moving parts as the Haydn Planetarium.

We can visit the past from the present. We have at our disposal a time machine and it does our romantic notions a disservice. Take your 1976 point of reference along when you drive 1949's best and you will burst your balloon.

Not with the Cobra. Our imaginary curve tops out in 1967 or so, when it strikes an impenetrable ceiling, a bullet-proof thatch of social pressures. Just about the time the Cobra raised the sports-roadster curve to what will remain its high point, there was a societal revolution.

It was a sneaky little war, fought on several fronts. The federal bureaucracy took over automobile design, the insurance people gutted high performance drivers, Detroit stabbed the oil people in the back. Powerful cars became immoral, limited production cars were mostly illegal and open cars were unfashionable.

Reinforcing this, racing changed. The rules and the venues changed. The open roadster built for the Mille Miglia was replaced by the mid-engine coupe for Le Mans. Where once Cunningham and Reventlow commissioned artistry, we had Jim Hall getting aerodynamic weapons delivered in plain brown vans with Michigan plates.

So much for our ever-rising curve. Two conclusions:

1) The Cobra was the sports-roadster, the thinly disguised road racing

car, brought to its ultimate perfection, and

2) We shall not see its like again.

How this happened is more than names, numbers and technical tidbits. Writing as a storefront sociologist, a visceral historian, it strikes me that the Cobra was created by the convergence of three parties, two of them motivated by more than money.

The Cobra triad was comprised of AC Cars, Ltd., Ford Motor Company and Carroll Shelby.

AC has been building cars forever. Always small, always different. The cars are a sideline, actually, and one gets the feeling AC builds cars because AC builds cars, as the Zen folks say.

The details of the AC contribution begin with, yes, the Ferrari barchetta. Italian sports-racing cars commenced as widened formula cars with cycle fenders. About the end of World War II, the artists in that country discovered the envelope body and did some lovely things with it, not the least of which were the roadsters Touring produced for Ferrari.

A couple of years later, England became the sports car center, the hub of that center being a few creative builders of specials. One builder was named Tojeiro and his high point was a roadster which looked near as sin to Ferrari's Touring-bodied roadsters.

AC had been building dated sports cars and wanted something new. So AC bought Tojeiro's special and it became, with detail changes, the prototype AC Ace, powered by AC's venerable engine. The Ace used Tojeiro's chassis design, a ladder frame with independent suspension provided by links and transverse leaf springs. Not the best way, but it worked. The Ace looked great and handled well, so AC did a deal with Bristol Aeroplane and offered the AC-Bristol, with one of the world's most complicated pushrod hemi-head sixes. Gobs of power, however, and the Ace-Bristol was the hottest thing in its class.

Then Bristol decided it didn't want to make engines for cars anymore.

Meanwhile, on this side of the pond, Ford Motor Company was entering its Feisty Period. Ford was doing well in the market. Ford executives were discovering Europe, the Jet Set and the prestige attached to high performance products from across the water. The top brass was ready for proposals which would make Ford a revered name for something other than the assembly line. And Ford engineers, smarting under the lash of having the hot rod image seized by Chevrolet, had come up with a nifty little V-8, a thinwall wonder, great power potential, small size, in sum the best engine swap material anybody ever had.

Now. The idea itself is not new. The man who snaps his fingers and exclaims, "Let's put a powerful American engine into a light European chassis with sexy body" is following the brainstorms of the great. Railton did it. Allard did it. Facel Vega did it. Shucks, if you want to invoke exotic memories, Miles and Sam Collier did it.

It works.

In the Cobra's case, Carroll Shelby did it.

Shelby is an interesting man. He was a pretty fair driver in his day. More important to this narrative is a different talent, the talent which actually determines who drives Grand Prix and who drives his own car while his wife pays the household bills.

Driving acumen isn't the controlling factor. There were a whole bunch of guys racing borrowed M.G.'s in the early days. Carroll Shelby was one who was invited to drive for the Wealthy Sportsmen importing the Ferrari and Maseratis. There were a lot of semi-pros like that, but Shelby was one invited to drive for A Team, namely Aston Martin. This isn't to knock Shelby's driving skill. It is to illustrate Shelby's other talent, that vital quality which somehow makes other people want what you want.

Well. Here was AC with this neat car and no engine. Here was Ford with the itch for glory, the urge to race itself into our hearts, and with this neat engine and no car. Here was Carroll Shelby with a great present, a ticky

heart and a need for a future. Hey, he said in effect to Ford, could I have some engines? Please, he said in effect to AC, might I have some cars? Sure, they said. He put them together and there it was, the AC Cobra powered by Ford, one suspects the correct title is.

This is simplifying like mad. There was money involved, naturally. The details are recorded in somebody's account books and we outside will never know, but odds are Ford backed the deal with cash while Shelby contributed energy and know-how. Why not? He was exactly the front man the project needed.

Anyway, they got some AC cars and some 260 V-8's and put them together at Shelby's new plant in California. Development leader was Ken Miles. The perfect choice. Miles was a fierce driver, backed by an incredible amount of engineering lore and just plain intuition. His homemade cars were always two jumps better than the expensive racers of the Wealthy Sportsmen, which meant Miles always worked twice as hard at getting good rides. Then presto! Here was Shelby and Ford and all that computer time and parts and money. Make it work, they said.

Miles surely did. The 260 V-8 with Ford's own four-speed gearbox weighed something like four pounds more than the Bristol engine and gearbox. Power and torque were doubled. The engine fit with scarcely more than a few dimples in the firewall, while the drivetrain, differential mounting, etc. needed lots more beef. The frame ditto, and there were minor suspension changes and wider tracks fore and aft. The aluminum body stayed mostly as it was, save for wider fenders with lips and a longer and smaller radiator air intake. The latter change improved the looks while providing more air flow at speed with less drag: a nice double benefit.

While Miles and crew were performing all this technical wizardry, they retained the original's English charm. The Cobra was a true roadster, with demountable side curtains that flapped, with a windshield readily removed and with a fragile fabric top sort-of held in place by 1234 snaps,

none of which quite fitted right when you tried attaching the top during a rainstorm. The doors were held closed, more or less, by those funny little chrome-box style latches dating back to at least the M.G. TA. Great searing blasts of heat came through the firewall in summer, your toes turned blue in winter, the heater made pitiful noises and dumped water on your feet . . . all part of the mystique, namely that the true sports-roadster was as light and spartan as the law allowed, everything having been done in the interest of speed and style.

So. What did they have? The first Cobra was delivered in February 1962. The nearly stock engine was rated at 260 bhp and true curb weight was 2020 pounds. *Road & Track* tested the car and were they astonished. The Cobra did the standing quarter mile in a careless and casual 13.8 seconds, going through the speed traps at 112 mph. Top speed, which was observed and thus accurate, was 153 mph. Wow. They couldn't believe it, but there it was.

The three sides of the partnership all came up winners. AC Cars had a dependable market and built-in sales and distribution networks. Ford had the hottest car on the road, both in fact and the public's eyes. Shelby had something worth doing. Ford dealers fought for dealership rights, everybody with $5995 to spend bought a Cobra, the Shelby team drubbed the Corvettes right off the bat.

There are two types of factual history involved here and both will be treated with quickness.

First, the technical side. Ford expanded the 260 into the 289 just about the time Cobras went into production, so the 289 became the standard Cobra engine. There were street versions, with a slightly different camshaft being the only change, and there were competition options like big-valve cylinder heads, hotter cams, higher compression ratios, a quartet of dual-throat Webers and something like 325 bhp. The first 125 Cobras had the Ace's worm-and-sector steering unit, the geometry of which had never been matched to the geometry of the front suspension. Plus it was heavy on the arms. Shelby and crew then came up with a rack-and-pinion system lifted from the M.G. Midget that was lighter, more precise and allowed the front wheels to point in the proper direction at all times.

New model time, so to speak, came when Shelby was running Ford's international racing effort and the team needed more speed so as to deal with Ferrari. The international rules allowed special bodies, provided they were fitted to the homologated chassis of the make and model in question. Pete Brock designed a lovely and aerodynamic coupe body for the Cobra. They called it the Daytona coupe, they built six and they are beautiful, if not exactly what one would call a production car.

The major Cobra change came in 1966. For reasons to be dealt with shortly, Shelby and Ford decided they needed more power, i.e. cubic inches. Easy. Ford had developed a truly monstrous NASCAR engine, the 427, good for an easy 500 or so bhp. The engine, that is. The Cobra chassis, semi-homegrown 1954 special that it was, simply wasn't enough for the new power.

In effect, they set the 427 on blocks, draped the body over it and filled in the space between with a new frame: wider, stiffer and with larger tubes. Ford's computers cranked out a scientifically correct geometry for a more normal suspension, fully independent with locating arms and spring/shock units. The body was widened down the middle, provision was made for oil cooler and brake duct vents and the radiator intake was made larger,

*On the opening pages and the pages following: a 289 roadster and a 427 roadster.*

plainer and more aggressive.

The SCCA was still being sticky about options and extra equipment back then, so the Cobra catalogue showed two versions of the 427: normal and competition, the race version with hood scoop, headers and side-exhausts, differential cooler and engines of varying specification, some with aluminum heads, dry sumps, NASCAR cams, all sorts of internal tweaks and a claimed 490 bhp. At least. When the market for these machines was saturated after the sale of perhaps nineteen cars, minor modifications were made to make them street-legal. With the addition of signal lights, a road-going windshield, top and side curtains, an occasional bumper if ordered, rear wheel flares, less raucous exhaust and slightly detuned engine, the competition became the S/C—street competition.

The 427 was a racing engine, rather like Chrysler's Hemi in that it was built only for competition and sold to the public reluctantly and only because the rules made them do it. Damned expensive engine, too. At some point in the Cobra's production run, the 427 was replaced with the 428, Ford's big dull passenger car engine.

I can find no public mention of this running change. That isn't to say Shelby kept the switch secret, which is to say that's exactly what I suspect happened but have no proof. Odd. Probably by this time Ford had lost interest and reckoned to save a few bucks. Also odd is that I don't remember ever seeing a 428 Cobra offered for sale. Do all the 428 owners believe they have the 427? Have they all swapped engines?

*Left and below: the Pete Brock-designed Daytona coupe, one of the six built.*

Whatever, Cobra production began in 1962 and ended in 1967. During that time, according to the records, Shelby, Ford and AC jointly produced 630 of the 289's, including seventy-five with the 260 engine, and 510 of the 427/428's, of which twenty-six were the S/C version. (Collector's note: One of the more popular things for 427 Cobra owners to do is convert their cars to the racing version. One would suspect there are twice as many S/C 427's existing now as were originally built.)

Competition. To list all the entries and results of all the races in which Shelby, the Ford team and myriad private owners took part would be to use up the rest of this book. No way. Nor do the details matter much.

Suffice it that the first Cobra entry was Bill Krause in the second Cobra built, at Riverside in October 1962. The car waltzed away from the Corvettes, then broke. In 1963 the team raced itself into invincibility. In 1964, thanks to the Daytona coupe, Cobra tackled Ferrari and the international races—looked good at Daytona, won Sebring, took fourth overall at Le Mans, won the manufacturer's title in the SCCA pro series.

One might say all this was practice. Ford's own people had been dabbling in racing and hadn't done well. Shelby was assigned the Ford team and Ford won the FIA Manufacturer's Championship.

There they were, in the Big Leagues . . . with nothing for the Cobra to do. The rules had changed. The entrants didn't need even to pretend that their cars were fresh from the assembly line. They could build honest racing cars. They did. Ford and Shelby combined the enthusiasm of a street fighter with the resources of a moon shot. They had teams of drivers and engine dynos and wind tunnels and metallurgists and devices which ran the car at full chat for twenty-five hours with a thermo-couple in every crevice, in short, the show-no-mercy science they needed to win.

The Cobra, that brutal open roadster, that bellowing front-engine monster, was shown no mercy. Nothing personal, you understand. It was simply that Cobras were only good for winning SCCA races and Ford's top men wouldn't know Lake Garnett from Lake Michigan.

Came then the effects of the federal safety acts. For 1968, thanks to the social critics, the politicians looking for an issue for which they could claim credit, and special thanks for the public's resentment for years of being bullied by car dealers, cars were guilty until proven innocent.

All cars sold for road use had to be crash certified. Destructive testing, the lab guys say. Sure, Ford could have done it. Other limited production cars were somehow kept on the market.

Ford didn't want to.

Why should they? Ford had hot Mustangs for the younger set, all those international trophies for their own emotional kick, Panteras for the Beautiful People, Indy and NASCAR for the masses . . . I am getting carried away. To be fair about this, we must remember that Ford markets for the millions. Building a couple of hundred hot sports-roadsters per year is not what Ford Motor Company is there for.

The three partners quit winners. Shelby wrapped up the real-racing effort, built one prototype road car and took a long look. He decided not to bother. Shelby went off to sell racing tires, deodorant and chili powder. Ford raced sedans, took their lumps and then took their Mustang and made it into a lump. AC had the United Kingdom rights to various bits, so they built Cobras with 427-style chassis and 289 engines and commissioned an elegant two-place convertible with 428 power. The Cobra is out of production even there, now.

What harm the loss of the Cobra was, was emotional. Appearance is more important than reality, so all the trendy types zoomed off to buy slick mid-engine coupes, à la international racer. Never mind that it's hellishly hard to live in a car with the engine placed perfectly and the people wedged anyplace left over. The masses were cajoled—well, make that gulled—into buying little sedans with stripes and streamlined mirrors.

In that line. One cannot avoid noting that Ford Motor Company kept the rights to the Cobra name and now sells little coupes with Cobra emblem, plastic tackies and more stripes than anything this side of a silent movie chain gang. Comment on this seems inappropriate.

On the bright side, there were those who knew the high point of roadster history when it growled past. So the Cobra was out of production, so what. Cobras still stomped Corvettes in SCCA racing, they still stopped traffic and they still were delightful toys. Ford parts were available. So were AC parts, AC having that affectionate regard for customers which dis-

*Left: a 427 roadster from 1966. Pages following: a 427 S/C roadster from 1967.*     141

tinguishes the small English firms, which indeed may keep them alive. New outfits producing Cobra parts sprang up immediately when Shelby himself stopped making them. Zip, there was a Cobra owner's club. Normal retail asking price of any Cobra stayed level, then went up. Hasn't stopped rising yet.

Enough history. What's a Cobra like to drive? Let me tell you.

Before starting, however, we must bear in mind that the Cobras were the most powerful, highest performance cars in an era of high performance cars. As discussed, high performance is relative. Because the hot cars of today are not nearly as hot as the hot cars of ten years ago, a projectile like a Cobra performs right off our current scale. The Cobra is not merely quick. It's quick beyond comparison. To say that a stock Cobra is to a turbocharged Porsche 911 as the Porsche is to a Datsun B210 is to say that a broken leg smarts more than a sprained ankle.

Well. The stock 289 is a normal sort of incredible performer. The engine fires and idles with no fuss and a pleasant rumpity-rumpity-rump. Then Wham! the Cobra leaps into action in a great surging series of bounds. Terrific feeling of control. Just enough power to be more power than one needs, so the driver is always conscious of a car that will do anything it's asked to do.

There's an odd sensation to the clutch, presumably because there wasn't

much room for motion, so provided instead was lots of leverage and a short throw. There is very little feel. Lift the foot and the clutch takes hold. The gearshift is a delight, for technical reasons not explained in the literature. The standard American four-speed transmission for use behind a V-8 is a clumsy unit and comes with a great clumsy oar of a gearchange. It is balky and obstructive and only the most dedicated of dragstrip artists would tolerate one.

The Cobra 289, though, Ford trans or not, has short throws. It's precise and light. Only the knowledge that the writer was using the hot-knife-through-butter business as a mock cliché years ago prevents me from saying the Cobra 289 shifts like you-can-guess. Same for the location of the lever except that—Dammit Sirs—it *does* fall readily to hand.

Brakes. Discs all 'round and no power assist. Without becoming tiresomely technical, suffice it that drum brakes activate themselves and disc brakes don't. Discs need extra force. When there is no booster device—as there isn't on the Cobra—the extra force comes from the driver. The first stop becomes an experiment. Will one shut down in time? Yes, you must push down firmly, is all.

The Cobra is basically a 1950's chassis and the car never lets you forget it. Freeway ride is surprisingly smooth and the car tracks beautifully. One does need to flex the arms in the tight stuff, however, and the need to use

142

muscle makes it difficult to be as precise as the car looks. Again, this is the sort of thing a beginner notes on the first drive and promptly begins to forget. By the end of the day one is drifting through tight turns, whipping in and out of driveways, etc. So the steering is heavy, so what? If this is a dated car, then the rest of the world has gone in the wrong direction.

The Cobra 427. A monster. VROOOM! it says when the key is turned. There is no idle. It bangs and stutters and coughs and lopes . . . you think it's going to be hard to get this beast rolling, eh? Not so. Just because it won't idle does not mean there's no power at idling speed. Despite the bangs and snorts, there is so much torque at 600 rpm you can let out the clutch and lurch down the road without touching the accelerator. We motoring journalists are accustomed to reporting on cars which have so much power they don't need a transmission. This 427 Cobra has so much power you don't need a gas pedal. Clunk into second, then third, then high, all minus use of the right foot and there you are, 40 mph. Downshift, then touch the pedal and the whole damn thing goes VROOOM! again, the car is rocketing along at sixty in first on a narrow road and there are three more gears to go.

If ever a road car was faster than a speeding radio wave, here it is. Figures of speech are worth no more here than are times from a stopwatch. A standing quarter in a Z car is keeping your foot down and watching the instruments. A standing quarter in the 427 is being shot from a cannon.

One demonstration is worth a thousand thrilling words. A former 427 owner remembers how he treated skeptical passengers:

"I'd tell people how fast the car was and they wouldn't believe me. Okay, I'd say, get in the car . . . . Then I'd take a ten dollar bill and tape it to the sun visor in front of the passenger seat. Soon as the car moves, I'd say, reach up. If you can grab that bill, it's yours to keep . . . . I'd wind up the engine, drop the hammer and give it full power through the gears. Some people, guys who'd never been in a fast car before, screamed . . . . I never had a passenger who could raise his arms over his head when the 427 was pushing him back into the seat . . . . Nobody ever grabbed that ten dollars."

And nobody ever built anything like the Cobra—before or since. That the magic stopped is not anyone's fault, not Ford's, nor AC's, nor Shelby's. Not even the dunderheads who wrote the laws which made the Cobra impractical to manufacture were truly evil, for they took away something they didn't know existed.

But oh, what they missed! Over the mountains on a Sunday morning in a constant flow of tactile sensations, the music, the sun, the crisp air, g-forces, feeling of total command. A time machine, yes, the Cobra was a time machine. We shall not see its like again. We are all the poorer for it.✥ 143

# THE TOSS OF A HAT-IN-THE-RING: RICKENBACKER

## A Saga of the Car That Should Have Had Everything Going For It

Eddie Rickenbacker was coming home. And with him the French Legion of Honor, the Croix de Guerre and three citations, the American Distinguished Service Cross and seven citations. Behind him lay twenty-six German planes officially shot down in combat, the record of the American army. Behind him, too, further back, stretched a record of wins in races and exhilarating drives in the likes of Duesenberg, Peugeot and Maxwell. But ahead of him . . . what?

For the immediate future, there were the hero's welcomes—a "monster banquet," as the press called it, at the Waldorf Astoria in New York, and, not to be outdone, a three-day celebration a coast away in Los Angeles—with similar adulatory fetes at points in between. It was early 1919. World War I was over. Captain and Squadron Commander Edward Vernon Rickenbacker—affectionately he would be referred to as Captain Eddie the rest of his life—was twenty-eight years old.

"Although the American ace of aces has received attractive offers from motion picture producers and from publishers he has not yet decided what business he will engage in," reported *Automotive Industries*. Neither of those, Captain Eddie quickly concluded. Nor did he entertain notions of returning to motor sport. Instead—as he recalled in his autobiography—with the hoopla dying down, he retreated to New Mexico and the serenity of the desert where thoughts he'd harbored during "quiet days on the front" returned. He decided to manufacture an automobile. Meanwhile, in Detroit, someone else was thinking exactly the same thing.

The relationship between Eddie Rickenbacker and the car which bore his name is a subject to be approached gingerly. And, interestingly, it was even then. An article by W.A.P. John appearing in *MoToR* of May 1923 exemplifies. Opening with comments by a "vociferous gentleman" otherwise unidentified that "the big hero of the war, plastered with more decorations than a Polish wrestler" had sold his name to a party also unidentified who promised to "raise the jack and form the company, and give [Rickenbacker] a job with a good title and a swell salary," it continued in

apologia—and almost embarrassingly so—to prove that this indeed was not the case. One is left with the impression that Eddie Rickenbacker not only created the Rickenbacker car, but heaven and earth besides—a feeling conveyed also by many of the advertisements the company itself produced. Appropriate credit for heaven and earth lies elsewhere of course—and so largely does the Rickenbacker.

Eddie Rickenbacker was a celebrity, a legend, a "public utility," as *Motor West* put it, for whom speaking requests mounted "like compound interest." His war story was told a thousand times in the popular magazines of the day. As a representative figure for a burgeoning automobile company, there was no one quite like him. But in no way is this meant as a diminution of Captain Eddie's contribution. If he had done nothing else—and he did, as we shall see—but lend his name and presence to an automobile, he certainly chose wisely in the vehicle on which it was proffered. And it is certainly a measure of his stature that no narrative of the Rickenbacker automobile can begin without him.

But in reality the Rickenbacker automobile story truly starts with Byron Forbes ("Barney") Everitt. He was almost twenty years Rickenbacker's senior. At the moment, his Everitt Brothers was flourishing on East Jefferson Avenue in Detroit as the second largest body building plant in the world. But memories lingered of his years as a manufacturer, particularly his days with the E.M.F. Barney Everitt was thinking cars again—and the word Eddie Rickenbacker had received in the desert was the same. The two men found each other, and Barney Everitt started making a lot of phone calls.

Probably the first two were to his old partners, the M and F of E.M.F. The former, William E. Metzger, had subsequent to the initialed company, organized with Barney as president the Metzger Motor Car Company but had virtually retired thereafter. He wasn't interested in the Rickenbacker proposition. Walter E. Flanders had, previous to lending his initial and his experience to E.M.F., helped put Henry Ford on the road to

The Model B Touring Phaeton from 1923, one of four body styles offered and priced at $1685, certainly one of the better automotive buys of the season.

*An early 1924 Model C Opera Coupe, with the "vibrationless" Rickenbacker six-cylinder engine, and the air cleaner introduced in '23, but not yet braking at all four of the car's wheels.*

production—and afterwards had rescued Maxwell from the debacle of the fallen empire of United States Motor in 1911. He was looking forward to retirement. Barney Everitt talked him out of that—and into Rickenbacker instead, as a director of the new company. Initially, Walter Flanders hoped his tenure might be short, but he changed his mind when he saw the Rickenbacker prototype.

Walter Flanders was no engineer, but he knew production like few men ever had in the industry. Neither was Barney Everitt an engineer, but he knew business. It was largely his uncanny sense for it that had resulted in the three partners to E.M.F. becoming millionaires with the sell-out—on Barney's terms—to Studebaker. Eddie Rickenbacker was no engineer either, but he was, well, Eddie Rickenbacker.

Into the technical gap strode, first, Harry L. Cunningham who would officially be titled secretary and treasurer. His credits stretched back to Winton in Cleveland and the Ford "999" in Dearborn. After a racing career and work with Henry Ford, he had transferred his loyalties to E.M.F. and then to Flanders as sales engineer for Maxwell. Chief engineer for Rickenbacker would be E.R. Evans, lately of the Canadian Metzger Motor Car Company and more recently a freelance consulting engineer. Joining him as experimental engineer would be Ray McNamara, a veteran "driver and pilot in endurance contests" and former engineer for Maxwell.

Then, as assistant general manager, there was Roy M. Hood, erstwhile

purchasing agent for E.M.F. and Maxwell; and, as comptroller, A.L. Miller, who'd taken care of matters financial for Maxwell on the West Coast. Lest the organizational incest seem total, one hastens to add C.M. Tichenor as production manager, who'd done same for Pierce-Arrow and had been involved in Liberty aircraft engine production, and sales manager W.J. Drumpelmann who had been "associated in an active way with many of the industry's conspicuous merchandising successes," by name Chalmers, Olds, Hudson, Essex and Saxon. Both had missed affiliation with E or M or F along the way. Still, the new Rickenbacker organization somehow had the look of an alumni reunion.

The Rickenbacker Motor Company officially came into being in July 1921, with application filed in Lansing on the 25th for the $5,000,000 concern. Scarcely a word had issued forth about the company in public print prior to this date, although by that summer its reality was known by all participants—and each was by now at work bringing it into being. Already it had been decided that Eddie Rickenbacker's principal asset to the firm would be in the direction of public relations and sales—and he had despatched himself in December of 1920 for what he called a "refresher course" courtesy of his friend Cliff Durant as vice-president and general manager of the California company handling Sheridan distribution in that state. His title at Rickenbacker would be vice-president and director of sales—and his salary, one veteran of the company remembers, was set at

*An early 1925 Model D Coach-Brougham—the Rickenbacker's most popular body style, accounting for about sixty percent of total production—proudly noting what else the car had.*

$25,000 a year. A healthy sum in those days.

Barney Everitt, as president and general manager, remained in Detroit to get the machinery of the new company going, while in the shops of his Everitt Brothers plant, the Rickenbacker engineers worked to do the same for the new car. In August of 1921, as Eddie Rickenbacker was winding up his refresher course on the coast, a few more details about the company were released, though precious little about the car itself. And there was some confusion too regarding the financing of the company, with conflicting reports from varied sources, all agreeing only that it was Barney Everitt's money which was largely underwriting the enterprise.

Initially the Everitt Brothers plant was envisioned as the home for Rickenbacker, but minds were changed when its production capacity of a hundred cars a day loomed as too modest in light of the reception to the project simply the preliminary announcements had made. The name Rickenbacker was magic, and the names behind the new company were among the most respected in the industry. Detroit was agog. More room would be needed certainly, to supply the demand for this still mysterious car which sight unseen seemed to have everything going for it. Consequently, in September, "a property transfer of the first magnitude," as *Automobile News* put it, was consummated. Rickenbacker bought the Michigan Avenue plant of Disteel Wheel, with its 200-car-a-day capacity "and where expansion can be both great and easy." It stood in readiness.

"Oft expectation fails, and most oft there/Where most it promises . . ." Not so with the Rickenbacker. Captain Eddie was soon declaring himself "permeated with pleasure" after taking the first order from newspaper cartoonist Clair Briggs. The New York show was in progress, and the Rickenbacker, with touring, sedan and coupe models on display (priced $1485 to $1985), was universally acclaimed "worthy of its name," a slogan advertised far and wide. (Equally promoted would be the "Hat-in-the-Ring" insignia of Captain Eddie's flying squadron which now became the company's emblem.)

Departures from the ordinary made the big news for the Rickenbacker car and chief among these was its engine, a three main bearing six displacing 218 cubic inches and developing 58 bhp at 2800 rpm. A speed of sixty was assured and—most significant—it was guaranteed without vibration, virtually unheard of in its price range. The Rickenbacker did it with two flywheels at either end of the crankshaft. It was an idea that, Rickenbacker promotion said, Captain Eddie had happened upon Over There. After shooting down a German plane in combat, one which during battle had impressed him with its "marvelous maneuverability," he had asked on his return to the airdrome that the motor be rescued for his inspection. "Why, there is a flywheel on the rear end of that crankshaft," he exclaimed. A picturesque story, no doubt true, though the idea of the tandem flywheel was not, having been patented earlier by George Lomb. 147

Sporting *"speed and dash in its very appearance . . . for those thousands of youthful friends of Rickenbacker,"*
*the Model D Roadster from 1925 priced at a thrifty $1595.*

Nonetheless, according to all reports of test drives, the Rickenbacker was indeed a smooth running car with no period of vibration, a factor which impressed journalists and was the Rickenbacker's chief selling point during its maiden year.

Frame and suspension design were noteworthy too. Frame channels were wide and exceptionally deep—eight inches—for rigidity and elimination of weaving. ("Comparatively, Brooklyn Bridge does not provide such a factor of rigidity and strength," the ads said.) Springs were semi-elliptic, thirty-six inches in front and an unusually long fifty-seven in the rear, the frame cradled between them. Most other specs on the car were standard—though admirably crafted. Rickenbacker bragged that their rear-wheel brakes were "full anti-rattle equipped," but said little else about them; there wasn't that much to say. But in a corner of their exhibit at the New York show was a front axle display equipped with brakes. Nobody paid it much mind.

By March production in the factory was ten units a day, the thousandth Rickenbacker issued forth in May and production, then at thirty cars daily, was scheduled to be increased to fifty.

If ever a man was omnipresent, Eddie Rickenbacker was in those days. Whitman Daly, who was working in the paint shop of Everitt Brothers where the cars were finished, remembers seeing him often: "I don't know why he came in, probably just to see and be seen. He seemed a plain everyday fellow, friendly, nodding to everybody in the shop. He always wore a homburg and a long black coat, kind of looked like an undertaker—and he never *ever* took his coat off." Whitman Daly wasn't sure why. But a reasonable explanation, in retrospect, might be that it would have slowed him down. With coat on, he was ever ready for a quick getaway to his next port of call. In the first year and a half of Rickenbacker production, he crossed the continent twice and the Atlantic once (for a combined business-trip/honeymoon; he'd found time to get married), visited the forty-four distributorships that formed the nucleus of the organization now, two-thirds of the four hundred sales outlets and, via community luncheons and such, met an equal fraction of new Rickenbacker owners.

By August they numbered 2500, and the press marvelled at the figure "in view of the apparently great difficulties many thought would face the new concern because of the unpropitious time, commercially speaking, of its launching." The postwar depression hadn't yet bottomed. By year's end, the output neared five thousand, a five percent cash dividend was declared, and E. LeRoy Pelletier, "famous as one of the industry's greatest creators of selling atmosphere," joined the company as director of sales promotion and publicity. (He was, you guessed it, an E.M.F. graduate.)

It had been, all things considered, a very good year, begging to be celebrated in song. And it was, with words and music by Leo Wood, a ditty titled "In My Rickenbacker Car," boasting such long-to-be-remembered lines as "She won't jar your vacation for there's no vibration. . . ." Where it placed on the charts, no one can recall.

"Builders of Hat-in-Ring Car Push Work To Keep Up With Schedule" was the Detroit *Free Press* headline. As "one of the youngest and most successful automobile manufacturing institutions in Detroit," it had a big job to do. Cars produced in January numbered 500, February 750, March 1040—and now the company was predicting 15,000 for the year.

In March, too, Rickenbacker received authorization to issue $2.5 million in additional stock, in May Barney Everitt jovially reported that current assets were almost double liabilities, in June the second cash dividend was declared, distributors now numbered eighty-three with six hundred thirty associate dealers, and the company announced that a million dollar insurance policy from Lloyds of England had been procured for its vice-president. Captain Eddie, about to begin his fourth swing around the United States since the December previous, had decided it would be faster to do it by plane.

The Rickenbackers for 1923 were pretty much the same as those the year previous, though in May the company declared that henceforth production would center upon closed models, with open cars built on order only. The trend toward closed car preference in the industry had been noted as early as the automobile shows of 1922; still, industry reporters found the Rickenbacker announcement rather unexpected.

Had they not been aware—and *Automobile Topics* airily noted that everyone in "the better-informed trade circles" was—the news the following month (dateline June 27th) would have dumbfounded.

Four-wheel brakes. It was quite a revelation—the Rickenbacker was the first medium-priced volume-produced American car to install them. Duesenberg had pioneered their use in this country, as everyone knows—as had, obscurely, the Kenworthy "Line-O-Eight," the Heine-Velox and the Rubay, for all of whom the death knell had sounded prior to or near the Rickenbacker announcement date. Duesenberg was in a class by itself. What galled the Rickenbacker company—and they said so politely in print—was the fact that Packard had beat them to the brake announcement by sixteen days. Packard's were mechanical like the Rickenbacker's (Duesenberg had hydraulic), but Packard offered them on eight-cylinder cars only—which were, after all, a price class removed from the Rickenbacker. After Rickenbacker came Buick's announcement in August, followed by its sister car, the Oakland; then GM's Cadillac—and in a rush after that, Marmon, Chalmers, Elgin, Paige, Locomobile and others. Call it the domino theory, a hop on the bandwagon, whatever.

Anyone who cared to be aware would have known about the Rickenbacker brakes for months or even years previous. Captain Eddie had wanted them all along, both his racing experience and his frequent trips to Europe convincing him they were inevitable for production cars in this country. Indeed the very first Rickenbacker laid out on the drawing board in 1919 had them. But it was decided then to hold them in reserve, to develop them further, the company reasoning that the public is ever loath to accept the revolutionary readily. The vibrationless engine was enough to offer the marketplace initially. So four-wheel brake development continued—in semi-secrecy. Doubtless the Packard announcement answered the question of when was the most propitious time to spring the Rickenbacker surprise.

Whether or not it had been a mistake not to introduce sooner, there's no way history will ever really know, though there is something to be said for the contention that America wasn't ready for the idea in 1922. Indeed, many chroniclers of Rickenbacker history, including Captain Eddie himself, place a great deal of blame for the Rickenbacker decline upon the introduction and the concomitant public campaign by companies not offering four-wheel brakes that the system was unsafe.

Certainly, Rickenbacker did have the task at the beginning of educating the public as to the efficacy of the idea, including offering the comment of a European engineer that American brakes had heretofore been "criminally crude." And being first in its price class with the idea might have made for a stigma, although clearly the Rickenbacker system—each wheel was individually adjustable and provision for front/rear balance was also provided—was laudatory and probably superior to most variations offered by companies rushing to the braking bandwagon after the Rickenbacker announcement.

Benjamin F. Capwell, who was with·Hunt Motor in New York at the time, recalls that Rickenbacker's brakes caused no trouble, save for drivers following behind in two-wheel brake cars. Initially a bumper sticker advising "beware—four-wheel brakes" was devised, then the warning legend was transferred to the tire cover on the rear-mounted spare. Sometimes Rickenbacker owners were anxious to prove the point though. B.F. Capwell again: "We had one owner, a doctor in New York, who wanted his brakes even more sensitive than was standard, as he wanted to demonstrate how fast he could stop to his doctor friends at some outing. So our brake expert tuned them to perfection. On his first application on 56th Street over near 10th Avenue, the front wheels slid over the belgium blocks and the vibration caused the two headlamps to break off their brackets and hang loose, dangling from the wires. He didn't complain, just had to pay to have the two brackets brazed."

But an automobile accident of a tragic sort had meantime befallen the Rickenbacker company. It killed Walter E. Flanders. In his obituaries, the press recognized him as "a potent yet practically unseen factor" behind the Rickenbacker venture, and the impact his death had on the company cannot be tangibly measured. The 10,000th Rickenbacker left the factory on July 6th, with considerably less fanfare than previous production marks. In August W.J. Drumplemann left his sales manager job to take over the northern Ohio territory for Rickenbacker. A replacement for him wasn't found until January; it was A.J. ("Jack") Banta, whose credits included stints at Locomobile, Premier—and Maxwell.

By year's end, the Rickenbacker concern seemed to have gathered itself together. Production for the year was about 10,000 units—lower than anticipated but praiseworthy nonetheless—and Barney Everitt planned for double that the following year, a figure above it being "incompatible with

A six-cylinder Rickenbacker (above), the late 1925 Model D Coach-Brougham—and the Rickenbacker with two cylinders added (below),  a 1926 Vertical 8 Super-fine.

that degree of quality which satisfies the pride of the maker and the expectations of the buyer." Barney had a deft way around words too. Then Captain Eddie returned from a five-week trip to Europe and a tour of its auto shows to add a few well chosen ones himself, including allusion to the Rickenbacker company's million dollar cash balance. Barney had betimes announced that stock offerings had been oversubscribed and a million dollars of the authorized issue had been withdrawn from the market because Rickenbacker found itself "abundantly financed and operating on a profitable basis."

Things perked up. By early the year following—1924—advertising wordsmith Pelletier was in full swing. His previous efforts running to the likes of "Socially, it is good form to drive . . . economically, it is good business. . . ," "If you'll try it—you'll buy it," and "The more you know about motor cars, the more you will appreciate . . ."—LeRoy let loose for the new selling season with, "To be seen in a Rickenbacker is to be classed with the cognoscenti and cultured." As *Automobile Topics* related, he thereafter "wore out two envelope openers getting at mail . . . from all sections of the Country . . . in praise and criticism of the usage of a new word in advertising copy." Ned Jordan, who was flinging around some impressive verbiage himself in promoting his car, was moved to comment:

> Of all the words I ever wrote,
> And I have written plenty,
> There's none that ever had the punch
> Of this one COGNOSCENTI

In May Captain Eddie was exclaiming that business "is good, normally and wholesomely good. It is real business—not bloom or bluster." That month, too, Rickenbacker very quietly—only *The New York Times* reported it—opened trading again in the company's capital stock.

Now that the brake system was old Hat-in-the-Ring, the company made known—also in May—that something new again had been added to the Rickenbacker. The Skinner Oil Rectifier—or the 9th Fundamental, as LeRoy Pelletier would have it: "vaccination which prevents you having small pox is better than any cure the doctor can prescribe after you have contracted the disease." The Rectifier was a preventive, immunizing "the motor against many ills and preventing 'Crank-Case Dilution'." It was, in essence, a miniature distillery where all surplus gasoline, water and acids formed in the cylinder and carried by the oil were broken up into their component parts, distilled, purified and then led back to their original sources to be used over again. It wasn't a Rickenbacker design—patented instead by R.S. Skinner and built under license, Packard, Willys-Knight and Stearns also subsequently employing it a while. And it looked great on paper. In practice? Well, B.F. Capwell says it best: "The idea was fine, but the float valve that was supposed to open and return the rectified oil to the crankcase would sometimes carbon up and stick. At those times everything went into the intake manifold and you laid a smoke screen all over town. Fortunately, I had one of these cars and soon realized it was a very troublesome feature. Sometimes a sharp blow to the side of the tank would do the trick but more often it wouldn't. Rickenbacker soon modified them."

In June of '24, Rickenbacker, according to *Automobile Topics*, demonstrated "its ability to discover popular trends in their very earliest stages and take advantage of the market while it is still swayed to interest by their novelty." The company introduced the Vertical 8 Super-fine. LeRoy Pelletier couldn't contain himself: "A Prince of the Purple might drive this car himself without losing caste!" It was an altogether splendid automobile. A nine bearing crank L-head of 268 cubic inches and 70 hp, probably its most unusual feature was the location of the camshaft, completely immersed in oil at all times in an oil-tight compartment separate from the crankcase. It was otherwise similar to most straight-eights in being arranged as a central and outside four but, in a departure from the norm, with the engine also carbureted and fired as two fours. The Vertical 8 also sported dual ignition, dual muffler—and of course the dual flywheel. The price range was $2195 to $2795.

Sprouting now too were a few seeds of discontent. In August Drumpelmann sold his distributorship, and in December Banta resigned as sales manager. By year's end, Rickenbacker had produced but 7187 cars. It was nothing to brag about, and the company didn't, nor did it publicize its complete financial statement for the year. *The New York Times* would report that Rickenbacker had made a net profit in 1924 of $230,107—but that was before taxes. After, the figure was a deficit of

$147,763. Something had to be done.

Barney Everitt recognized it—and his proposed solution, advanced in October of '24 was merger: his company, Peerless of Cleveland, Gray of Detroit and the Trippensee Closed Body Company (the latter having resulted via consolidation with Everitt Brothers). But it was not to be. Whitman Daly remembers that happy rumors ran through the factory for about a week that the deal was at the paper-signing stage. It wasn't. The merger plan fell through because of "local pride," so trade circles said. Cleveland which had lost the automobile industry championship to her neighbor across Lake Erie was not about to align herself with and be controlled by Detroit interests. That in any case was the conclusion of the Cleveland bankers controlling Peerless. Besides, that company was doing splendidly as an independent anyway.

Rebuffed but otherwise unruffled, Barney Everitt concluded finally that he, too, could carry on very well alone. His engineers had beefed up his six (to 68 hp) and his eight (to 84 hp)—and in January he announced that Rickenbacker had been strengthened as well by the acquisition, via an exchange of stock, of Trippensee. In a letter to his 12,000 Rickenbacker stockholders, Barney Everitt cautioned them to "retain Rickenbacker securities and ignore circulated rumors." Better news that month was that Rickenbacker had hired as "chief test pilot" the one and only Cannon Ball Baker. As headline-grabbing a celebrity as Captain Eddie then, he proceeded to run up a series of records with the Rickenbacker that were publicized from coast to coast.

But one very large mistake was upcoming. It was made in July—a sweeping reduction in price on the Vertical 8 from two to six hundred dollars depending upon model which was, as the Rickenbacker's own press

EVERITT BROTHERS
Harper and L.S. & M.S.R.R.

Automobile Painting and Trimming
Phone Market 3240

**Workman's Daily Time Report**

Name W. C. Daly    No. 517

Feb-27—1922

PIECE WORK

| No. Pieces | Make of Car | Operation | JOB NUMBERS | | | | | Price | Amount |
|---|---|---|---|---|---|---|---|---|---|
| 5 | Rickenbacker Tourings | Slush | 118 | 120 | 121 | 123 | 119 | 20 | 1.00 |
| 2 | Sedans | Slush | 76 | 65 | | | | 25 | .50 |
| 6 | Coupes | Prime Outside | 31 | 39 | 38 | 28 | 29 | 35 | 2.10 |
| | | | 19 | | | | | | |
| 3 | Tourings | Prime Outside | 163 | 164 | 166 | | | 20 | .60 |
| | | | | | | | | | 4.20 |
| | | | | | | | | | |
| | | | $ 5.40 | | | | | | |

DAY WORK    NOTE: If Pieceworker—time spent on "Day Work" must be Ok'd by Foreman

| Department | NATURE OF WORK | Hours | Amount |
|---|---|---|---|
| Paint | Painting door pockets, blowing out & mixing paint | 3 | 40 | 1.20 |

Piece Work 8½   Hours $ 4.20
Day " 3 " " 1.20
Total 11½ Hours $ 5.40

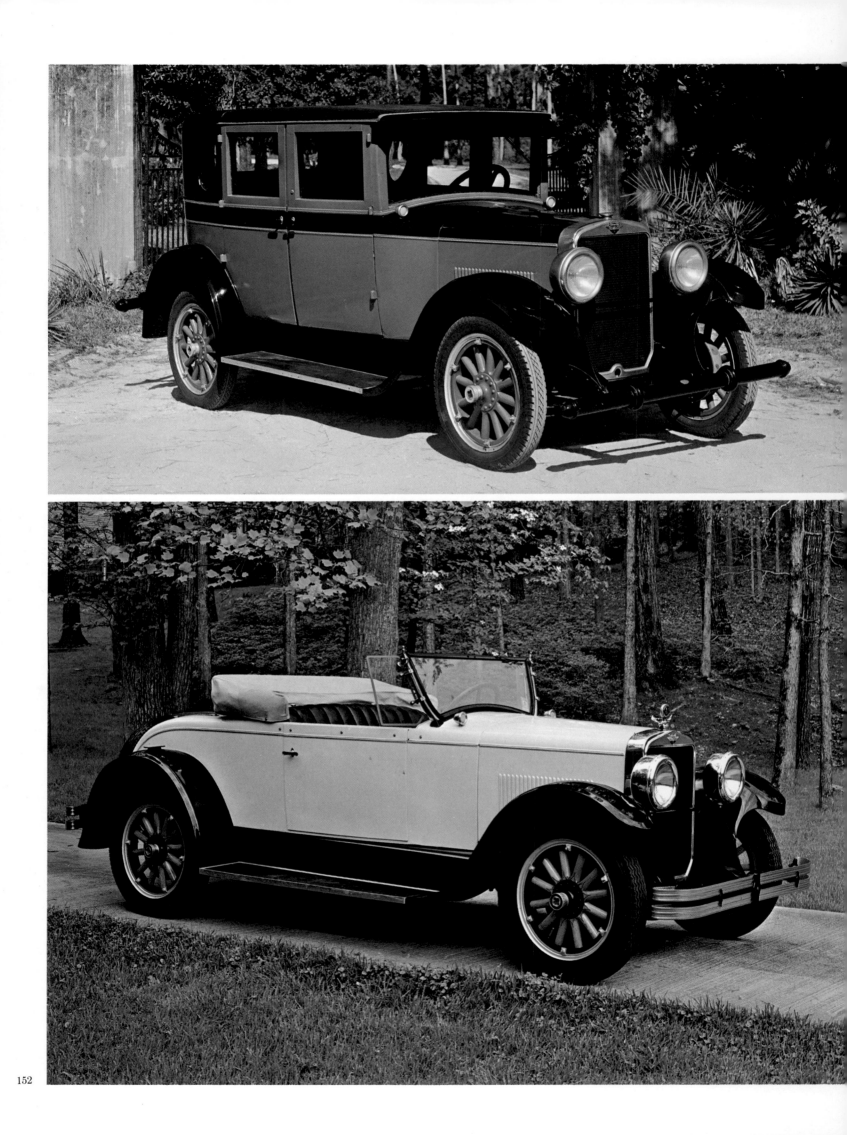

*Two of the "Wonder Six" Rickenbackers from 1926, a Model E Brougham and Roadster (left).*
*The Super Sport, above, the ultimate Rickenbacker, as depicted in the brochure produced to widely tout the same.*

release stated, startling to say the least. Unfortunately, it rather startled Rickenbacker dealers too, whose stock on hand had been bought at the previous wholesale prices. Rickenbacker dealers now numbered nearly a hundred, with some six hundred associate distributors in North America (as well as agencies on four other continents), and it's safe to say not one of them was enamored of the decision. Quite the contrary, they would be bearing the financial loss. A disenchanted dealer network bodes unwell.

In September a minority interest in Rickenbacker was purchased by a banking firm, from which was expected about two million additional dollars working capital. A financial report released by the company showed a combined net profit for Rickenbacker-Trippensee of $247,563, $230,107 of which was attributed to Rickenbacker. Trippensee was soon to prove an albatross. Plans for '26 called for a 30,000 unit production—the plant had that capacity and Barney Everitt had apparently changed his mind about the cut-off point incompatible with quality. Production for 1925 had totaled 9214 cars, an advance on '24 to be sure, but one made at the expense of the dealers. And if they had felt showered upon that year, it seemed that Rickenbacker was looking to drown them the next.

Two nice things happened at Rickenbacker in 1926. The first was a letter from a very satisfied owner concluding, "I am surprised a gas car can be made to so nearly approach the excellent driving qualities of the Stanley Steamer." From Freelan Oscar Stanley, that was quite a concession. The second—and historically more significant—was the Super Sport introduced at the New York show. Touted as America's fastest stock car, it was guaranteed to do ninety; Captain Eddie had put up ninety-five with four passengers. Its engine was the Vertical 8 boosted to 107 bhp, but it was the car's looks that excited the most. The Rickenbacker company was anxious always to surprise, and for '26 attention was turned from engineering to styling, an area in which the firm had heretofore been markedly conservative. "Put an evening gown on the lady" was the assignment—and in that context the result was as eye-catching as Dior's New Look would be two decades later. Torpedo-shaped rear deck, aerofoil bumpers, cycle fenders of laminated mahogany, brass bound and with wood inlay ornaments, bullet-shaped headlamps, safety glass all around (probably its first application throughout on an American production car)—and the conspicuous absence of running boards. It might not have been the most beautiful car in America—as the Rickenbacker company averred—but it was unquestionably one of the most striking. Its price: $5000.

The Vertical 8 Super-fine and the "Wonder Six," as it was now called, were continued with refinement—and in January of 1926 sale of Rickenbacker stock was suspended. Merely a formality, Barney Everitt said. Captain Eddie was noticeably silent. By June Barney was exclaiming that

"recent sensational price reductions . . . had caused an unusual influx of business." But Rickenbacker dealers were furious. In truth, the Rickenbacker distributor network had never been a strong one administratively—and since this was largely the responsibility of the company's vice-president, Captain Eddie must bear his share of the blame. In public relations he was a master, in public image he had no peer. But in day-to-day business detail he had faltered. And it doesn't really matter much how commendable the car, even other mistakes which might be put right, without a healthy dealer network, any automotive enterprise is doomed.

In September, after weeks of intramural bickering, Captain Eddie said simply, "Here's where I get off." He resigned, the press said, to pursue his aviation interests. But the reality was that his leavetaking was but part of a plan for a rigorous reorganization. It was too late. LeRoy Pelletier was convinced of it, he left too. So did Harry Cunningham.

As valiant efforts go, Barney Everitt's was an heroic one. His company was in receivership—"entirely friendly . . . instituted as a means of straightening out some kinks in the readjustment program"—and the new Rickenbackers came in December, dubbed 6-70, 8-80 and 8-90, with engine refinements and fresh styling termed "European Type," though the designations were British to a fault, literally so, as witness Gainsboro and Marlboro. The others were Inverness, Exeter, Oxford and Buckingham.

It was all over quickly. By February of 1927, Barney Everitt asked permission of the receivers to sell his firm's assets. "It will be one of the biggest public auctions ever held in Detroit," the *Free Press* commented brightly. It would also be one of the most oft held. Ultimately, what remained of the company was parceled out, the engines, together with certain jigs, tools, dies, et al. going to Jörgen Skafte Rasmussen who used same in production of two Audi models in Germany until 1932 when the Great Depression made big American cars a less than attractive proposition in Europe.

The Rickenbacker represents one of the more interesting might-have-beens in American automobile history. Certainly it deserved to survive. It was, in many respects, an industry leader—and one would like to think that was not its downfall. Probably it wasn't. What manufacturer, after all, who started a new company during the Twenties survives today? Walter Chrysler had the advantage of the entrenched Maxwell company when he introduced his Chrysler—and he soon bought out Dodge and brought out his Plymouth. And that rather sets the mind to dreaming. Granted, Barney Everitt's combining of the Rickenbacker and Trippensee companies worked to the Rickenbacker's disadvantage, but what if his original merger idea had succeeded? Gray was probably not the most salutary entry for the low-priced end of the market—but what a combination Rickenbacker and Peerless would have made. ✤

153

# AMILCAR OF ST. DENIS

*Thoughtful Engineering, a Dash of the Frivolous and a Healthy Helping of That Intangible Quality That Makes Some Cars Very Special*

Out in front of the Ritz Bar, where the opulent Hispano-Suizas and Rolls-Royces lined the rue Cambon, there appeared one day a young American and a tiny two-seat French automobile. "You call that thing a car?" asked the Ritz's famous bartender, Frank. "That's a child's toy; that's more like the size of a side car than a regular car." The scene was repeated frequently. "You here again, Mr. Side Car? What will it be this time?"

Eventually the young man, a twenty-one-year-old Floridian-in-Paris named Horace Chase—nephew of Palm Beach architect Addison Mizner —decided to have Frank mix a special drink. "What will it be?" he answered the loquacious bartender's inevitable question. "Well, in Florida, I used to mix Bacardi and lemon juice and a little Cointreau. Let's try that but use brandy instead." Horace pronounced his brainchild a tasty concoction indeed and those at the bar who eagerly sampled it agreed. Frank, as the drink's craftsman, was pleased too and he christened the new cocktail at once. He called it a Side Car, thinking of Horace's distinctive little vehicle in the street out front. The machine was an Amilcar.

Built in a thriving Paris suburb—as were eighty percent of France's approximately 350 marques during the Twenties—the Amilcar was perfectly attuned to a fabulous era and city, a time and place immortalized by Ernest Hemingway as a "moveable feast." Thoughtfully engineered, a little frivolous, the Amilcar possessed undeniable charm and a healthy dose of that intangible quality that makes some cars stand out while others—perhaps equally as good—pale by comparison. For a fleeting time during the peak of an immortal decade, it was a great success.

The Amilcar was a direct outgrowth of that uniquely French passion for tiny light cars and cyclecars which—prompted partly by the government's low tax of one hundred francs on vehicles weighing less than eight hundred pounds and their low selling prices—had begun before the Great War. Long after cyclecars had disappeared from the United States and fallen into general disfavor in Britain, the French were still happily piloting their nasty belt-drive Bédélias during the mid-Twenties and building flocks of other cycle and light cars, the latter known as voiturettes. Both the first Amilcar and the first Citroën were descended from one of those little machines, the Le Zèbre, built by a Parisian firm founded in 1908 or 1909.

By 1919, however, when the Le Zèbre's makers, Borie and Company, sold out to the son of a wealthy Paris clothesmaker named Emile Akar and a reflective, gray-haired Le Zèbre executive, Joseph Lamy, the marque was in trouble. Its chief designer, the brilliant thirty-nine-year-old Jules Salomon, had been lured away from the firm by André Citroën, for whom he had designed a new small car that threatened to dominate the low-priced market, the Citroën Type A. By virtue of Citroën's genius for mass production, the new car would undersell the Le Zèbre and cars like it and be more up-to-date as well. In addition, besides the new competition, Le Zèbre found itself burdened, like other manufacturers, by the postwar rise in raw material prices.

With the marque's future a troubling questionmark, a robust thirty-six-year-old Le Zèbre technician and salesman, former military flying instructor and would-be race driver, André Morel, had a meeting one day with a colleague of Salomon's from Citroën. At the Excelsior Restaurant, the two men traded dreams. Morel—who had spent a decade as test driver at the pioneering French automaker, Berliet—wanted to become a champion racer. The engineer, a charming and talented man named Edmond Moyet, was then working nights at home on a new automobile that he wanted to have produced. The two men had found a common ground, it seemed, and lacked only one thing—capital. The most likely source Morel could think

*On the pages preceding: an Amilcar C4, circa 1922, a longer wheelbase variation of the CS with 1044 cc engine; a CGS3 from 1924, the "3" designating the rear passenger seat.*

of was a wealthy friend of his, Emile Akar, who was then manager of an extensive chain of grocery shops—they delivered door-to-door via dog-drawn carts—known as the Planteur de Caiffe, as well as being a Le Zèbre investor as noted earlier.

Morel arranged a meeting among Moyet, Lamy and Akar—and the latter was intrigued. He provided 100,000 francs for the construction of Moyet's little car and two examples were soon built. Lamy then had Morel and a companion demonstrate the newly-minted machines—simply dubbed Borie cyclecars—to Le Zèbre agents, untroubled apparently by any possible conflict between the new model and the Le Zèbre itself. He needn't have worried. Several Le Zèbre concessionaires quickly invested a million francs in the project. This together with the two million more raised by Akar and Lamy was used to found the Société Nouvelle pour l'Automobile and, having relinquished their interest in Le Zèbre, Akar and Lamy assumed control of the new company, Akar as general director, Lamy as sales director. At a small atelier near the Bastille at 125 rue de Chemin Vert, the production version of Moyet's automobile was born.

A light car with a pressed steel frame that ended at the rear quarter-elliptic spring mounts—there being no chassis at all for the rearmost quarter of the car—the machine was powered by a splash-lubricated engine similar in appearance and design to both that of the Le Zèbre and the Type A Citroën, Salomon's influence obviously. A side-valve four-cylinder unit displacing 904 cc and developing 18 hp, the new car's

powerplant was constructed in unit with a three-speed gearbox—again a Le Zèbre and Citroën technique—with engine, gearbox and the multi-plate clutch sharing the same oil. Unlike most small French manufacturers, who used proprietary engines, this powerplant was built in-house. Shaft driven but lacking a differential, the new two-seater with a 92½-inch wheelbase could achieve 50 mph.

In all, Morel's backers were pleased. They happily displayed their wares to a few friends in Paris' automobile circles and it was one of these, Maurice Puech—an associate of the formidable and eccentric Gabriel Voisin—who coined a suitable name for the new car: an anagram formed of Akar and Lamy. The machine would be called the Amilcar.

By mid-July of 1921, the first Amilcar—designated CC—was rolling out of the factory at the rate of five units a day. It was more expensive than a comparable Citroën—9200 francs versus less than 8000—but it was well received and attracted considerable attention at the Paris salon. Across the Channel, road testers from *The Autocar* said there was probably no main road hill in all England that the little car could not climb, and they liked the effective and chatter-free rear wheel brakes (operated by foot pedal or hand lever), though were less pleased with the harsh ride and body rattles of its sporty coachwork. To French engineer J.A. Grégoire, however, it was the healthy rasp of the engine's exhaust—"slightly less deep than a Bugatti's which rattled windows but so much better than the clickety, asthmatic Salmson"—that was its strong commercial point.

156

*Above right and left: a sprightly CGSs from 1926, built under license in Italy by the Compagnia Generale Automobili, and marketed in that country as the Amilcar Italiana.*

In 1921 an automobile engineer named Marcel Sée—who together with his cousin Gilbert Nataf had begun a bodyworks called Margyl, an anagram of their first names—joined Amilcar as technical director and Morel found an immediate and sympathetic ally in his campaign to become a famous driver. Engineer Moyet thought racing a good thing too, but Akar and Lamy, who held the purse strings after all, demurred. Morel, however, was not easily dissuaded. In November that year, he took a CC to Lyon and put up a flying kilometer at better than 90 km/h—which merely whetted his appetite. In 1922 he secretly prepared a boattailed Amilcar for a hill climb also at Lyon and established second fastest time of the day there, behind a Voisin. Lamy had not found out about Morel's first outing, he did the second. But he also could not help but notice the rush of orders which followed the event. A solid businessman, Lamy would be at the track for Morel's next appearance.

For 1922 Amilcar introduced an engine enlarged to 1004 cc, developing 23 hp, installed it in the CC chassis and called the result the CS. It seemed ideal for racing and Morel soon entered one in a club event at Lyon. Afflicted with valve spring problems, he placed second behind an 1100 cc Spidos and was greeted at the finish line by Lamy himself, now bitten by the racing bug. "We could have won," cried the sales director. The Amilcar racing program was established then and there.

For the company's official competition debut, Amilcar elected to contest the world's first twenty-four-hour road race, a thoroughly dangerous

event around a roughly triangular circuit lacing its way through the Saint Germain Forest near Paris, dreamed up by an ex-French air force fighter pilot named Eugene Mauve. Numerous entrants showed up, all there hoping to capture a worn and peeling gilded fruit stand about three feet high that gave the race its name, the Bol d'Or (Gold Bowl). This time out, Morel won, averaging 37 mph and establishing a world's speed record for twenty-four hours. Later that summer, a team of three Amilcars was entered in the Grand Prix des Cyclecars at Le Mans. Two of them finished the race, not first and second but third and fourth behind a pair of rapid little overhead cam Salmsons. The battle between Amilcar and its chief nemesis—a racing and sales competition destined to last nearly a decade—had begun.

The remainder of 1922 proved more fruitful for Amilcar. In June Morel set a new 1100 cc record for the flying kilometer at 120 km/h and then went on to victory after victory. By year's end, he had realized the dream he and Moyet had discussed two years before; he was named Champion of France for the 1100 cc class. Back at the works, business was prosperous.

Forty-seven first places in competition and the arrival on the Amilcar scene of English motor sports enthusiast Vernon Balls—he would both import and race Amilcars until 1931—kept the factory happy during 1923. Meanwhile, engineer Moyet and two of his colleagues who had quit Citroën to join Amilcar—Maurice Dubois and Emmanuel Cohen—were hard at work on something special. It arrived the following year, one of the two models for which the firm would be best remembered. Its success in the marketplace was immediate. It was a car which many would come to think of as a poor man's Bugatti.

The Amilcar Grand Sport or CGS was more powerful, sturdier and generally more refined than its predecessors. The abbreviated frame of the earlier machines was retained but reinforced at the front where stronger vanadium steel half-elliptic springs replaced the quarter elliptics of the earlier cars. And the new machine was equipped with a feature Moyet and Dubois had labored to perfect: four wheel brakes. Patented by Moyet and based on a hollow kingpin which carried a pushrod, the front brakes of the CGS were practical and effective. A lever actuated by a brake rod or, on later models, a flat steel ribbon, pressed the pushrod upwards against a cam, forcing the shoe against the drum.

Power for the new car was provided by an enlarged four-cylinder engine of 1074 cc, developing some 28 hp. Most important perhaps, the new engine—aspirated by a single downdraft Solex—relied on pressure rather than splash lubrication. Sustained high speed driving and the added braking power had taxed the splash lubricated unit beyond its endurance; during initial road testing, Amilcar test driver Van Parys dubbed the long straightaway near Magny et Vaxin as "the cemetery of the big end bearings."

Bodywork for the CGS was distinctive, a boattailed two-place staggered seater with a third place available, if ordered, in the car's tail, the latter model called the CGS3. At first fenders were composed of an angular, board-like contrivance but this was replaced by cycle fenders eventually. In both cases, a pair of crossed steel rods forming an "X" were affixed to the fenders at the car's front as braces. Racing versions of the CGS would dispense with fenders altogether.

The CGS proved a car of instant appeal thanks to its good looks, sporting image and reliable performance. French actress Eva Le Gallienne owned a CGS, and so did that royal motoring enthusiast, Alfonso XIII of Spain. Emulating the American named Fowler who earlier had created an international incident by flying his plane beneath the Arc de Triomphe, Horace Chase drove his CGS through the chained-off memorial. And, some time after that prank, he accompanied a friend, Alice de Lamarr, to Amilcar mecca, the factory itself. As enthusiastic about Amilcars as any devoted *Amilcarriste,* Miss Lamarr later wrote a friend: "They were all lined up on display in a large barn-like shed rather like an airplane hangar. We fairly shouted with delight. . . . There were black ones and red ones and blue ones and tooled aluminum jobs with mahogany trim, and in all manner of styles they were incredibly chic. . . . The car . . . was a very good bet for exploring the byways of Europe in those early Twenties when the roads were none too good. They were so light in weight you didn't have to get a horse to pull them out of the mud or sand if you got stuck."

While appreciative drivers were flitting about streets and country lanes in their CGS's, competition remained foremost in André Morel's mind. By the end of 1925, Amilcar claimed to have won 102 first places in various events during the year and to setting five world's records, including the flying kilometer at 147.42 km/h. If the races in which the little cars competed lacked Grand Prix stature, it should be remembered that, by contesting the smaller displacement classes at local events, Amilcar was making itself very well known to the thousands of people who frequented such contests—an obvious sales benefit.

In fact, the CGS sold so well that in 1925 Amilcar was forced to find larger quarters and moved to the industrial suburb of St. Denis. Thirty-seven hundred cars were built that year, production increasing to 4800 in

*A C6 from 1926, the special version of the competition Amilcar CO built for sale to private entrants, and raced successfully by Vernon Balls and Goldie Gardner among others.*

1926. At Sée's urging, heavy investments were now made at the St. Denis works, including chemical and metallurgical research facilities and extensive engine test benches. Sée's Margyl bodyworks was also purchased, giving Amilcar the capability to construct complete cars. By the end of 1926, some 1200 employees were turning out thirty-five Amilcars per day.

By then, Amilcar's competition efforts had expanded and matured. A racing department had been founded in 1924 and with a one million franc initial budget, a special race shop had been established. Morel, Charles Martin, Arthur Duray and Marius Mestivier formed the original team drivers and they were supported by ten mechanics. Besides a new spate of hill climb wins in 1925, three cars were entered in that year's Bol d'Or—a red, a blue and a white machine—and Morel again won this event.

Back at the drawing board in St. Denis, Moyet was dreaming grander dreams than even the successful CGS. He was at work on a new car, one designed exclusively for racing and intended to set the racing world on its ear. Moyet knew that in 1926 Grand Prix cars would be limited to a 1500 cc engine displacement and that this would lead to increased emphasis and attention on the next lower 1100 cc class. Now, he used all his experience to design the most sophisticated 1100 cc racer built to that time. It was, as *The Autocar* called it, the "first purely racing car of 1100 cc as distinct from sports models adapted for racing." It was a machine designed to incorporate a device that threatened to revolutionize engineers' conception of racing engines, the supercharger.

Moyet's new racer—a sort of miniature Grand Prix car—was based on a jewel-like six-cylinder powerplant of 1096 cc. The overhead valves were operated by gear-driven double overhead camshafts which were ball-bearing mounted. The crankshaft, machined from a solid steel billet, rested in seven main roller bearings and the connecting rods too were roller-bearing mounted. Careful thought was given to the induction and exhaust systems with the intake manifold providing a straight shot for the fuel-air mixture into the combustion chambers which boasted inclined spark plugs to permit oversize valves. The exhaust valves emptied into a graceful, businesslike manifold that led to the car's straight exhaust pipe. Affixed to the front of this engine, enclosed in a heavily-ribbed case and cooled by its own oil supply, was a Roots supercharger. At 6500 rpm—most of these racers had two tachometers incidentally, one driven off each camshaft—this engine developed 75 bhp. Lubrication was by dry sump.

The race car chassis was based on a stiff frame suspended with half-elliptic springs at the front, quarter elliptics at the rear and with a wheelbase of 74 inches. A flat pan covered the bottom of the car to minimize air resistance there. Bodywork for this machine—the Amilcar CO—was straightforward and simple: familiar Amilcar radiator shell, a long louvered hood fastened with leather straps, cramped two-place cockpit and a streamlined tail that enclosed one of the car's two fuel tanks, the other located just in front of the firewall. This was a low vehicle, the top of its hood just 33½ inches above the ground, and light—1385 pounds. Unlike the CGS, the new racer had a four-speed gearbox but like the sports car, it lacked a differential, a calculated omission that did nothing to hinder the machine's nimble handling.

The CO immediately lived up to its promising specifications. In the fall of 1925, it won its class at the Paris hill climb held at Gometz le Chatel. More auspicious almost, the Amilcar was actually the second fastest car there, only a 1500 cc Darracq outpaced it by one-and-a-fifth seconds. Early the next year, Morel established new records for 1100 cc cars in the flying kilometer at 197 km/h and the flying mile at 195 km/h. Charles Martin set a new record for the standing kilometer at 126 km/h. A team of

*With only about fifty C6's being built, Amilcar's sporting CGS line—a CGSs from 1927 shown here—remained the marque's most prolific production car during the Twenties.*

*Amilcar's first touring model—designated the E—came in 1923, followed by the G in 1925,   the latter in a supercharged version winning the Monte Carlo Rally in 1927.*

three cars was then sent to England to contest the 200-mile Brooklands race in 1926—and finished one-two-three in class. A year later, in the same event, Morel finished second overall, averaging 1.45 seconds less than the winning Bugatti.

In 1927 a special CO with narrow bodywork and only one seat became the first 1100 cc automobile to better 125 mph, accomplishing the feat near Arpajon at nearly 128 mph. This car, the MCO Record, went on to establish numerous Class G (up to 1100 cc) records during 1927 and 1928. A slightly oversized version displacing 1174 cc also set world records in Class F as well, the same car also occasionally—and handsomely—defeating 1.5-liter Bugattis in road races.

From the beginning, the six-cylinder Amilcar racer had made a great impression on competition enthusiasts—Salmson could not of course sit by for all this and developed their own interesting eight-cylinder 1100 cc to compete with the Amilcar, which it did with indifferent success—and in 1926, the company produced a special version of the CO for sale to private entrants. This model, the C6, lacked the CO's roller bearing crankshaft —though it still stood up well to maximum rpms—and was less powerful, its supercharged engine producing 62 hp at 5600 rpm. Fitted with road equipment, the C6 sold for a rather steep **£725** in England, not substantially less than a 1.5 Bugatti, and its commercial market was thus rather

limited. Some fifty of these cars were sold.

If the C6 was not available in quantity to the public, the CGS certainly was. Improvements during its six years of production included greater oil capacity, slightly more power (about 35 hp), enlarged brakes, a four-speed transmission and the very special CGS model called the Surbaissé or CGSs. Towards the end of its production, a few CGSs cars were available with Cozette superchargers and developed 54 hp at 4500 rpm with a top speed of nearly 100 mph. (Tops for a normal CGS was 65-75 depending on body styles.) All CGS models were popular and the car came to be sold and built under license in other countries.

In Germany, the CGS was made by the Erhardt Automobilwerke and marketed—with some tasteless and unneeded hubcaps—as the Pluto. Supercharged versions bore the title, Pluto mit Kompressor. In Austria, the Viennese firm of Frosee and Friedmann built and sold the CGS as the Grofri, and Amilcars were assembled in Italy by Compagnia Generale Automobili as the Amilcar Italiana with graceful bodies and attractive flaired fenders. The marque was imported into the United States too by Maybach Motors in New York; seldom could cars of greater contrast in size and type have been offered at the same showroom. Some 1500 Amilcars were exported to Australia, though most of these were not CGS's but CC's or the less sporting touring and sedan models which Amilcar had

*The Model L was a more powerful G and provided the basis for Amilcar's M series of sedans produced from 1929 through 1934, an M2 faux cabriolet from 1930 pictured above.*

first offered as early as 1923 and which comprise an important if less exciting side of the firm's history. These cars ran the gamut from the staid and conventional to innovative and even revolutionary and the company's increased emphasis on them marked a dividing line in Amilcar history that, once crossed, led steadily to uncertain marketing, diminished sales and, finally, to ruin.

The first Amilcar touring model, unlike the CC or CS, had a full length chassis. With a 116-inch wheelbase, it offered four wheel brakes, a 1485 cc engine, four-speed transmission and—for the first time in Amilcar history—a differential. This model, the E, was available from 1923 through 1925, by which time its displacement had increased to 1587 cc and its top speed from about 60 to 70 mph. The G, a smaller sedan with 102-inch wheelbase, joined the Amilcar line during the latter year, powered by a slightly detuned CGS engine though with a stronger frame and larger capacity radiator than the two-seater. Fitted with a Weymann-type fabric body, the G proved a reliable little car and when *The Autocar* tested one with 60,000 miles on the odometer, they found only some gear noise in the indirect ratios gave a hint at the car's age. Probably the most popular touring Amilcar, the G could achieve 36 mpg and 58 mph. Its ultimate possibilities were proven when, in January 1927, a supercharged version won the Monte Carlo Rally.

Despite the reflected glory of that victory, however, 1927 dawned gray and gloomy on Amilcar. The French industry generally was uncertain of its future. De Dion-Bouton, the oldest carmaker in France and one of the oldest in the world, was then in liquidation. All the cyclecar builders were out of business. Rumors of general collapse were rife, so prevalent that Louis Delage felt impelled to issue a press statement denying that he had either sought outside financial help or was about to amalgamate. Other French manufacturers were seeking help or joining forces. Chenard et Walcker, Delahaye and Unic got together in a cooperative grouping, each concentrating on producing a car that would not compete with the others'. Surveying the French industry in March 1927, *The Autocar* concluded that "the prosperity of the last eighteen months was undoubtedly artificial and now that it has passed away, the weaklings are feeling the pinch."

If not a "weakling," Amilcar—just six years old—found itself at least shaky. It had invested heavily during that time of "artificial prosperity" and though its cars had sold well, the racing program had proved dangerously expensive. So had Sée's expansion. In addition, times and the public's ever-inscrutable taste were changing. Within a year, veteran automotive journalist W.F. Bradley would predict that, "As far as France only is concerned, the open car appears likely to go out of existence except as a sporting job. All the demand is for closed bodies." And Citroën was    161 doing a good job of meeting that, turning out 500 comfortable little cars every day. Amilcar was not even remotely in the same league.

Not only were there external pressures on the company, but it also faced some internal shakeups as well. Moyet—who had suffered a fractured skull in a motorbike accident at Montlhéry during an Amilcar record-setting expedition—returned from a long convalescence to accuse his old associate Dubois of trying to usurp his power. Dubois, who had contributed much to Amilcar, was forced to leave. Then Lamy and Akar—whose calm and resourceful leadership and interest in their employees' well being had made the company a good place to work—found themselves unable to meet their financial obligations and were forced now to give up control of the firm they had started.

In July 1927, Amilcar was reorganized under new control and became the Société Anonyme Français d'Automobiles with an announced capital of ten million francs. A board of directors headed by Albert Neubauer, a well-known figure in Paris automotive circles, now assumed overall responsibility for Amilcar. Given the increasing French ardor for closed cars, the new Amilcar board elected to head the marque away from two-seaters, even though this meant competition with giant Citroën and Renault. It was also an effort to convince the public that, whatever image Amilcar might have had as a sports or miniature car, the company would now market a grown-up product. In 1929 the CGS series was discontinued, and a more powerful G was added, an 1188 cc 26 hp model called the L. Of this new Amilcar, *The Autocar* now wrote, "Slowly but surely, the car once considered 'a baby' is being regarded more seriously both by manufacturers and buyers." The L, the magazine went on, was "easy to start and

control. It is responsive and powerful when hills heave in sight . . . . The car holds the road splendidly and is stable on corners." This machine, built for only one year, provided the framework for the M series, which would be produced for the next five years. Neither the G nor the M, however, was the sort of car that had made the marque famous.

If the two-seaters were out, racing was not, at least not immediately. Though it had been de-emphasized by the factory, competition still played a role in the overall Amilcar scheme of things during 1928, and on August 26th, a blue MCO set new records for the flying kilometer and flying mile at Arpajon, turning in speeds of 206.895 and 206.027 km/h respectively. In September a C6 established new records for the five kilometer, five mile and ten mile distances, some of which would stand until the 1960's.

In 1929, however, both André Morel and Charles Martin left Amilcar, understandably disappointed at the company's ultimate decision to abandon racing. José Scaron, an Amilcar agent from Havre, and other amateurs continued to drive their own cars in competition and set an occasional further record at Montlhéry or Brooklands, though, on the other side of the Atlantic, the entry by Thompson Products of a six-cylinder Amilcar in the 1929 Indy 500 ended ignominiously in retirement. The heyday of Amilcar racing was over.

The records set by Amilcars during 1928 had done nothing to improve the firm's financial state, and in October it was announced that Amilcar was about to join forces with Durant Motor Corporation, Amilcar to market the Durant and Locomobile cars in France, Durant to manufacture parts for and sell the Amilcar in the United States. It was not to be. Billy Durant, unfortunately, had invested heavily in the stock market.

*From introduction in 1924, the CGS was improved through the next half dozen years—a 1926 car shown here—and was exported to or built under license in at least that many countri*

When the Crash came, he was largely wiped out—and his hoped-for deal with Amilcar never had a chance.

Whatever the disappointment on their part, Amilcar's directors were far from defeated and moved to salvage the future on their own. At Sée's urging, they proceeded with plans to build a wholly new and more luxurious Amilcar. Called the CS8, it was a machine that represented a complete break with the company's past, a roomy touring car with a 120-inch wheelbase and a completely new single overhead cam straight-eight engine. But just as its production got under way, the first waves of the Depression struck Europe and the ranks of new car buyers, especially buyers of medium-price cars, were vastly depleted. Amilcar, new to the market, could not recoup its investment and the CS8 was phased out in 1932. Obviously desperate now, Amilcar swung to the CS8's opposite extreme. In an effort to meet changing times, the C was introduced, a tiny 621 cc car which was offered for sale along with the larger M3. Produced in slightly bored out variants never exceeding one liter, the C was built until 1934. By then, business had continued its dreary, steady downturn and the firm was forced to give up its St. Denis shops and move to a tiny factory in Boulogne. There Amilcar was reorganized as the Société Financiers pour l'Automobile and most of its old personnel left, seeking employment at the larger French automakers. Marcel Sée became director of the reorganized company and tried again with an expensive new car—La Pégase or N7, the first Amilcar ever to use an engine other than the company's own, in this case the 2.1-liter 70 hp Delahaye unit. It was built through 1936. Both Citroën and Delahaye offered more car for the same or less money, and the bitter lesson Amilcar learned was that it simply had not been able to es-tablish itself as a meaningful force in the luxury car market.

In 1937 Amilcar was taken over by Hotchkiss and the idea now was a new small car powered by the under-one-liter Amilcar C engine. After an initial prototype failure, J.A. Grégoire of Tracta fame was hired to oversee the project. By the end of 1937, a prototype had been completed. Similar in appearance and conception to the Adler Trumpf Junior—though smaller—with its front wheel drive and torsion bar rear suspension, the new Amilcar B 38 or Compound was based on what Grégoire called the first production automobile frame to be made of aluminum alloy. The engine drove through a four-speed gearbox that could pull this phenomenally lightweight—1675 pound—four-seater along at some 65 mph. Less than a thousand of the machines were delivered to customers when another worldwide calamity intervened in Amilcar history, World War II. It spelled the end. Hotchkiss did not try to revive the Amilcar when peace, finally, came.

By then, the great days of the Amilcar company were only memories cherished by a generation of French enthusiasts who had loved the marque, by those who had once owned a CGS or seen a supercharged six-cylinder racer as it whined to victory up some twisting country lane in a hill climb. For those people, the real Amilcar story had ended even before the war—ended as it had for onetime Amilcar engineer and World War I fighter pilot Pierre Chan—on the sad day Amilcar left the factory where its most famous models were built. "For me, the Amilcar was dead after St. Denis," Pierre Chan has said. One needn't really view the Amilcar story from the comfortable distance of time to believe him right. Those who lived the story knew. ✠

*The ultimate CGS Amilcar, the CGSs or Surbaissé (which translates "lowered") arrived in 1926 and remained on the scene until the Great Depression struck, the car pictured from 1929.*

# THE BENTLEYS BUILT BY ROLLS-ROYCE

## *The Song May Be Ended, But The Melody Lingers On*

It actually seems that there is a certain element among Bentley enthusiasts which likes to pretend the marque literally died in 1931, upon acquisition by Rolls-Royce. Like a proud family which tends to overlook the fact that one of its members has been committed, these types regard the Derby- and Crewe-built Bentleys as subjects definitely not for discussion. This is silly of course, for in fact the Bentleys that Rolls-Royce built are outstandingly fine automobiles, in virtually every way *better* than their predecessors, and through the years have been the embodiment of just about anybody's idea of what a truly great high performance passenger car

should be. They may not appeal to the vintage crowd, and they may have lost their separate identity in recent years, but no one who knows them can say that they are not bloody good cars, because they are.

W.O. Bentley's own account of how he lost control of his company to Woolf Barnato and friends, and how they in turn sailed it into receivership, the brief efforts of acquisition made by Napier and the company's eventual purchase by Rolls-Royce, make for interesting reading. It was a very sad tale from Mr. Bentley's viewpoint but, as it turned out, it did the marque Bentley a power of good. For the first time, the company was financially

Clockwise from the left: a 1934 3½ Litre Tourer by Vanden Plas; a 1936 4¼ Litre Drophead Coupe by Park Ward; and a 1936 4¼ Litre Sport Coupe by Gurney Nutting.

secure and, even more pertinent, it was going to start building cars that, it was hoped, sizable numbers of people could be interested in buying. As it happened, the new Rolls-built Bentleys did sell a little better than W.O.'s old originals did, but that's getting ahead of the story.

For a time after its acquisition—for £125,000, or something over six hundred thousand dollars in those days—nobody at the Rolls-Royce works at Derby seemed to know quite what to do with their new property. Obviously a car of some sporting character was considered to be desirable, but one perhaps with an added measure of refinement and comfort compared with their uncompromising, thundering, fire-breathing predecessors. After a couple of indecisive years had slipped by, the management at R-R also began to realize that they'd better get on with it and produce *something* before Bentley's potential customers' brand loyalty wore out and they drifted off to Lagonda and Alvis.

Although still at the peak of his engineering accomplishments, Sir Henry Royce, now in his late sixties, was a very sick man. To avoid the bitter British winters, he had since 1911 been spending the colder months at his Villa Mimosa near Le Canadel in the south of France, working as hard as ever, but his health was slowly but surely deteriorating. Among other projects which were occupying him during the early Thirties was the design of a small 2364 cc six-cylinder car for Rolls-Royce, code named "Peregrine." It is difficult to understand what the reasoning was behind this project. It was the very antithesis of the fundamental Rolls-Royce concept of large, smooth, quiet, slow revving, understressed engines propelling big, roomy cars. Because it soon became increasingly evident that the performance of such a car was going to be considerably below R-R standards, some means of improving it was deemed desirable, and it was finally decided a blower might be helpful. Amidst the struggle with supercharger problems, an unblown chassis was completed, bodied and sent to the Continent for a

10,000-mile test. A depressing exercise. It was soon discovered that the Peregrine would go through one set of bearings after another at a sustained 5000 rpm, and high revs were absolutely necessary if any kind of performance was to be got out of such a small engine. An oil cooler might possibly have helped, but would only have made the thing still more complicated—and costly. Its performance remained disappointing and it still didn't have its supercharger. The power output of the Peregrine was only on the order of 70 to 75 bhp. It was not what one could call a success.

But then someone there—it's never clearly been established just who—had a stroke of insight. It was obvious really. Why not try a current production 20/25 Rolls-Royce engine and transmission in the small, light Peregrine chassis, and call it a Bentley? The combination, to everyone's surprise and relief, worked beautifully. It was fast—much faster than the Rolls-Royce—very quiet and handled exceptionally well. In the words of W.A. Robotham, who joined the company as an apprentice in 1911 and eventually ascended to the R-R board of directors: "It was better than we had any right to expect." Dealers liked it, and so did the R-R production people, because it presented comparatively few problems to build in series. Even Sir Henry, who was not at all that free with compliments, gave it his enthusiastic blessing. It was even thought to be a bit *too* good by some at first, one of the Sales Department's requirements being that the new Bentley *sound* like a sports car—something akin to the Bentleys of old.

Sir Henry did recognize that for such a dual personality as this new car would obviously have, some means should be devised for varying the stiffness of the suspension, depending on whether one wished to dawdle about or really get on it. Such devices had been attempted before but so far none of them worked very well. So the legend goes, one night he sat himself up in bed, sketched out a design for such a system on the back of an envelope, and handed it to his nurse, asking her to get it into the morning

*Clockwise from the left: Eddie Hall's Bentley of the '34, '35 and '36 Tourist Trophy races; the Nikky Embiricos 4¼ Litre Coupe; and its sister car, also by Van Vooren.*

*Two 4¼'s by Vanden Plas: a 1937 Tourer; a 1936 All-Weather Tourer (above and above right).*

mail. He was dead the following day. This variable ride control, adjustable from the driver's seat, was fitted to all subsequent Bentley and Rolls-Royce models—up to but not including the current T-Series/Silver Shadow cars.

It didn't take long for the new Bentley's true sporting potential to be realized. E.R. "Eddie" Hall, a popular and quite successful driver of the period, took delivery of one of the first production 3½-liter chassis, which he had quickly fitted with scanty coachwork—and entered it in the 1934 Tourist Trophy race in Ireland, this initially to the considerable consternation of the people at Rolls-Royce, who were not at all anxious to see their new offspring publicly thrashed by other factory teams with years of racing experience. Through cajolery and threats, Hall finally talked them into it, and in a matter of months had the Bentley name alive in competition again, with Hall putting up a terrific performance in the T.T., finishing second on handicap, but actually outrunning the entire field of very serious Aston Martins, Lagondas, Frazer Nashes, Rileys, etc. He did it again the following year, with the same car, and to drive the point fully home, he did it all over *again* in 1936, the car now fitted with a hotted-up 4¼ engine. For three successive years, he recorded the fastest speed of any entrant in Britain's most prestigious road race, surpassing in that first—1934—race, incidentally, by some eleven miles an hour, the highest lap speed ever recorded by the old Bentley team at the peak of its form. One would assume that any argument now about whether this new Bentley was a sports car or not was surely and permanently settled.

In 1936 the 3½ engine, after being fitted to 1177 production chassis, was opened up to 4257 cc, to become the 4¼ Litre. (The 3½ Litre model was also still marketed for a short time.) There were no other significant changes, but a few were soon to demand the attention of the development staff at Derby.

*Gurney Nutting coachwork on the 4¼ Litre, a Sedanca de Ville from 1939 (below left).*

An increasing number of reports had been coming from Bentley owners in Germany that the new high speed autobahnen were causing the oil to overheat, resulting in a loss of oil pressure, and in some cases outright bearing failure. These were brand-new motoring conditions for Bentley, Rolls-Royce or anybody else for that matter, and typically the engineers at Derby set to solving the problem immediately. Their first impulse was to recommend that those owners who took their cars regularly to Germany have them fitted with longer rear axle ratios. This was fine for Hitler's new highways, but if the cars spent much time in England, the owners objected that they had to spend most of their motoring in the indirect gears. In 1938 an overdrive gearbox was therefore made available. It was a better solution, but still only makeshift (no pun intended), as all it really was was the old four-speed gearbox now with a direct third and an overdrive fourth. Still, it cooled the cars down on the autobahnen.

While they were wrestling with the high speed problem in England, a wealthy young Greek racing driver who lived in Paris was finding his own sensational solution to it. Nikky Embiricos had engaged Louis Paulin, a young Frenchman famous for his experiments in *Le Streamline*, to design for him a lightweight 2+2 coupe with very low drag characteristics. The result was built by Carrosserie Van Vooren on Embiricos' new 4¼ chassis—and what a magnificent automobile it turned out to be. It weighed between two and three hundred pounds less than a normal coachbuilt 4¼, drove through a remarkably tall rear axle ratio for those days—2.87:1—and had a top speed of around 120 mph. At about 25 mph per 1000 rpm, it would probably run the legs off any other touring car of that period and in fact later on did establish a number of international records. If anything, it was too fast for its own good, the touring car technology of the time not yet being up to such high sustained speeds . . . the treads had shown a distressing tendency to detach

themselves from the rest of the tire.

All the same, the engineering staff in England was soundly impressed by the Embiricos car and asked to try it out on the Continent. Thus an outing in January of 1939 was arranged, and a second car, a Van Vooren saloon, was also laid on. The trip involved three days of very high speed motoring in France and Germany, all brilliantly successful. As this outing had been carefully publicized, inquiries soon began arriving back at the factory, old and new customers alike wondering if they could buy something similar to the fabulous Embiricos Bentley.

Rolls-Royce had a superb answer waiting in the wings—the superlative but stillborn Mark V. It was a completely new chassis, destined for formal introduction in 1940. The engine of the Mark V was quite similar to the current Rolls-Royce Wraith, and it also featured coil sprung i.f.s. as did the Wraith, but of a completely different type. A divided driveshaft minimized any possibility of vibration and the frame, also quite different from the Rolls, was immensely stiff and strong. Synchromesh was now on all but bottom gear, and optional close ratios were available. A batch of perhaps thirty-five cars was sanctioned for an initial production run, but only seventeen, possibly nineteen, were produced before the outbreak of World War II. Even so, the impression made by the Embiricos car on Rolls-Royce management had already left its mark. A very high performance, four-door prototype was planned, and the result, of course, was the famous Corniche.

Through joint collaboration between H.I.F. Evernden, Bentley's chief of body design, M. Paulin and Van Vooren again, a prototype four-door saloon was built on the Mark V chassis, having more satisfactory seating capacity at the rear than the Embiricos car had, with a very striking, wind-cheating body. It was now well into the summer of 1939, and as the new car was put through her considerable paces on the motorways of France and Germany, the evidence was everywhere that Europe was about to catch fire again after twenty years of unsteady peace. When it did, the Corniche was caught in it, bombed to smithereens as she stood on the quayside at Dieppe awaiting a ship to take her out of France. For the duration, Rolls-Royce and Bentley would have far more serious matters to attend to.

As early as January 1944, some of the R-R automobile staff began to consider postwar car production again. Several prototype engine designs of four, six and eight cylinders had already been tested before the war in experimental cars which they managed to find the time to build. These were, strictly speaking, Rolls-Royce engines. It had already been decided that the postwar Bentleys, though they would be somewhat smaller overall, would share as many R-R production components as possible. One of these prototype war babies, called "Scalded Cat," consisted of a Bentley-sized chassis and body with a new experimental six-liter, straight-eight engine with overhead intake and side exhaust valves. (This valve arrangement was adopted mainly to minimize the increased length when consideration was given to producing a straight-eight.) The Scalded Cat was, in fact, a sensational performer, but regrettably this engine never went into a Bentley. It later did see service in the enlarged Rolls-Royce Silver Wraith, built from 1950 into 1956 for heads of state only, which was called the Phantom IV. It went into other sorts of vehicles too, fire engines and gun carriers and such.

As it happened, the i.o.e. six that powered the new postwar Silver Wraith of 1946 also worked even better in the new Bentley Mark VI, principally because of the Bentley's smaller size and weight. The Mark VI was a lovely car, a bit cramped by today's standards, but the combined power, handling and quiet produced a vehicle that was absolutely unique in its time. It was, in fact, all that the Mark V was expected to be seven years before. Its top gear performance, like all those R-R-built Bentleys before

*A 4¼ Litre Saloon by Park Ward and a 4¼ Litre Tourer by Vanden Plas, both from 1939 (above left and right); a 1949 Mark VI Drophead Coupe by Mulliner (below).*

it, was the equal of or superior to any car built anywhere, and vastly better than any other production car built in Europe. *The Autocar* raved over "... a new thrill which mere words cannot convey. It is a completely docile, silent town car, and a fast touring hill-devouring vehicle rolled into one." *The Motor* agreed, praising its "outstanding accelerative and hill climbing ability, very quiet running, light yet precise handling qualities and particularly powerful brakes." The Bentley was undeniably still a thoroughbred to the bone.

The new Mark VI was also the first Rolls-Royce product to be fitted with a standardized steel body, stamped and welded up for the company by Pressed Steel of Coventry. Bodiless chassis were still available on special order, but the vast bulk of Bentley's Mark VI production from this point on was made up of Standard Steel Saloons. Rolls-Royce was probably the first to recognize that the postwar era would no longer favor the specially coachbuilt car, and it has been observed by some historians that the bread-and-butter Bentley was very likely responsible for keeping Rolls-Royce cars alive during the Silver Wraith years—Silver Wraiths were still sold as chassis only.

The standard production body of the Mark VI was a very elegant affair, and it remained unaltered through the increase in engine displacement in 1951 (from 4257 to 4566 cc). The latter soon became known as the Big Bore/Small Boot model, to distinguish it from the Big Bore/Big Boot of the R-Type which followed in 1952. The R-Type was really only the Mark VI Standard Steel Saloon with a larger trunk—not much of a model change—but except for its comparatively limited interior space, there was hardly any reason to change it. Drive a mint Mark VI some day if you get a chance. You'll see why.

While the Standard Steel Saloon quietly went its graceful course, the lily

was really painted when the extraordinary R-Type Continental made its appearance in 1952. The project was instituted in 1950, when Evernden and J.P. Blatchley were directed by management to produce a high performance companion to the R-Type, which "would not only look beautiful but possess a high maximum speed coupled with a correspondingly high rate of acceleration together with excellent handling qualities and roadability." They certainly did all of that. The code name at the beginning was "Corniche II," and of course that's exactly the kind of car they were striving for. Fortunately for the original owners who would take delivery of them, *this* Corniche got into production. In September of 1951 the prototype—affectionately known throughout the world wherever Bentley is spoken as "Olga"—was taken to the track at Montlhéry in France and after some juggling of differential ratios, she began reeling off laps at around 120 mph, or about 25 mph faster than the standard Mark VI could manage. This was, mind you, at 20 mpg, in complete silence and sybaritic comfort. How about 50, 80 and 100 mph in the indirect gears? Once again, there was a Bentley that could do what no other car in the world could do, and today ownership of any of the 207 Continentals produced immediately marks a man as an undoubted connoisseur.

Both the Bentley R-Type and the R-Type Continental were continued up to 1955, with another slight engine increase to 4887 cc in May of 1954. By then, though, no matter how refined the Standard Steel Saloon was, there was growing need for improvement, in styling and internal room particularly. It had, after all, been in production since 1946. The result was the new Bentley S-Type, introduced along with the Silver Cloud Rolls-Royce in April of 1955. The cars were more alike than ever now, the stern realities of production costs forcing commonality of parts to the extent that, but for the radiator shell and the occasional appearance of the name or logo, they

*Clockwise from the left: "Olga," the prototype for the R-Type Continental, by Mulliner; a 1955 R-Type Standard Saloon;  a Series S Standard Saloon from 1959.*

were virtually indistinguishable from one another. It is of perhaps passing interest that the new Cloud actually got the old R-Type Bentley engine this time, with its 4887 cc six, twin carburetors and moderately higher output. Automatic transmission was now standard equipment, there was more braking area (though the wheels were reduced by one inch to fifteen inches) and a new six-port aluminum cylinder head allowed them to breathe a little more deeply. But, to be really honest about it, the Bentley had lost the unique and separate identity that it had always enjoyed and that, until then, had been so carefully protected.

Possibly the nicest feature of this new S range was the absolutely superb styling of the new Standard Saloon. Though chassis and body remained separate entities, those few coachbuilders who still existed were hard pressed to improve on its design, and very few of them ever did. This was also the first occasion on which a standard production body went onto a Rolls-Royce. There was a Continental version of the S, though the only difference now was a slightly higher compression ratio and a longer rear axle ratio.

In August of 1959 came the S.2, creating retroactively the S.1 before it. There was a big change under the skin this time. The venerable i.o.e. six —one of the smoothest and sturdiest engines of all time—finally expired, being replaced by a big (for Rolls-Royce) 6.2-liter aluminum V-8 of American design (GM), which bolted conveniently onto its American-designed automatic transmission. Outwardly, the car had hardly changed at all, but the performance was considerably increased. So was fuel consumption, but one has always tended to doubt that Rolls or Bentley owners ever counted pennies when filling up. The Continental version continued, though now the only difference from standard specs was in tire size and axle ratio.

174 The S.3 appeared along with the Cloud III in October of 1962. There was

no difference at all now between the Rolls and the Bentley. The Continental name was continued but all it meant this time was smaller tires. Outwardly, the cars were identical, though the S.3/Cloud III quad headlamp arrangement did distinguish it from those before; it also served as grist for endless argument over whether the company had sold out, "gone American," or simply was keeping up with the times.

One last *beau geste* was made with the Continental Flying Spur, a lightweight four-door saloon on the S-Series Continental chassis—all of them coachbuilt, and considered by many to be one of the finest sedans built since World War II. The standard S-Type Bentley was a thoroughly nice car, in many ways an exceptional car, but it was no longer *more* of a car than its contemporary Rolls-Royce. So it was with the S-Series that the Bentley really died, even though its memory still lingers on as a sort of mirror image to Rolls-Royce products up to this day, through the S.2 and S.3, all lovely cars, but without that uniqueness and spirit which always made a Bentley a Bentley.

The present range, the T-Series, represents the most recent Bentley/Rolls-Royce design, the Silver Shadow being its R-R counterpart. Introduced in 1965, it was not greeted with manic enthusiasm at the time and, as far as one can tell, it is still in little danger of it. Smaller overall than the S-Series, the car is stupefyingly complicated, an absolute bastard to service and withal doesn't seem to do anything much better than a number of higher priced American sedans, even though it costs four times as much. But if this seems somehow disrespectful or unappreciative, one should hasten to acknowledge that there is no car built anywhere in the world today which still receives such attention to detail in its finish, uses finer materials in its construction or that carries with it the massive social impact of any new Rolls-Royce or Bentley. Still, it is devoutly to be wished that there was more than this to praise the Bentley for today. ✥

*Bentleys of the Sixties and Seventies: an S.2 Continental Flying Spur by Mulliner from 1962 (above); a Series T Saloon produced in 1971 (below).*

# THE FOOL THINGS

*Remembering the Halcyon Days*
*When America Wasn't All Too Sure*
*It Liked the Automotive Idea,*

*With Paintings by Leslie Saalburg*

*1899 Locomobile Steam Stanhope*

In America, the mayor of Warsaw, Georgia found it politic any expedient to offer a public apology when he bought one. In England, the
Marquis of Queensbury, rather unsportingly, petitioned the government
for sanction to "shoot on sight" anyone speeding past him on one. In
France, novelist Hughes Leroux tried exactly that, firing his revolver twice
in the direction of one whose charge he had just escaped. He missed.

Somehow, the automotive idea survived too.

"In various ways the automobile is a valuable invention, which promises
far more than it has yet fulfilled," the New York *Herald* allowed in April of
1900. "Presumably its future is secure, but it ought to be so regulated as to
give the present generation a fair chance of surviving to witness its
triumph." What was the matter with the automobile? For one thing, it was
quite as much disposed "to start backward as forward under the mismanagement of a driver who has lost his head or never had one." For
another, there were the factors of "Frightening Horses" and "Running
Down Children." For yet another, the fool things were providing a
needless multiplication of new perplexities to add to the problem "of existence in this city [which] is already quite complicated enough."

Outlawing them was tried, particularly in pleasure areas, with varying
degrees of success. President Clausen of the New York Park Board made
an "opera bouffe" of himself, as one sympathetic journal noted, in trying
to keep them out of Central Park, his "general testiness ill becoming a civic
official at the dawn of the twentieth century." The good fathers of Boston

managed to exclude the vehicles from that city's parks, but only during
certain hours of the day—10:30 a.m. to 9 p.m.

There were the small victories. In Hackensack, New Jersey, Dr. William
L. Vroom was declared not guilty in a lawsuit brought by John L. Guyre
"for damages for the loss of his wife" who was thrown from her buggy in
January (and died in August) after Dr. Vroom's out-of-control automobile
jostled the Guyre horse into panic. Dr. Vroom demonstrated that he was
275 feet away from the horse—and in complete control. The jury agreed
with him.

But there were always the forebodings of defeat. Betimes, in Manhattan, one of the New York aldermen was trying to jostle through a resolu-
tion prohibiting the use or presence of gasoline anywhere in the city. Fortunately, no one agreed with him.

It remained a struggle, though one slowly being won. Numerous courts
ruled similarly to the one in Indiana that "in this progressive age modern
improvements in the method of travel cannot be subordinated," and
horses had best get used to the idea. This was a godsend. Earlier,
proponents of the automobile had given as among its advantages the fact
that it could not run away like a horse. By early 1900, automobiles were
running away all over the country—in Indianapolis a belligerent equine
nudged one down a hill.

It was principally a matter of education. Into the tutoring gap strode
magazines devoted to this wondrous new invention, deploring the popular

*1899 Oakman Hertel Runabout*

*1900 Columbia Mark XIX Electric Surrey*

conception of the motor carriage as an "airy, fairy" contrivance, "a thing of gossamer, almost imponderable, regulated by a magic touch button and gathering its power from 'airy nothing.' " It was all easily explained really; in the automobile, the horse was *in* the vehicle, that's all. Nothing frightening about that.

Quite serious it was, this matter of education. The daily papers in rural communities might make sport of it—the Reading (Pennsylvania) *Telegram* suggesting that "in view of the tendency of automobiles to run into stone fences," inventors turn their talents to coming up with a fence-jumping attachment for their latest models. The motor press, however, sagely counselled that inventors should think instead of ridding the automobile of its horse-wanted appearance, the slavish imitation of horse-vehicle forms was irksome and impeding the automobile's progress.

Another obstacle was the almost universal ignorance of the public regarding the nature, capabilities and handling of the motorcar. "It must doubtless be admitted," *The Horseless Age* said, "that the owner of an automobile, who is not blessed by nature with an instinct for things mechanical, is in a desperate case, and a weekly visit to a repair station is probably his only hope." The magazine offered to open its news columns to motoring readers with experiences to relate and "wherever sketches are needed to make clear the writer's meaning, we would urge that they be made. No matter how rough they are, we will see that they are properly reproduced."

Gradually, with more daring, the automotive press began suggesting what seemed to it to be inevitable. When wealthy New York residents, in increasing numbers, began using their motor vehicles exclusively in the

*1901 Packard Model C Roadster*

city, one magazine stoutly declared that leaving the horse in the country was only proper: "It is there, and there only, that poetry may be associated with him. In the city he is a nuisance and an object of pity, a menace to the public health, and a dumb servant compelled to work under conditions not natural to him, and to which he cannot properly adjust himself." Another journal waggishly suggested that the costumes being designed for the new motoring scene might be appropriate too for members of the horsey set, "as they are necessarily more or less exposed to wet and grime in exactly the same manner as is the automobilist." Tit for tat.

But, beware, the automobile press warned, that manufacturers in their eagerness to supply an enthusiastic clientele not be "guilty of gross exaggeration in the advertising of their machines." The "perfect carriage," it advised, had not yet been built.

There were lots of imperfections on the market now. The first exhibition of motor carriages in the United States—organized by the Massachusetts Charitable Mechanics Association in 1898—had served fair warning that an industry was on its way. By November of 1900, when the Automobile Club of America brought together forty automobile manufacturers to exhibit their wares in New York's Madison Square Garden, there was no doubt. Some 300 examples of less-than-indefectibility were displayed.

A quandary did exist, however, as to just what the motive force of a motor vehicle should be. Automobile licenses issued in Chicago that year totaled 378, 226 of them for electric machines, 92 for steam, 60 for gasoline power. Significantly, the Windy City required that any automobile accidents be reported to the city electrician.

Automobile magazines, on the other hand, noted that in Paris, where the

International Automobile Congress was ongoing, the overwhelming prominence had been given the gasoline vehicle. And in Swampscott, Massachusetts, Prof. Elihu Thomson—of the General Electric Company yet—expressed his opinion that steam was the power best adapted to the motor vehicle.

Which was good news for the Locomobile Company of Bridgeport, Connecticut. It had been feeling some heat lately. One of the company's clients was immeasurably displeased. As Rudyard Kipling wrote a friend; "[My Locomobile is] a Holy Terror. . . . I suppose she will settle down some day to her conception of duty but just now her record is one of eternal & continuous breakdown. She disgraced us on June 26th when I took two friends over 13 miles of flat road. The pumps failed to lift. . . . Also she took to blowing through her pistons. We overhauled her on June 27th. . . . On June 29th we laid out a trip 19 miles out & back. I took the

wife. She (the Loco) betrayed us fully 12 miles out—blew through her cylinders, leaked, and laid down. It was a devil of a day. It ended in coming home by train. The wife nearly dead with exhaustion." The hero of the short story in which he subsequently wrote about his experiences with the Locomobile was called First Class Engine-Room Artificer Hinchcliffe.

"Our 1903 Locomobiles are the result of many years of study and manufacture," the company said in the catalogue for its steam car line. By 1904 Locomobile had gone gasoline.

The problem with electrics was that they didn't go far enough between charges nor fast enough fully charged. Charles J. Glidden might power himself up Fifth Avenue in New York in his Mark XIX Columbia electric surrey "with goggles over his eyes and linen duster and all the appurtenances of speed," but Hiram Percy Maxim, who was the car's designer and happened to see him do it, knew how fast he was going

*1901 Columbia Mark VIII Runabout*

positively . . . because I had measured it numberless times. Mr. Chidden was running at slightly less than twelve miles an hour!"

Columbia had another idea, or more accurately the idea was that of Albert A. Pope who counted Columbia among his automotive enterprises. It was a gasoline car, and it joined the electric by century's turn.

Not that all this should infer gasoline carriage builders found the going any easier. There was the matter of the Selden patent ("the antiquated document . . . galvanized into new life," as one trade magazine scoffed, and which threatened to monopolize the gasoline vehicle industry), and there was the equally urgent problem of staying in business.

Max Hertel couldn't solve that one. In 1898 his Oakman Motor Vehicle Company in Greenfield, Massachusetts glowed with promise, he had just finished his factory and had looked around and decided he needed more space for "an increase in production" he was sure was forthcoming. What

Max didn't figure on was that potential customers might desire a motor vehicle a little more formidable than the two bicycle-type frames with an engine and body perched between them that he was providing. Max printed a lot of catalogues—and built a few cars and that was it.

Success had its sting too. There was no doubt—in his own mind at least—that Alexander Winton built a good car. He had sold twenty-two of them in 1898, which made him America's largest producer of gasoline vehicles—and by 1900 when sufficient others had joined him to form a budding industry, he was its dominant influence. This made him fair game for the critics. He seems "to hesitate to add 5 or 10 pounds weight where it is actually needed," P.B. Rawson carped. "The chain transmits direct to the differential on rear axle, instead of to a gear box adjacent to it." A journalist who fashioned himself as Dr. Henry Power cavilled that "the old, rather faulty, method of water cooling, has been retained, and [he has] not

*1903 Autocar Rear Entrance Tonneau*

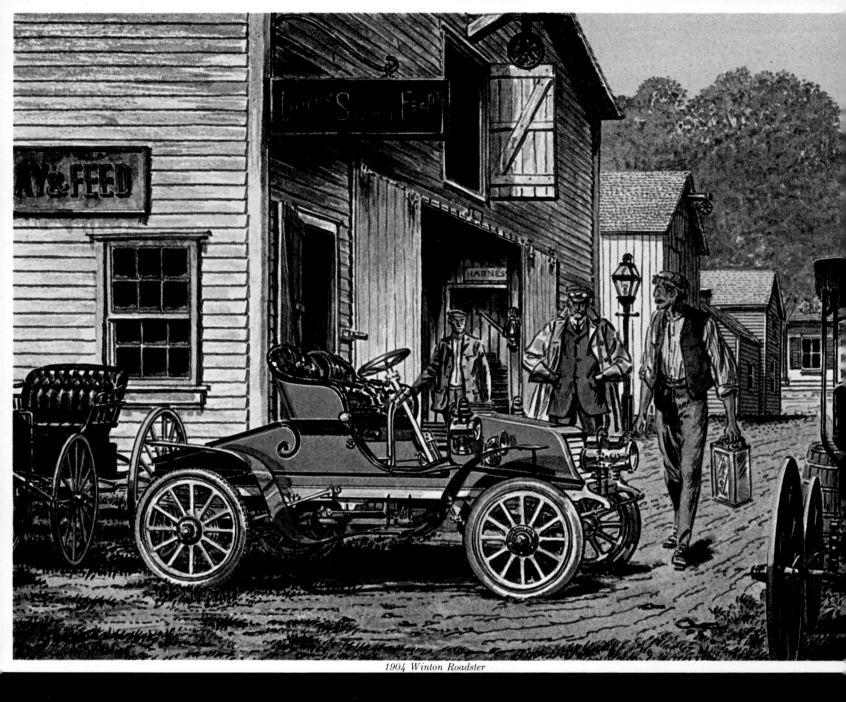

*1904 Winton Roadster*

yet considered the problem in light of modern physics." And a fellow writing simply as "Expert" summed up the Winton coachwork succinctly: "Too low to the ground and too flat-sided, needing more swell to the seats. It seems as though the front box should carry more. Lighten up the back end of body, balance more the front and put on wooden wheels a little higher than ones now on."

Louis S. Clarke received a rather better press for his Autocar. He had built his first vehicle in 1896, his second in 1898, but was careful to keep them experimental and didn't consider serious production until he moved his company from Pittsburgh to Ardmore, Pennsylvania in 1900. When he introduced his new car for 1903, the press delighted in "all of the good features of the late models" being retained, "but all those details of the 1902 machines that proved wanting [having] been modified and im-

proved." Among these were the relocation of the engine from under the body to under the bonnet, a three-speed transmission instead of two, and the "wide range of speed, viz., 250 to 1,200 turns per minute." Motoring journals even accepted without blinking the Autocar claim that all its parts were interchangeable. If they were, Henry Martyn Leland didn't deserve the Dewar Trophy he won a half decade later.

And if the press was resolutely enamored of the Autocar efforts, it was positively ecstatic when it heard that J. Frank Duryea—whose pioneering provided so much news-story material in the Nineteenth Century—had allied himself with the well-known armaments firm of J. Stevens in Chicopee Falls, Massachusetts for the purpose of building a car to be called the Stevens-Duryea. The first came in 1902, and by early '04 a racer varia-tion was coursing the Ormond-Daytona sands for a mile in 57.2 seconds,

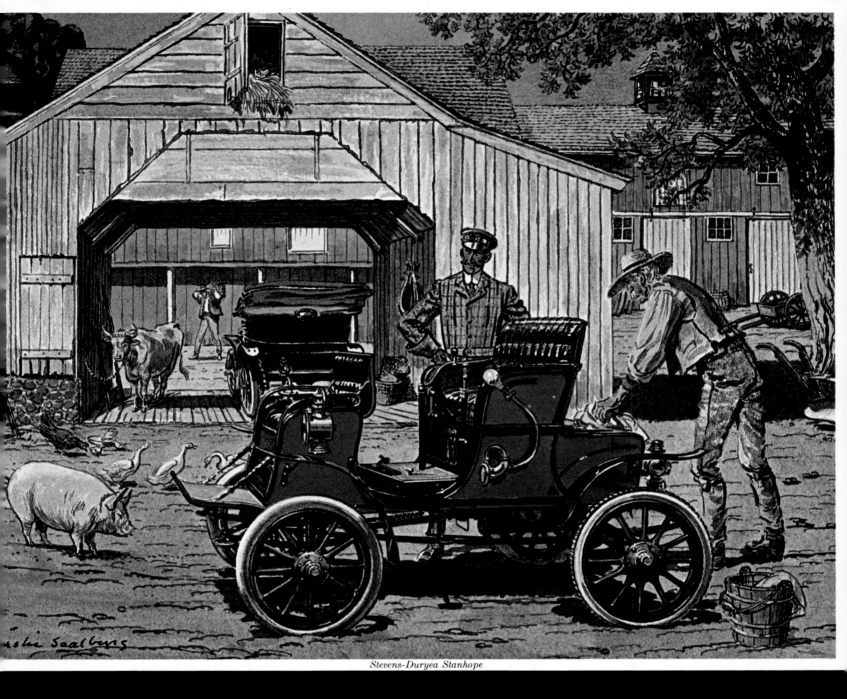

*Stevens-Duryea Stanhope*

Now *that* was muscling in on Alexander Winton's territory . . . he thought. It was bad enough those ambitious rascals from Michigan—Ransom Olds with his Pirate and Henry Ford with his 999—were challenging his speeding Bullets, but when J. Frank Duryea joined in—and then James Ward Packard! Too much. The latter had had the audacity several years previous to tell Winton how to build a better car. When Winton replied to the effect that his alleged expertise seemed to suggest that he try himself, James Ward Packard did. And now the Packard was challenging the Winton in the marketplace too—as well as the race track.

Intramural bickering. It was bound to come, as inevitably as the automobile. The motoring public, gradually coming to like the automotive idea, paid it no mind. The delight of motoring was taking hold, there would

United States; as 1904 turned into 1905, that number had jumped to 77,-000. From Europe had come word that Jules Verne and Emile Zola were saying very nice things about the automobile, Rudyard Kipling be hanged. In Reading, Pennsylvania, six citizens met on a corner one day and discovered each owned an automobile and decided to have a race—stone fences be damned. In New Jersey, Princeton University students beat Harvard and Yale to the organization of an automobile club. At the Waldorf Astoria, John Jacob Astor joined a lot of other luminaries "to start the agitation" for a highway to run across the whole of the U.S.

And there was another large movement afoot. When, in 1901, an innkeeper in Yonkers began providing amenities and special accommodations for motorist visitors, it was quickly decided this was a very good idea. They called them automobile hotels the

# THE GLORIOUS DELAGE, A BITTERSWEET STORY

## Commitment and Obsession –The Rise and Fall of the French Empire Builder Named Louis

*The exquisite Delages of the marque's early years, a Type F from 1910 (left) and an R4 from '14 (below). To all outward appearances, the Delages of this vintage might seem simply big cars in miniature, but as the press noted in 1911, the Delage was "far from being a mere reduction of some high powered brother." Quite the contrary. It was designed specifically as a high speed yet strong small car. That it proved to be exactly that might be suggested by the use of Delages in World War I. The 1913 R4 (right) was discovered many years later sporting camouflage paint and army buttons throughout.*

"What sort of man was Louis Delage?"

The answers to this question have seldom varied. People who worked with him rarely painted a fetching picture of the man. Moral types spoke sourly of his princely pursuit of expensive women. A former member of his executive staff summed up the consensus in a handful of words: "The Delage men were not *attachants*," he said. Not attractive, not likeable. "Neither the father nor the son were people you would particularly want to know."

Reflecting upon all the empire builders who have coursed automotive history, one concludes that, as a class, disinterested charm is rarely among their attributes. The sort of trip they are on leaves little time or energy for anything but the job to be done. Their will to achieve and acquire sets them apart from the mass and in judging them it seems reasonable to do so on their own terms—on the quality of the result of their commitment or obsession.

In the case of Louis Delage, this task is simplified by the fact that we know he ran his company with a rather iron hand from its founding in 1905 until its liquidation in 1935. It was a reflection of *his* personality, and of none other. He was a graduate engineer who surrounded himself with men of the same high professional qualifications. From his administrative offices to his factory floor, he built a managerial staff that was packed with engineers of quality. Thus, in a young industry overrun by visionaries and adventurers, he built an extraordinarily rational and efficient modern manufacturing organization, and this was the solid base for the product.

The product itself was consistently extraordinary for two things. One, obviously, was engineering quality, which remained on a lofty level throughout those thirty years. The other thing—and it also marked Delage cars from start to finish—was the founder's feeling for the automobile as thing of beauty and art object. His earliest, small and inexpensive runabouts possessed a chic that puts them in an enduring class by themselves. As the trends of design and market moved to bigger, more powerful cars, that pertness was blended with elegance and majesty, Delage cars becoming leading standard-bearers of all that was implicit in the term *la belle voiture française*. Delage chassis, along with the few made by Hispano-Suiza, attracted the bulk of the most inspired work of France's finest coachbuilders. These latter deserve the fullest credit for *their* products. But the personal taste of Louis Delage was a constant factor in determining the type of coachwork which was proposed to his chassis-buying clientele and that which was adopted for his catalogue models.

Then there was Louis Delage's passion for racing and his conviction that there was nothing like a successful competition program to embellish the image of a marque. He was loyal to this passion and conviction until 1927, when he won the Grand Prix racing World Championship with a team of some of the most sublime machines of the type ever to be conceived and realized in metal. Others had designed them, but they were expressions of *his* will. He quit racing then, because the almost quarter of a million dollars

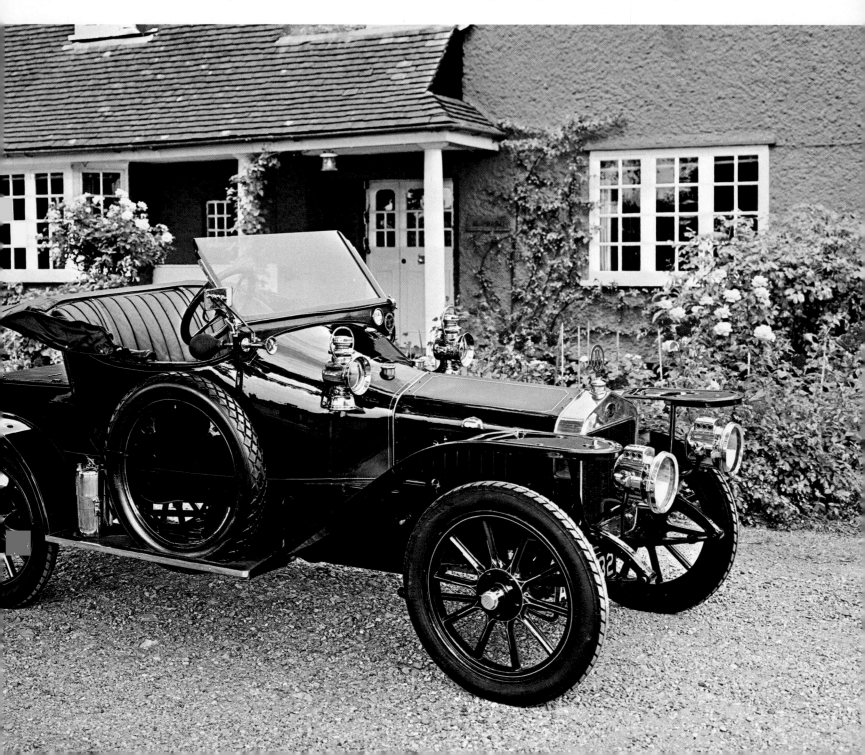

which that year's campaign had cost him came close to ruining him. But Europe was thunderstruck by his crushing and gorgeous affirmation of technological superiority and there can be no doubt that it played a major part in minimizing the early effects of the Thirties depression upon Delage sales and therefore upon the financial health of the firm.

In surveying the career of Louis Delage, one is reminded of E.L. Cord and Sir William Lyons—two other automotive empire-builders who, like Delage, had uncanny good taste, knew how to offer a great deal of quality at competitive prices, and knew how to infuse their marques with a prestigious sporting image.

Louis Delage had the feet of clay of all mortals and made an occasional very bad decision, often in his very own discipline of engineering. His downfall has been attributed to his "compulsion"—dating from the early post-World War I period—to rival or surpass his super-glamorous next-door neighbor, Hispano-Suiza. But a glance at his total production indicates Delage never neglected for long his bread-and-butter line of vehicles. He was like a scaled-down General Motors, presenting a range of small to large cars—all of well-known quality—but under a single name—his own. One of the paradoxes of the Depression, on both sides of the Atlantic, was a giddy rush by manufacturers toward the super-luxury car market at the same time that that market shrank to the vanishing point. Delage was merely one of the many to commit this folly and this alone doubtless did not account for the failure of the firm. The Depression simply winnowed out the weak from the strong and Delage, who had only made some 38,000 cars in his three decades as a constructor, had not the strength to survive.

Cognac, France had been his birthplace, and his birth date, March 22nd, 1894. Some writers have stated that he was born to wealth—this perhaps because of the rich elegance of the marque he created—but his family merely enjoyed the bourgeois rank becoming his father's position as assistant station master of a small provincial town. His parents could afford to send their son to the Ecole des Arts et Métiers at Angers, from which fount of engineers he graduated in 1893, in time to do his military service. That year and the next he passed in Algeria and on his return home he followed his father's counsel and got into railroading, as a works boss based in the station at Bordeaux.

But it was the automobile, struggling out of its chrysalis, that fascinated young Delage and in 1900 he moved to Paris and set himself up as a consulting engineer, living off odd jobs picked up within the horseless-carriage trade. In 1903 his background was sufficient for him to find a job as chief draftsman and tester for a little enterprise that had been building cars for four years. It was the budding automotive division of the big Peugeot industrial complex and its headquarters were at 83, rue Danton in the suburb of Levallois-Perret, northwest of Paris. By the end of the following year, Delage knew almost as much about the automobile as anyone in the infant industry and had arrived at a vision of its future. He found financial backing, resigned from Automobiles et Cycles Peugeot and, on January 10th, 1905, went through the legal and administrative ritual necessary for the founding of Delage & Cie. Later in the day he demonstrated his ability as a judge of engineering talent.

In early 1904, Peugeot had hired Augustin Legros as an engineering draftsman. Legros had obtained his engineering degree in 1899, had

186

worked briefly for Clément-Bayard at Levallois and, subsequently, wanting to broaden his experience of the world, journeyed to England, where he worked for Daimler at Coventry for two years. Then he returned to his family home in Levallois and, Peugeot being in the neighborhood, soon found himself working under Delage.

The night of January 10th, his own company now a reality, Delage invited Legros to join him as a designer of the cars to be built by the new marque. Legros, just twenty-five, enjoyed working for the thirty-one-year-old Delage. He agreed to the proposition, found a qualified man to take his place at Peugeot and, on the 13th, installed himself in Delage's walk-up living room/drawing office on the fifth floor of 62, rue Chaptal.

The new business thus began with these two men—and when it ended thirty years later, Legros still was second in command of the company. From the mid-Twenties onward, he was in charge of the firm's entire production activity. It is perhaps unfortunate that this clear-thinking man was not also burdened with its financial management, but that sector always remained the private preserve of *Le Patron*, the boss.

In his memoirs, Legros recalled looking out the window of his garret office in the rue Chaptal and beyond the gardens of the English hospital there to the fine factory of Carrosserie Belvalette. He dreamed that someday, if he could put enough of his taste, care and best judgment into the effort, someday Delage might have a factory equally beautiful and grand.

The two men worked on the design of the cars they would produce and on the logistics of getting them into production. It was not until mid-June of 1905 that Louis Delage rented a shop in a rickety wooden barn at 83, rue Anatole-France. The shop contained six machine tools: four lathes, a drill

press and a milling machine. But cars had to wait, in favor of job work that would bring in needed cash.

However, the first two Delage prototypes were finished in time for the opening of the eighth Salon de l'Automobile de Paris that December. The Type A was equipped with a 1059 cc single-cylinder de Dion engine and the Type B with a 496 cc version. On the opening day of the great show and marketplace, it became clear that the current vogue considered these engines to be too big or too small. The young entrepreneurs feverishly produced another chassis fitted with the 697 cc de Dion. It hit the mark.

Many years later, a distinguished Parisian newspaperman, Victor Breyer, wrote ". . . it was at that epoch that I met Louis Delage for the first time. At that time Charles Faroux, under the name of 'The Masked Chauffeur,' edited the automotive section of *L'Echo des Sports*, of which I was the director. Although Delage's financial situation eliminated any possibility of paid publicity, we gave the public a detailed description of the Delage car with complimentary comments which legitimized its conception and construction, because this ensemble of happy solutions was of real interest for the future. Neither my partner nor I was sufficiently stupid or pretentious to claim any part of the credit for the success of Delage."

The famous magic of Faroux's opinions certainly did no harm, however, and a good stack of orders, with cash deposits, was harvested at the Salon. And, as a complete surprise, a wealthy admirer pressed a loan of 150,000 francs upon Delage on the condition that the latter give the former's car-happy son a job. Delage & Cie. was decidedly in business.

One of the *Patron*'s first acts with his newly acquired substance was to rent a storefront at 2, Place du Général Leclerc and to establish his business office there. The office was just a few steps from the barn-workshop, where production went on furiously. But Delage took time away from immediate practical goals to participate in the Coupe des Voiturettes de L'Auto.

On the fifth day of eliminations, one of the little Delages was eliminated definitively when it skidded and wrapped itself around a tree. The other, however, finished a magnificent second to a victorious Sizaire et Naudin, ahead of the fearsome Lion Peugeots which managed no better than third and fourth.

This quite brilliant performance by a marque less than a year old took place in November, a month before the next Salon. It created enormous, resounding publicity for Delage who, at the show, found himself swamped not only by eager buyers but also by equally eager seekers of dealerships. Racing did indeed improve the breed.

The little workshop became totally inadequate and, around the spring of 1907, Delage bought three-quarters of an acre in Levallois, at the corner of rue Baudin and rue Jules-Guesde. And, in October, he had another go at the Coupe des Voiturettes, but only finished seventh, which still was not too bad for a field of fifty-six starters. Then, at the time of the Salon in December, Henri Davène de Roberval, board director of the large gear and machine tool manufacturing firm of Malicet-Blin, became Louis Delage's silent partner. The substantial capital which he infused into the little company spurred its development and machine tools and gears suddenly became available at friendly prices.

All went well as 1908 unfolded, and Delage prepared three cars for an extremely important and historic race, the Grand Prix des Voiturettes held at Dieppe on July 6th. And the victor, among thirty-one finishers, representing the cream of European light cars, was Albert Guyot in one of the Delages, while his teammates came in fifth and twelfth. The press and public reacted with near delirium to this victory against top international competition and suddenly the big new factory was far too small to meet the demand for Delage cars. A new two-story building was built the length of the rue Jules-Guesde. By year's end, Delage had 43,000 square feet of floor space under cover—nearly an acre—and had inscribed his name indelibly in motor racing history.

Louis Delage had only begun. In 1909 most automobile "manufacturers" were assembly specialists, buying their components from scattered sources, and only a very few dreamed of making their own engines. Delage & Cie. already were a bit unusual in that, from the start, they designed and built their own frames and a great deal of the hardware to go with them. Being dependent upon de Dion or any other outside source for engines rankled Delage and Legros. The expansion of the rue Baudin plant and of cash reserves made it possible to take action.

Thus far, Delage cars had been fitted with one- and two-cylinder engines, but now the vogue for fours was coming in. Ernest Ballot was manufacturing excellent fours and Louis Delage—a *very* hard business-man—entered into negotiations with him. The ultimate result was that Ballot would provide fifty percent of Delage's annual engine requirement. At the same time, Ballot would give Delage a complete set of engineering drawings for this powerplant and the know-how for its manufacture, with the right to build it without licensing fees. In addition, all of these engines for Delage cars, whether made by Delage or Ballot, would bear the Delage nameplate. This put Delage in the engine manufacturing business at virtually zero cost, while at the same time creating an important new, if ephemeral, market for Ballot.

As for coachwork, virtually no car manufacturer in Europe at this period built his own bodies. He was a *constructeur* of chassis and even his catalogue bodies were subcontracted to specialists in coachbuilding. It was in 1909 that Legros was contacted by a young master woodworker named François Repusseau who, with a blacksmith and an upholsterer as partners, was just setting up a coachbuilding business in Levallois, next door to Peugeot. To get the thriving Delage business, Repusseau permitted Legros to beat his price down to 300 francs per body. Then Delage himself intervened, extracting a price of 280 francs from this naïve beginner. No profit was left for the coachbuilder and Repusseau's partners deserted him. He stuck with Delage, however, until early 1914 when Peugeot, needing to expand, offered him 200,000 francs for his lease. He took it, and went on to become an important force in the French auto industry. Looking back from his

Louis Delage enjoyed driving and liked his cars to be driven, a lot. As demonstration, during the Twenties— when the two cars on the pages preceding, a 1925 Type DI Formal Limousine by Castraise and a 1927 Type DIS Torpedo by Kelsch, were built—he spearheaded a series of treks on the Continent that were eye-openers. The Autocar suggested that such excursions were not a good idea, an inconvenience or danger perforce to citizens and other road users. In a letter that revealed much about Louis and his Delage, effectively advertising both, he replied grandly: "Whilst automobile construction, design, and the study of automobile improvements absorb me to such an extent that I have become one of the greatest motor travellers of the period, I have still remained a reasonable tourist. . . . An enumeration of our 'slaughter' is the best proof that can be given. During the whole of the journey of more than three thousand miles, I killed four unfortunate hens and one goose. . . . You will naturally ask how I have been able, while driving prudently, to make daily averages of 520 miles, without remaining at the wheel an abnormal length of time, for our average daily running time did not exceed fifteen hours. You yourself have furnished the answer to this question, and also shown your complete knowledge of motoring and motoring conditions, when you state '. . . The fact that the same driver should have had the wheel throughout the trip is a remarkable proof of the ease with which the car can be controlled.' This sentence is the key to the success of this demonstration. I think I can claim, without false pride, that the car I have sought to perfect, in conjunction with my engineers, for the last three years, is the most flexible, the easiest to drive, and one which gives the least fatigue at present in existence. Although the powerful engine enables a speed of sixty miles an hour to be maintained with ease, it is owing to extremely rapid acceleration, and particularly to the brakes on all four wheels, that a very high average can be maintained without reaching a very high maximum speed. It is because of these two factors . . . that the average speed always remains very close to whatever maximum the driver may set for himself. If you add to this the fact that the manufacturing details of this car are now so perfected that for the past two years our clients assure us with perfect sincerity that they are able to cover thousands of kilometers without the least stop for repair or adjustment, you will understand that any driver who is willing to sit at the steering wheel for fifteen hours a day can do just as well as I have done, without being a nuisance or a danger to anybody." Louis invited the magazine's editors to come to France for a day's drive, an offer he would repeat about a decade later when the fabulous D8 series was introduced, a 1930 D8N Coach by Chapron pictured above and a Type D8S Drophead de Ville by Pourtout from 1933 pictured below.

position of wealth many years later, he confided to Legros that the sale of his lease and shop equipment provided the only money that he had made in five years of being coachbuilder to Delage.

It seems to have been in late 1909 that Legros, with myriad other responsibilities to attend to, designed his last chassis. To take over his duties in the design sector, Ing. Arthur-Léon Michelat was hired. He had come from the Hermes company in Liège, Belgium, where the now-forgotten Hisa car was made from 1906 through 1914.

The year 1910 brought further reinforcements to the firm's engineering department. Ferdinand Demolliens was hired with the title of technical secretary, to serve as liaison between Legros and the factory. Then the gears, which were supplied by Malicet-Blin, of gearboxes and rear axles began attracting attention for their high noise level. Costly hand finishing made for only mediocre improvement and Legros convinced Delage that he should invest in his own gear-cutting and heat-treatment facilities. This was done and Ing. Maurice Gaultier was hired to run that department.

The quality of the product benefited importantly from all these changes in 1910 and sales were booming more than ever. But Levallois was an industrial backwater of the metropolis and was awkward for clients and agents to reach. This disadvantage was overcome by the acquisition of the ornate, dark red brick building at 60, boulevard Péreire Nord in Paris. Here Delage installed his sales headquarters and, in the vast garage behind the handsome building, his service center and spare parts warehouse. Soon after this, all of the firm's administrative offices were moved to this more fashionable and impressive Paris address.

Sales kept improving, prosperity was rampant, and again it was necessary to expand. In 1912 Louis Delage found a piece of land on the boulevard de Verdun at Courbevoie, just across the Seine from Levallois. Its area was just in excess of eleven acres and it bordered upon the factory properties of Berliet and Hispano-Suiza. By the end of 1912, the first of the new Delage factory buildings was completed there and Gaultier was installed with the title of production manager. Delage had been eager to liberate himself from his dependence upon Ballot, and during this year Gaultier masterminded the creation of plant facilities which assured the firm's self-sufficiency in terms of engine procurement. The Levallois fac-

tory was sold to the Meunier chocolate firm and later became the main plant of the famous Jaeger instrument company.

Through 1912 Delage had specialized in light cars with engines of one to four cylinders and generally modest displacement, with a ceiling of 2.1 liters. In 1913, with the prestige of his marque constantly growing, Delage decided to upgrade his line with the introduction of a 2.5-liter Six. In terms of displacement, this was still a small car but its number of cylinders and their smoothness made it a distinct move toward the luxury car market. The price of this Type AH chassis was highly competitive—only $1825 in London (£365), including import duty. Legros frowned upon this move and the gap widened between the two men.

Such minor problems were swept aside by the outbreak of war in August 1914. The greater part of Delage personnel was swiftly mobilized into the armed forces and only a skeleton crew of skilled workers remained, kept busy for the next year producing liaison vehicles for the military. In the meantime, the plant had been commandeered for conversion to manufacture of artillery shells and projectiles. At a certain point, a scandal erupted over the criminally faulty manufacture of munitions and it was production manager Gaultier who had the pleasure of taking the five-year prison rap. Louis Delage never was accused directly of any wrongdoing but this very grave incident left an enduring taint upon his name, particularly in government circles. Appointment to the *Légion d'Honneur*—normally automatic for a man of his stature—never came his way.

In the study of French automotive history, one notes repeatedly that car manufacturers, supposedly totally committed to the war effort, were very busy during those years with their postwar projects. In referring back to 1915, Legros wrote: "For the postwar period Louis Delage had decided to justify his motto: 'Make but one thing, but make it well.' Towards this end he had adopted the plan to build a single model of chassis, with a tax rating of 17 CV (about three liters), a six-cylinder engine and Perrot front brakes, which had been perfected on our race cars for Lyons in 1914. . . . On his return from the army, soon after me, Arthur Michelat was assigned to commence this project. In informing me of it, Louis Delage took from his desk a piece of paper which he urged me to keep, and on which he had written: '1) Twelve months after the resumption of normal operations we

will have just one model on the market; 2) Twelve months after, that model will have no competition. 3) Twelve months after that, whatever the size of the model, 3,000 units.'

"A few months before the Armistice, since I did not seem to be very convinced of his plan, because his 17 CV Six would appeal to a very limited clientele, Louis Delage, always sure of being right, affirmed to me that the figure of 3,000 cars per year would certainly be exceeded. On the paper which he had handed me three years before he wrote, '4,500 cars. This 19.3 1918—L.D.'

"Unfortunately the future would prove me right. A few years after the war the 17 CV had to be replaced hastily by the 11 CV Four, a more popular model which permitted Louis Delage to rediscover the prosperity of 1913 and to modernize his factory and tooling."

As a matter of fact, the new Six grew from 17 to 20 CV (4524 cc) while still in the prototype stage. Michelat left Delage in anger during the early stages of the project, which was turned over to an ex-Fiat engineer named Lovera, and another newcomer, Ing. Fregal Escure, joined the engineering staff. The new Type CO was presented at the first postwar Salon, held in October of 1919.

A few weeks previously, Delage himself, and with W.F. Bradley as a witness for the British Automobile Association (the across-Channel market was very important to Delage), accomplished the run from Paris to Nice in one of the new cars in just under sixteen hours. This time and an average speed of 41.5 mph in spite of unspeakable road conditions were sensational and helped to pull crowds to the Delage stand at the Salon. Although the market was saturated with used war surplus vehicles, it was a seller's market for new cars. But orders for the CO were not sufficiently numerous to keep the Courbevoie plant working through 1920.

Still, Louis Delage was euphoric. He had grown very wealthy just before the war and extraordinarily wealthy during it. He bought a splendid, huge town house at 140, boulevard des Champs-Elysées, which he transformed into a sumptuous administrative headquarters and showroom, the latter being one of the most lavishly elegant in the whole world of the Roaring Twenties. The business offices of Delage & Cie. were moved to this swank location and the property on the boulevard Péreire became a splendid

demonstration and service center. The stage was set for Delage to become a marque of *grande classe*.

*Le Patron* did not neglect his own lifestyle, however. Before the war, he had purchased a very nice chateau at Le Pecq with part of his loan from Clément-Bayard. Now he bought a fine villa at Saint-Briac, a town house at 42, avenue du Bois, and a sea-going yacht, *l'Oasis*.

This postwar period of nouveau-riche affluence brought little mechanical novelty to tempt the window-shoppers at the Salon, but this was made up for through sheer, eye-stopping glitter. One of the most striking features of many marques was the exquisite finish given to entire chassis and above all to engines. Delage was among the leaders in this costly nuts-and-bolts glamour and his production chassis were sparkling jewels.

But he did provide something of a novelty with his Type CO. In 1914 he (through engineer Michelat) had utilized four wheel brakes on a GP car and in 1919 he was to make them standard equipment on a touring model. He did so stubbornly, out of personal conviction of the merits of the principle and long before the public had been conditioned to this radical innovation. His competitors missed no opportunity to warn the populace of the grave dangers of four wheel brakes.

This was at least a small factor in the sluggish sales of the CO. To stimulate them, in September of 1920, just before the Salon, Delage and Bradley staged another spectacular, this time doing a 3120-mile tour of France in six days and two hours. At the Salon, Delage introduced the DO, a four-cylinder version of the do-one-thing-well CO. In all, only 212 DO's found buyers and the CO, between 1917 and its ultimate retirement in 1921, only 1390.

Ing. Lovera having returned to Fiat, Delage hired in 1919 Ing. Charles Planchon to head his engineering department. Planchon was Delage's cousin, had worked with him and Legros at Peugeot in Levallois in the old days and in the period following had accumulated vast experience on the engineering staffs of Charron, Clément-Bayard, Gnôme et Rhône and Panhard. His first assignment at Delage was to create a more popular replacement for the CO. Assisted by Escure, he produced the 2116 cc four-cylinder L-head Type DE. It was ready in time for the 1921 Salon and

"Eh bien, cher ami, on conduit son Alfa, on est conduit dans une Rolls et l'on donne une Delage a sa maitresse." This remark, rather loftily uttered by a millionaire enthusiast of the Thirties, made a telling point. One drives an Alfa, one is driven in a Rolls, and one gives his mistress a Delage. The very sensuousness of the car that Louis caused to be had made it a particular favorite of elegant women during the age when elegance was the required norm for those who could afford it. Moreover, as historian David Scott-Moncrieff has written, no car ever built was more proper for a woman than a Delage: "Merely to be seen in one can, like one of those nonsensical and fabulously expensive hats, make quite a plain girl look radiantly beautiful!" And the Delage was, all prices considered, quite the bargain for one's favorite paramour. To procure anything comparably chic among the other glamorous motorcars on the market would have meant the outlay of at least two thousand dollars more than a Delage's price tag. For this reason, the marque was a runaway winner in its class in the Concours d'Elegance which were the rage of the day. But the Delage's reputation was by no means all to its favor in the marketplace. John Bolster, a strapping enthusiast of speed sport and a motoring journalist of authority, felt constrained to practically apologize for his ownership of a Delage. "Pansy," some might call it, he remarked one day, but his very selection of the marque constituted "an endorsement of its qualities as a car of character, to say nothing of its being one of high performance." His particular car put up a timed speed of 98.9 mph during a test made in 1931. And, as The Autocar remarked later in November that year, "Even to-day, when 100 m.p.h. has become commonplace for racing cars, extending even to the smallest, there is something almost faintly fantastic about such a speed for a comfortable, touring-type car which can be used just as effectively for general purposes, including town work." Racing had helped. As the press was careful to point out during introduction time of the D8 series, there could be no direct connection between the 4050 cc straight-eight touring Delages and the phenomenal 1500 cc supercharged Grand Prix racers, "although no company can embark on an intensive racing programme without very favourably influencing its normal production." The Delage was a worthy in performance all right—"all the speed that can possibly be wanted, and extremely rapid acceleration . . . obtained with practically no noise at all"—it simply looked very lush and well-mannered doing it. As these cars —the 1932 Type D8 Coupe de Ville by Fernandez on the preceding pages and, from the top on these pages, the 1933 D8 Drophead de Ville by Fernandez & Darrin, the 1936 Type D6 70 Drophead de Ville by Coachcraft and the 1937 Type D8 100 Seven-Passenger Town Car by Franay—so pleasantly attest.

during the following two years 3600 copies were sold.

There were still a few hundred CO's that could not be sold, which prompted Delage to take the great step to overhead valves. A pushrod head was designed for this engine and the chassis was christened the GS—for *Grand Sport*—the big engine now producing 80 bhp instead of the 65 or so of the side-valve original. But the model name did not appeal to the carriage trade for which this chassis was inherently suited and the series was withdrawn before a hundred units were built. Renamed the Type CO2—a good name for a fire extinguisher—some 200 chassis were built and disposed of.

Eager to get back into sales-sparking racing, Louis Delage decided in 1922 to build a sports prototype based upon the short-wheelbase DE. For this project, he engaged Henri Toutée, an engineer from Chenard et Walcker, who produced a pushrod version of this side-valve engine. In original form, its horsepower output was thirty-two; with the Toutée conversion, it was seventy-five—ten more horses than the Type CO. This modified DE chassis was called the 2LS and, detuned, became the prototype for the 11 CV Sport which, from 1924 to 1927, was marketed as the Types DIS, DISS, DIS 5 and DIS 6—a total of 938 being built.

The marginally powered 2.1-liter DE was replaced at the 1923 Salon by the pushrod DI of the same displacement. Unsold DE's were given a wider track and more ground clearance, renamed the DIC, and shipped off to the colonies. The day after the Salon—October 19th—Louis Delage transformed his firm into a public company with a capital of one million francs. During the following year, this was increased to five and then to twenty-five million. Another highlight that year was the departure, in a rage, of Pierre Delage from his father's office. It was said that Louis expected just one thing of his only son, and that was blind obedience, and that Pierre's sole sentiment for his father was defiance. The son moved to Tangiers, Morocco, where he opened and operated a commercial garage until early 1928. He then passed a year with Amilcar at St. Denis and then, in 1929, returned to the paternal lair.

It became clear in 1923 that the CO2 was another drug on the market and that getting rid of the existing stock would be a heavy chore. The 4.5-liter L-head engine dated back at least to 1917, since which time a certain amount of progress had taken place. Something had to be done about this segment of the market and again Delage and Legros could not agree. Delage's ambition was fixed more than ever on building a supercar, without regard for cost and capable of rivaling or even humbling the greatest marques—read Hispano-Suiza. Of course *Le Patron* got his way.

Ing. Maurice Sainturat, after a long background with Richard Brasier and Delaunay-Belleville, had just designed a rather progressive and impressive prototype chassis for Hotchkiss. Delage decided that this was the man to design his new super-car and to have it ready for Salon presentation in October of '24. Sainturat agreed to undertake the mission, providing that he be given total liberty and absolute autonomy relative to the rest of the firm's engineering staff. Louis Delage accepted those terms and provided the distinguished engineer with a complete and well-segregated design bureau of his own.

Paul Yvelin, then heading Delage's service department, says of this six-liter 100 bhp masterwork, named the *Grand Luxe:* "When one considers the three years consumed by the project, the cost of tooling, the unimaginable care in machining and assembly of a series of two hundred such splendid cars, it obviously was a costly folly and a beating in terms of return on investment." That it was. Of the 200 GL's which were built, 180 were touring versions of assorted wheelbase and twenty were short-chassis sports models, chiefly intended for the Berlin and London markets. Manufacture of the Grand Luxe came to an abrupt halt after two years, due to simple lack of demand for it. Sainturat's activities with Delage also terminated at this point.

While all this was happening, a crisis was taking place in the real Delage engineering department. Planchon had been its head and he had two chief assistants—Escure in charge of touring models and Albert Lory in charge of sports and racing models. Delage managed to fire his brilliant cousin, Planchon, in 1923. This left Escure alone and unsupervised with the design of the Type DI, which turned out to be a mediocre product. And then in 1925, Escure quit and went off to grow grapes near Bordeaux.

Legros proposed to Louis Delage that the time certainly had come to try to entice that remarkable talent, Michelat, back to the ranks. Whatever effect Michelat's return at that time might have had for the future is unknowable but it almost certainly would have been pronounced. However, Delage still regarded him as a deserter. Legros' next suggestion was that they bring back poor Gaultier, who was happily at liberty. This most serious and competent of engineers returned to Courbevoie in 1925 and promptly whipped out the Type DM, having first debugged the DI engine in time for rerelease at the October Salon. This machine and its variants turned out to be rather marvelous average cars of the day and remarkably troublefree. They were the best sellers in all Delage history. A six-cylinder version of the DI, the DM, had all the virtues of the two-liter Four, whereas its three-liter engine produced almost twice the horsepower.

The 1927 Salon was the setting for the introduction of the first all-original Gaultier design, the Type DR, in 2170 and 2516 cc variations. The DR was a very paradoxical machine. To begin with, there was no difference in catalogue price between the big and small engines. Then, very quickly, the small engine was withdrawn from production, many being replaced in clients' cars by the larger engine and at no cost. The additional seven brake horsepower did not change the fact that the DR was a gutless gas-hog with a most uncomfortably hard ride. In spite of these seemingly awful objections, however, it possessed some elusive charm which helped to sell 5400 units during its two-year model run. It was the second-best seller in the firm's history—a lesson which Delage failed or did not want to absorb. And it was doggedly reliable.

Meantime, the racing program that Delage had begun shortly after the war reached its culmination, producing the 1.5-liter supercharged straight-eight, crowning diadem of Delage competition history and the winner in 1927 of the Grand Prix World Championship. It all had been accomplished at crippling cost, but it did contribute to 1928 being a year of peak prosperity for Delage. A new annual production record for the firm of 3600 chassis was realized and Legros was able to obtain from Louis Delage the funds for factory improvements which had been forced into second place by the cost of the racing program. At this zenith of its history, the firm had about 2000 employees. Although the plant had no stamping presses, no foundry, and just one small, light forge, it did have 1400 machine tools, did all its own screw-cutting and sheet metal work, and made its own spark plugs and carburetors.

At the Salon in October of 1929, Maurice Gaultier's masterpiece was introduced—the big four-liter, straight-eight, 105 bhp D8. It was a solid, finely made machine which, in its silence, luxury, comfort and elegance, did indeed begin to invade Hispano-Suiza territory. But the just-beginning worldwide economic crisis robbed the D8 of the success that it should have had during the four years it remained in the catalogue. This aristocrat of chassis sold for around a mere $3000 and another $1500 would clothe it in a really worthy sedan body. This prompted Gabriel Voisin to say that he could not explain how Delage could sell such fine cars at such low prices. After the bankruptcy, Delage probably could have given Voisin a very expert explanation of just how it was done.

Of course, a sports version was offered—the 120 bhp D8S. It was breathtakingly elegant and exciting for both coachbuilders and critics. But only ninety-nine ever found buyers.

For 1930 two new Sixes were added to the line, both derived from the D8. The D6 was the D8 with two cylinders deleted and the DS was the D6 with its bore reduced by 7.0 mm. It was a bad year. Only 2000 cars of all models were built, many of them just piling up in the warehouse. During the winter Delage built a front-drive prototype, apparently using the straight-eight engine. Nothing came of it.

By 1932 things were going very badly. The DS, D6 and D8 were too expensive and simply weren't selling. Buyers, becoming more rare, became more demanding, dealers blamed the manufacturer for their lot, and the firm's cash reserves were more than perilously low. Gaultier had designed his new D6 11 to meet the crisis, but it could not be built without a heavy investment in new tooling. Then in April, Louis Delage was able to obtain a ten-year loan for 25 million francs. The D6 11, a modestly priced two-liter Six, was put into production and presented at the Salon, even though it had not been tested adequately.

Delage had had hopes of branching into aero-engine manufacture and had put Ing. Lory to work on the creation of a supercharged, twelve-liter inverted V-12. The prototype was finished in time for the Salon de l'Aeronautique that November, and hope bloomed anew. To have been competitive, it should have produced around 450 bhp but, when tested, it

The elegance would continue through the Thirties, but the Crash of '29 and its aftermath brought some stark realities home to Delage. And one of them was that the marque had best begin thinking bread-and-butter again. The result was the D6 11—the 1934 Coach by Letourneur et Marchand shown at left—an unassuming two-liter six with independently sprung front wheels, a box frame and a price tag in standard sedan form of less than three thousand dollars. It was a Delage in every respect, save scale of accomplishment. At seventy-five miles an hour, it was twenty or so less than its larger marketplace companions and at twenty to twenty-two miles per gallon, it was a good eight miles less thirsty. It was a quite marvelous vehicle to drive, a fine top gear car, so the press said, "beyond what is implied by that term usually." Alas, it was not enough to save Delage. The marque did not die, however, when Louis Delage was forced to give it up in 1935; Delahaye simply came into its life. On the pages following are three of the cars that resulted: a 1938 Type D6 Convertible Victoria by University Coachcraft on the left, and a 1939 Type D8 120 Torpedo by de Villars and 1939 D8 120 Deltasport by Letourneur et Marchand above and below on the right. Of the three, it was the car with torpedo coachwork that most emphatically caught the eye. Introduced at the last prewar Salon in Paris in October of 1938, it was greeted with frantic acclaim. With its chrome-flexpipe exhaust system and long, low voluptuous lines, the car immediately became the queen of international Concours d'Elegance—in the manner of Delages of happier days before. But it did not have the performance of its predecessors; though developed horsepower remained 140 bhp at 4000 rpm, the car had gained a weighty thousand pounds and the D8 120 was hard pressed to better much more than ninety miles an hour, a speed of which sporting Delage drivers could scarcely approve. Better for the marque's image was the good performance potential of the Delage six-cylinder engines which survived into the Delahaye period, Michelat's D6 70 for example. Bored out to three liters and with the addition of three Solex carburetors and an aerodynamic coupe body, the car was taken to Le Mans in 1937 by Walter Watney and surprised everyone with a fourth-place finish. The following year it retired, but for the Le Mans of 1939, with still further refinements and two cars built, Delage performed incredibly—by half. One car crashed, but the other led the race from the seventh to the twentieth hour, and finished second overall. And it repeated that finish in the 1949 running at Le Mans. If that did not provide the spectacular drama of earlier Delage racing efforts, it did allow for a respectable finale for a grand marque.

would yield no more than 370. To cap it all, the prototype was involved in an accident and had to be written off. Like the front-drive project, it represented money poured down a rathole.

In 1933 things really began to fall apart. Up against the wall, Delage was forced to sell his splendid building in the Champs-Elysées. All of the administrative and business offices were dragged back to Courbevoie. Using the new D6 11 as a base, Gaultier came up with two new models, the straight-eight D8 15 and the four-cylinder D4. This cobbling on a shoestring provided that many components, such as gearboxes and rear axles, be common to all three chassis. If they were right for the Six, they were marginal for the Eight and too heavy and costly for the Four.

It became increasingly difficult to meet the payroll. Rumors flew concerning the cessation of payments to creditors, and of outside takeover. Prospective clients were unwilling to risk down payments. The morale of the workforce sank and, with it, the quality of workmanship. Key personnel, including executives, began finding more promising employment.

In 1933 Louis Delage approached Robert Peugeot, proposing that his firm take over the entire Delage distribution and sales organization, which Peugeot declined. With liquidation looming before him, Louis Delage contacted Paul-Louis Weiller, head of Gnôme et Rhône. Weiller, the rescuer of a grateful Gabriel Voisin in similar circumstances, was interested. He offered Delage 100 million francs for his company's assets, including the marque and the name. But Delage had been married under the community property law and it seems to have been his wife who refused these terms. (The woman—who to this day remains something of a mystery—had not

an easy life. Her husband's public stable of actresses, dancers and such must have made even the good years painful for her.)

The suppliers were not being paid and on November 5th, 1933, the principal ones quietly and discreetly set up a corporation for the collection of Delage's debts to them. A sympathetic press made a great deal of bluster along the lines of DELAGE CARRIES ON, but no one believed this and it probably did more harm than good. And Delage's competitors, of course, missed no opportunity to hasten the company's ruin.

At this moment, a miracle took place. Arthur-Léon Michelat returned to Courbevoie. Legros apparently had finally persuaded *Le Patron* that this was the last-ditch hope. Gaultier, no doubt relieved, moved to Renault. And "Papa" Michelat, with his great good spirit and competence, transformed the depressed atmosphere. In record time, he conceived, designed and rushed into production the new D6 65, the D8 85 and the D8 105, all of which were introduced at the Salon in October of 1934. They were splendid, even if their detail finish was not. These cars were very well received and at the close of the show, the Delage road men took off in new demonstrators and blanketed France. Under unimaginably difficult conditions, they worked wonders and brought in orders from the dealer network. The dealers themselves rallied beautifully, many of them giving up their profit in order to breathe new life into their wonderful company.

But it was all too late.

In February of 1935, Louis Delage had a new desperate idea and created a fund-raising corporation called the Société d'Exploitation des Automobiles Delage. It was a humiliating failure. And then, on April 10th,

each *Inspecteur de Route* received the fateful telegram: RETURN TO FACTORY WITH SERVICE CAR—DELAJAUTO.

Ten days later the Delage assets were in the hands of the receiver.

But the Delage marque lived on until 1953. Following the firm's liquidation, certain assets, including the marque itself, were bought for two million francs by Walter Watney, owner of AUTEX, the agent for Delage cars in the Paris region. Watney promptly entered into negotiations with other automobile manufacturers. On August 22nd of 1935, he signed an accord with the fine old house of Delahaye, permitting that firm to deliver, under the Delage marque, cars assembled largely from Delahaye components. On September 18th there followed the creation of a Société Nouvelle des Automobiles Delage. The new corporation survived for a little more than two years when, burdened by unsold stock, Watney sold all of his Delage assets to Delahaye. This, in turn, led immediately to the creation of yet another corporation, the Société Anonyme pour la Fabrication des Automobiles Delage (SAFAD). Its directors were Messrs. Desmarais and Peigney, the directors of Delahaye and, merely for the prestige of his name, Louis Delage.

Four Delages were displayed under the big Delage sign at the October 1935 Salon. The D6 60 had a Michelat engine but otherwise all the cars were Delahayes bearing such Delage stigmata as radiators and bonnets. The Michelat engine became the base for the Delahaye-Delage D6 65, D6 70, D8 85 and D8 105. The D8 120, to come in 1938, was Delahaye engined. After the war, the D6 70 was bored out to provide the powerplant for the sole postwar Delage model, the D6 3 Litres. It was the end of the line.

And Louis Delage? During 1941 ex-Delage racing driver Robert Benoist was tooling through the French countryside in his Simca Cinq when, to his amazement, he recognized *Le Patron* plodding along the side of the road. He stopped, saluted the old man and offered him a lift.

"Out of the question," said Delage. "I am making a pilgrimage to Chartres on foot."

Like Charles V, he apparently had found in Faith what he had not found in Empire. He seems to have led a serious religious life and in May of 1947 he published, in a popular French magazine of the day, the account of his just-completed Paris-Lourdes-Paris pilgrimage by bicycle . . . at the age of seventy.

Toward the end of 1946, Paul Yvelin, now with Peugeot, was walking down the Champs-Elysées when, right in front of the old showroom, he ran into Delage. The old man was shabbily dressed and the lenses of his spectacles were broken. But he recognized Yvelin and came toward him with hand outstretched.

"How is my little runaway?" he chided. Then he added, "I think you did well to go to Peugeot. It's a good outfit. It's where Legros and I started out."

Then, no doubt with his head full of magnificent memories, he melted into the passing crowd.

. . . Louis Delage died on December 14th, 1947. Arthur Legros followed him on March 12th, 1953. Pierre Delage died in extreme poverty in March 1964. Madame Delage, blind and helpless for many years, died on November 1st, 1970. ✥        197

# CHRYSLER'S ALPHABET FROM C TO B TO L– THE 300 LETTERCARS

My wife never liked our . . . better make that *my* . . . Chrysler 300-C. The feeling was mutual.

Why this was so, I never really have figured out, but I think it had something to do with the natures of both parties.

The Chrysler 300's—real 300's, not the pallid claimants that came later, a distinction which will be made clear in due course—the real 300's were cars for men, and they knew it. No secret fraternity, no clubhouse packed with small boys swearing allegiance, ever had the loyalty factor of a Chrysler 300.

Case in point. I was cruising along at the ton or so one fine summer day in 1964 when I passed a Pontiac whose driver considered this to be a challenge. Which it was. We did a top-end number down the highway and I was doing fine until brown smoke began curling up from the floorboards and out from under the hood. The gauge was pegged. Stopping miles from civilization didn't seem sensible, so I eased off and cruised into the next town. I raised the hood and reeled back from the heat. The engine glowed a dull red. All the wires were smoking. A freeze plug had dropped out, the water followed and I had done a few miles with no water in the engine.

I located the parts store, bought a new plug and sat around until the engine stopped ticking. I hammered the new plug into place, filled the radiator and drove the car another 40,000 miles. No damage at all.

On another occasion, I had removed the intake manifold for some obscure reason. When I started the engine, number one cylinder went dead. The spark plug was broken, from the inside. Another plug, and the cylinder signed off again. The gap had been hammered shut. I had dropped a foreign object down the intake port. I removed spark plug and guide tube and fired the engine. Something went POIINNG! into the weeds thirty feet away. With plug re-gapped, number one joined the living and I never again had any trouble from that quarter, either.

This dumb loyalty and willingness to soldier on despite all worked in both directions. The car arrived with a terrible tremor in the drivetrain, between fifty-five and eighty miles an hour. Naturally, I drove at either slower than the former or faster than the latter. Mild bother, I felt. And the giant engine was placed in such a way that removing number eight plug required the heater fan and duct to be removed first. Ech! Tuning the engine was an all-day ritual anyway.

But then, I knew into what I was getting when I bought the car. First, there was reputation. In 1957 the Chrysler 300-C was the most powerful car on the road. Chryslers were known for speed, power, brute strength, pure engineering, NASCAR triumphs and vulgar displays. This was the car that launched a thousand social protests. When shrill voices carped about phallic symbols, tail fins, wasted resources and pushbutton appliances and things like that, they were talking about the 300-C. Naturally, I had to have one.

Then there was a personal sort of pedigree. My car came used. A lot. The first owner had been a racing driver who at one time had been a partner with a man who later was a partner with Jim Hall, so owning that car put me as close to my hero as I ever expected to come. The hood even retained a dent caused by a flying chunk of metal hurled from the air conditioner

# An Enthusiast Remembers When Chrysler Built the Fastest, Best-Handling Sedan on the Market ...and a Good Time Was Had By All

compressor when the absent-minded original owner turned on the a/c at eighty-five miles an hour. (No, he wasn't an especially good racing driver either, but never mind that.) The car came up for sale, I could almost afford it, I bought it.

Enter the woman in the case. She likes cars, but her taste runs to nimble little coupes that look good, drive easily, go for weeks between refuelings . . . and start every time, no magic tricks needed.

When I went and traded our newly-new Valiant with four useful doors, tidy shape and size, thrifty slant six and three on the tree for that great hulk of a garish, loud, thirsty and temperamental brute, she did not understand it.

Nor did things get better. The 300-C had Chrysler's famous Hemi V-8, in what was then a high state of tune. Two four-barrels, mechanical valve lifters, dual points and like that. Learning to make it run properly took me some time. And there was something about the starter that caused it to lose strength when hot. For me, the 300-C would drive ten miles with a literally red hot engine. It never failed to start. It never failed to get me home.

For her, driving to the corner store like as not meant walking home.

The reader may be wondering how I kept the car and wife in the same household. The three of us liked to travel. She'd be relaxing on the passenger half of the genuine leather seat, watching the scenery blur past. "How fast are we going?" "Ninety," I would say calmly. "Oh," she would say, suppressing a yawn.

Like a rock, that car was. At doing what it was made to do, the Chrysler 300 had no equal in its day.

To understand where that day came from and where it went to, we must go back a long way, out of the present efficient dullness. We will leap backward over Musclecars and Ponycars, over sports cars and personal cars and budget racer compacts. We'll start in the days when Bigger really was Better, when cars had social impact and when power was something only the well-to-do could pay for.

The prime movers were pride, skill and desperation. The catalyst was octane.

Progress is war's only useful product. In war time, all sides will pay for research and all sides suddenly get battalions of smart people learning things private industry can't afford to learn.

During World War II, Chrysler Corporation built a bunch of tanks and such. Chrysler engineers learned a lot about combustion and engines. So did the other carmakers and the oil people.

When things got back to normal, all Detroit was busy designing new

row of rocker shafts, and a massive head casting. Just in case, the block and crank, etc. were made equally big and strong. The result was huge. It was heavy. And with the same displacement of 331 cubic inches, the same compression ratio of 8.5 to one and an equally sized two-barrel carb, the Chrysler delivered twenty more horsepower than the Cadillac V-8.

Best of all, people bought Chryslers. The superior engine didn't make up for Cadillac's invention of the tail fin, but Chrysler did stay in business, something that was at times an open question. Even the bean counters liked the Hemi.

Forget the public for a moment. Racing had escaped from the county fair. There was road racing and there was sedan racing. There were influential Americans interested in good design. They were into racing, wanted to win, and they knew they couldn't do it without a good engine.

Briggs Cunningham was such a man. He ran a Cadillac sedan and a Cad-powered special at Le Mans in 1951, and did fairly well: eleventh and tenth. He wasn't satisfied, and after a preview of Chrysler's V-8, Cunningham and his team designed and built a series of Chrysler-powered sports cars. They didn't win Le Mans, but they did put the engine in the public eye, and exposed Chrysler engineers to a lot of useful information.

Along about this time, there were plans to open Indianapolis to stock-block racing. Chrysler developed a series of engines for that, and cranked 400 bhp out of the 331 Hemi, on methanol and with fuel injection. The rules never were changed, but one engine was crammed into a Kurtis chassis. The car lapped at better than 135 mph and ran 900 miles at speed, without so much as a plug change. Two de-stroked versions later powered Firestone's tire-testing chassis. The Hemi was the engine to have. One pushed a Bonneville streamliner to 235 mph, and there were more road racing specials using Chrysler power than anyone has managed to count.

More to the point of our story was the Mexican Road Race. Chrysler sedans were naturally entered in the earliest events, by private owners. Company engineers tagged along to observe, and followed that up with advice, then participation. In 1952 a Chrysler sedan finished third overall, only sixteen minutes behind the winning Ferrari. This prompted the factory to develop and offer as an option a, well, in those days they called them "export" packages, but what they were was competition equipment. The engine had a higher compression ratio, hotter cam with roller tappets and dual four-barrel carbs. The chassis had stiffer springs, better shocks, anti-roll bars and disc brakes from the Imperial. (Yes, disc brakes. Jaguar wasn't the only factory with new ideas.) The competition had been equally busy, however, and the best Chrysler could do was fifth in class, well behind the winning Lincoln.

Chrysler engineers were learning. For 1954 they commissioned a run of special New Yorker sedans, with handling packages and racing engines. Maybe more racing than was announced, as the official forms said the engines were simply the highest power option for the standard New Yorker. But truly stock high performance New Yorkers could manage 125 mph or so, while the optioned sedans retained by Chrysler for internal use would do 140 mph. The informed opinion at the time was that the 1954 racing sedans used the 1953 engines. No matter. The factory turned out fifteen of the special specials, which were later sold to private teams. One won that year's NASCAR Grand National race.

The stage is set. Chief engineer for Chrysler at that time was a man named Bob Rodger. He liked cars, he had been an observer during the Mexican adventures and he was the man upon whose desk was dumped most of the mail from people who wanted to buy a high performance car. He knew Chrysler could do it.

Luck was on his side. First, while the 1951 through '54 Chryslers were square and stodgy things, built to be big on the inside, small on the outside—now there was an idea ahead of its time!—stylist Virgil Exner had prevailed and the 1955 Chrysler line was longer, sleeker and infinitely more attractive. The top men had been pushed into styling, so to speak, so the idea of an even nicer version as a prestige model fell right into line.

Also it was useful. The sports car invasion had alerted U.S. buyers to cars as entertainment. As usual, Chrysler was a lagging third in the sales race. Chevrolet could afford a semi-sports Corvette, Ford could be preparing a semi-sports Thunderbird. Chrysler couldn't afford a two-seater, sports, sporting car or whatever, so Rodger and staff determined to build the fastest, best-handling sedan on the market. For all that, the first 300 could blow the doors off either the Corvette or the Thunderbird.

What Rodger got, first off, was permission to draw up some rough plans: 201

engines, to produce efficient power for bigger and better cars. They wanted to increase compression ratios, provided the gas companies could and would deliver octane ratings to match. The latter in turn wanted to produce better gasoline, provided Detroit could produce a demand for it.

The manufacturers sprang their overhead valve V-8 engines. They had more power. They also cost more to build, and they didn't have terribly high compressions. Clincher was, they would tolerate low octane. Can't trust the oil men.

Chrysler Corporation went one better. The hemispherical combustion chamber was not new in the Forties. Dates back to 1904 or so. The hemi, which means half a sphere but has been adapted to mean the engine itself, gives maximum power—and high efficiency.

But it wouldn't run right on low octane, that is, a Hemi with 8:1 c.r. would need better fuel than a conventional engine with 8:1 c.r.

Chrysler engineers gambled. They guessed that 1) the gas companies would come through, 2) that the parent Chrysler bean counters would agree to a better engine for more money, and 3) that the public would buy Chryslers if Chrysler offered more power.

They won. The Chrysler ohv V-8 was costly. Putting the valves at right angles to each other, on opposite sides of the chamber, required a double

what a high performance sedan would look like, how much special work would be needed, and so forth. The design team was something of an in-group. None of the men involved said this in so many words, but because the stylists, engineers, production men, etc. came from all over the corporation, the suspicion arises that the first members knew who in the company really liked cars, and invited those men to take part. (Exner was one of the team, incidentally, and he was the one who suggested removing all surplus chrome, to give a purebred look.)

You can't turn the *Queen Mary* around in a fish pond. The car had to be assembled from stock parts wherever possible, with only minor changes. The basic body shell was New Yorker, the smallest big sedan, as it were. The grille came from the Imperial. Rear quarter molding was Windsor.

The engine couldn't be as radical as the racing versions. Rodger fitted a solid lifter cam and dual fours. In this tune, the Hemi cranked out 300 bhp, which led to the model name. Suspension was easy. They just used the heavy-duty bits developed for the Mexican team cars, calmed here and there. The car's emblems featured black and white checks, a reminder of the Cunningham efforts.

They ran the first example down the line to be sure the special work could be handled on the production line. The workers clustered around it. They called the top men down from the corporate offices and they, too, clustered around the car.

Do it, they said. The official name was C300, and it was a very limited model. The hardtop coupe was the only body, the 300 bhp Hemi the only engine, a two-speed automatic was the only transmission and the colors were red, white or black. (Two of these limits were wiser than the decision makers knew, as we'll see later.)

Several of the few options were figuratively handmade. The stylists were still experimenting with placement of emblems when production began, and there were no holes drilled at the usual time. So on a few cars, the medallions went where the workers liked them. Wire wheels were listed, mostly because they kept the brakes cooler but also because there was a large pile of wire wheels left over from when Imperials had optional wires. When the supply was gone, so was the option.

Never mind that. The enthusiast press loved the C300 and told the readers so. Better still, Chrysler accepted the services of an unpaid salesman. Carl Kiekhaefer manufactured Mercury outboard motors. He wanted to show the public that his firm knew about power and reliability and he wanted to place his evidence before people who weren't yet boaters. He decided stock car racing was the way to go. He knew engineering and no sooner had Chrysler announced the new car than Kiekhaefer bought a bunch and created the Mercury Outboard Team.

Which was fine with Chrysler. It's safe to say that the stock Chryslers

were better than the stock Lincolns, as both came from the factory in the Mexican Road Race era. Chrysler had learned the hard way that racing mechanics are better than engineers at building racing cars.

Nor was Kiekhaefer a backyard builder. He set up a complete testing facility of his own, he began to stress and race the cars and as things fell shy of requirements, he reported back to the factory. And the factory made running changes, to their credit.

The 300's won. They won damned near everything in sight. A 300 took top time at the Daytona speed trials, and another 300 was second. The 300's won thirty-seven major races in NASCAR and AAA during 1955, and won the manufacturer's championship in both leagues.

This was better than mere brand loyalty. Win on Sunday, Sell on Monday is still a working proposition. But the workings are secondary. The owner of, say, a new Plymouth really believes that the speed of Richard Petty's car proves something about his own sedan. And it might, but you can't prove it.

The 1955-version stock car wasn't strictly stock, but there were limits to the changes the builders could get away with, and there was a direct link between power on the track and power off the showroom floor. Sure, a race-prepared Oldsmobile could cover a stock C300 with rubber dust, but a stock C300 truly was faster and more stable and stopped better, et al. than any other stock sedan on the market. The owners knew it and they could (and sometimes did) prove it.

A good time, then, was had by everybody involved with the C300, excepting perhaps a few owners who bought the most expensive car on the showroom floor and learned later about the rough idle, harsh ride and so forth. At the same time, an unprecedented number of owners wrote to Rodger asking how to make the car run best. The official manuals had come out before even the development teams knew that, so Rodger wrote his own set of tuning instructions, had them copied and sent them to the faithful. The records show 1692 C300's were produced during what was a rather short model year for the car. That was probably as many cars as they could build.

For 1956 some changes, mostly to do with mechanical improvements. The name itself shifted around. The factory wanted to mark the yearly model business, so the 300 had a "B" added to it, hyphenated, after the numeral. Actually this didn't confuse much, since the C300 had oft been promotionally advertised as the 300 only. Still, in retrospect, you can get into an argument about even the hyphens, as sometimes the official version has C-300 and 300B. We'll go with the vice versa.

The Hemi's displacement was enlarged, from 331 to 354 cubic inches, and horsepower ratings were either 340 or 355, depending on whether the engine had 9.0 to one or 10.0 to one compression ratio. That's what the factory said, anyway. From the safety provided by time, one can wonder about the latter figure and rating. Chevrolet made a big noise later about one horse per cubic inch and Chrysler never said anything. I suspect the 10:1 engines were strictly for racing. The factory also fitted special connecting rod and main bearings, along with a stronger crankshaft, the needs for which had shown up in racing. The transmission was two-speed PowerFlite or, late in the year, the new three-speed TorqueFlite. The manual transmission was a three-speed, presumably for racing, as one can't imagine any useful purpose for it on the street. Or on the showroom floor, as the stick mystique has always pretended that all sporting engines need at least four speeds. (They don't, but shattering that myth will have to wait for another day.) The official catalogue listed twelve rear axle ratios. That was openly a racing option. The sanctioning bodies kept their eyes on gears, and the selection was needed to match engine characteristics to the various tracks.

In 1956 Chrysler's 300-B did the job on the opposition again, sweeping that year's Grand National one-two-three and generally winning all the marbles. Top speed mattered then. Kiekhaefer took the team to Daytona Beach, the actual sand beach, mind. Tim Flock did the flying mile in 142.911 mph and had a two-way average of 139.549 for an "unofficial"

world's record for stock cars. Quotes supplied for the unofficialness because there never actually was a class for such a record. All it means was that there was no proof any stock sedan ever went faster.

Something of the same applies to Vicki Woods' woman's speed record of 1956, 136.081 mph—in one of the Kiekhaefer cars. The speed made the papers; being a record set by a grandmother didn't hurt there, albeit the bodies which recognize records have never given official status to the division of the sexes. Point is, the 300-B went some twelve miles an hour faster than the C300, same sand, same team, etc.

Looks were changed hardly at all. The Chrysler performance leader was a Chrysler hardtop, less chrome, three colors, Imperial grille and a few medallions tastefully placed.

Total production was 1050 for a full model year.

Sad. Mechanically, the 300-B was a better car: more power, stronger engine, better transmission, backed by a factory with the time and experience to iron out those little bothers. The body was as good looking as ever, and the marketing men had the full year to do their tricks. Still, the 300-B didn't sell like the C300.

Comes now the proof, and the high point of the story.

Hearken back to Virgil Exner and Chrysler's discovery of style. Exner

had a heap of ideas, not least of which was to carry the tail fin theme as far as it could be carried, i.e., from front bumper to taillight.

More history. In 1954 the Plymouth was the car people said they wanted: small, practical, thrifty. And the 1954 Buick, big as the average house, knocked Plymouth out of third place in sales. There was an internal struggle among corporate planners, marketers, stylists, accountants and so forth—won by men smart enough to realize that surveyees frequently give the answers they know responsible citizens should give.

Chrysler determined to build the car people said their no-account neighbors wanted: flashy, powerful and so forth.

Exner was ready. The general theme for the Chrysler Corporation line was that Suddenly, It's 1960. The fine print said the factory had decided to introduce for 1957 the cars formerly due out in 1960. What the body shape was, was a flying wedge, the feathers on an arrow, one long sweep. Terrific. The cars sold like crazy.

For specifics, one of Exner's experiments just prior to the designing of the 1957 line was a conceptual exercise. Exner's idea of a full-size sports car for a grown man. Key feature was a huge grille, with egg-crate insides. Virgil Exner went Ferrari one better, with a very clean shape that capitalized on a basic equation: size of air intake equals power output. No motorcar ever had a more aggressive front.

The 300-C's basic body was New Yorker hardtop, but the 300-C had its own hood, grille, trim, etc., something the factory had wished to do two years earlier but couldn't afford. The Cunningham-inspired checked flag motif was dropped, in favor of a round medallion, colored a patriotic red, white and blue.

The Hemi grew again, to 392 cubic inches. It kept the dual four barrels, the aforementioned ignition, solid cam and so forth. Once again, there was the actual engine, rated at 375 bhp, and an optional one with higher compression ratio, a 390 bhp rating and the inability to appear anywhere except on the race track. Still, 375 bhp was the most offered the public that year. Adequate, as they say.

The car itself was 200 pounds heavier. The front suspension received torsion bars, and spring rates at both ends were reduced. The ride improved, the handling was still two big jumps better than the normal sedan.

At what had become the annual Daytona Show, a 300-C ran the measured mile at 134.108 mph, slower than the 1956 record. The reduced speed may have been due to a secret: Chrysler engineers had been busy with a car using Bendix fuel injection. They flogged the car day after day. Obviously they should have been tuning this year's model. And later, when

*The lettercars, alphabetized. On the opening pages, the Chrysler that started it all, the C300 from 1955—and on the two pages following, the 300-B from 1956. Clockwise from top right on the next two pages, the 300-C from 1957, the 300-D from 1958 and the 300-E from 1959. On these pages, the 300-F from 1960 (left) and the 300-G from 1961 (above). On the two pages following, the 300-H from 1962. Chrysler Corporation thereon skipped the letter "I"—for fear, purportedly, that it might be confused with the Roman numeral —and proceeded with three more letters and three more lettercars, as illustrated on the final two pages (clockwise from the left), the 300-J from 1963, the 300-K from 1964 and the 300-L from 1965. And that was the end of the alphabet so far as the Chrysler lettercars were concerned. The sticker admonition appearing at the right on these pages, incidentally, was not an accessory installed by Chrysler Corporation, though the company probably didn't mind the accoutrement— and it sprouted on many a Chrysler lettercar's dash during the golden days that, it is a bit surprising to reflect, ended better than a decade ago.*

CAUTION
DO NOT LOWER WINDOWS
AT SPEEDS IN EXCESS OF
120 M.P.H.

Vicki Woods got to make a run for the "record," the clutch gave up. Liberated note: Later in the test sessions she ran another 300-C down the beach at 138.985 mph. The stock 300-C was at least as fast as the 300-B.

First, the good news. The 300-C—all-new body, astonishing looks, most powerful car available on the open market—sold well, to the tune of 2188 units. The obvious bad news. In June 1957, the Automobile Manufacturers Association banned speed—that is, bore down on its members to get out of racing, and to ease up on the claims, valid or no, of speed and power. Critics of advertising have long held what seems to ad people a touching faith in the power of their medium to persuade folks to do things. No right-thinking American boy, it was alleged, would dream of putting his foot to the floor if the billboards didn't lure him into temptation. Codswollop. Be that as it may, Chrysler dutifully fell into place and didn't talk about what had been a good selling pitch.

The obvious bad news actually disguised a worse sort of bad news, at least for the expensive performance car, the best of which the Chrysler 300's were. Plymouth had the Fury, Dodge the D500. Ford had a supercharger kit for racing sedans that really did get into a few private hands. And Chevrolet had fuel injection, one horse per cubic inch and one hell of a nice car. A few figures. The 300 which had started above $4000 was nudging a pricey $6000 by the Sixties. A high performance Fury could be had for $3000.

This was great news to the legions of young car buffs who couldn't buy the performance cars of their recent past. Think about numbers. We all know how popular and influential that first Thunderbird was. Beautiful. But it took Ford three years to sell 10,000 early 'Birds. They were not for the masses.

Something was happening. From the adoption of mass production until the Fifties—allowing for a few exceptions—expensive cars had more power than cheap cars and only the well-to-do could afford expensive cars. Kids had flivvers, with four cylinders. Dad had a Chevy, with six—and The Boss or whoever had a Buick, with eight. Those young men who wanted power bought old Buicks instead of new Chevies.

Buyers had always asked Wottle She Do? One day there were thousands of buyers who asked Wottle She Do? and How Much Is That A Month? Shoot, man, who can't scrape up $10 more per month for a four-speed and fuel injection? Youth market, mass market, call it what you will. Detroit got so good at building better engines, they invented the optional high performance engine. Sure, and we 300-C owners loved to meet Chevies on the open road, or in the mountains, but when it came to the Stoplight Grand Prix, we turned right a lot.

But I digress and anyway, this was the start of a trend, which means nobody noticed anything had happened until it was too late. (Does that sound as if I oppose high performance for low bucks? Not at all. Power to the People, I say.)

Now, back to the 300. The 300 series received a convertible version in the C. Same engine, front, specs, etc., but it used the New Yorker convertible body. Then there was the pushbutton shift for the automatic, carried over from the 300-B. Great transmission by the way. I for one liked the pushbuttons. They were in a little box, to the left of the instruments. You pushed 1, 2, D and so forth. There were critics who claimed it was bad to take your eyes off the road, but with a day or so experience, you didn't need to, any more than a good typist must always watch the keyboard. And shifts were faster than with a lever on the column. You can punch faster with your thumb than you can move your hand sideways, especially when there's not a chance you'll move too far, like from 2 to N. But one day the government breathed hard, all the factories agreed to standardize controls. Chrysler Corporation, being a poor third, had to do with what the bigger outfits did. A shame.

Basically, the C300 was a Mexican Road Racer, slightly disguised, the 300-B was a sedan racer-to-be, but the 300-C was a hot road car, suitable for enthusiastic and patient men. Stupendous tow car, too. I hauled my M.G. TC on its cast-iron trailer literally across the country, never even breathed hard. Try *that* with a thrifty slant six.

The 1958 model was the 300-D. (You guessed that.) Near as dammit to the 300-C, in looks. The taillight lenses were smaller, still with those great big fins. Only we insiders could tell C from D at a glance.

The mechanical changes amounted to . . . a lot of fuss in the papers. Chrysler introduced that Bendix electronic fuel injection system: 15 bhp for $400. The word now is that it was difficult to maintain. One wonders

how they knew. Not many 300-D's were built with e.f.i. and most were converted to carbs. Quickly. Yr. cynical writer wonders if it had to do with the AMA racing ban.

The normal engine was still 392 cubic inches, hot cam, two fours. *Road & Track* was impressed enough to test one, and did 0-60 in 8.2 seconds. Rather good, they said, pity they can't take the thing and reduce it to three-quarter scale. High praise that, from *R&T* in those days.

Oh, and another thing, the 300-D was sold in six colors: white, black, red, coral, tan and turquoise. They sold only 761 300-D's. New bodies sell better than old bodies, colors or no.

Perhaps. Now we begin to pick up the pace a bit, as some of the rest of the story is picky and some of it is painful.

The 300-E had the second series body, that is, the 1957 New Yorker with that great grille and yet another revised treatment of the taillights. That's what it had.

What it didn't have was the Hemi. The Hemi worked fine, you already know, and it was mighty expensive to build, you may remember. The bean counters won. Chrysler had a 413-cubic-inch V-8 with normal combustion chambers, heads, valves, block. They could build it for no more than the rest of Detroit spent, and they could fit it out with dual fours, hot cams and

deciding that my car was better or faster than your car.

Instead, we had drag racing, the only truly participant sport in automotive history. Literally millions of car nuts could take part, running within fair rules and scores of classes fairly designed to give everybody a fair shake. Top speed no longer mattered. Elapsed time was all.

Well, not quite all. There was also technical expertise. Car people are funny people. It's perfectly possible to meet a man who says 1) he is so good a driver that he hasn't made a panic stop in years, and 2) his car is superior because it has four-wheel disc, air-powered, cross-circuited, spot-calipered magnesium brakes. He doesn't need or use them, you understand, but he surely likes to think about all that engineering wizardry. We like technical wonderfulness, in short.

So. Drag racing was in, and Chrysler had some things to work at the drags. The normal V-8 got ram tuning. The intake manifolds for each bank stretched 'way the heck over to the other bank, with a carb on each manifold. The length of intake pipe determined the point at which the speed of the incoming air was aided by pulses in the column of air and created a positive pressure in the pipe. Free supercharging, as it were. The principle wasn't new, but Chrysler made it public. The 300-F had ram tuning. The normal 413 V-8 was rated at 375 bhp. There was a hotter version, with larger valves, hot cam and such and it was rated at 400 bhp. Behind it could—a word used deliberately—go a four-speed transmission.

Another case in which the desire for technical keen stuff overcame common sense. Big engines don't need all those speeds. Buyers of big engines did, however. Chrysler ordered four speeds from a French company. Each installation purportedly required the car to be pulled off the line, stripped of its automatic and fitted with the manual gearbox, then pushed back into line. Expensive and time consuming. Probably no more than fifteen 300-F's were sold with the four-speed installed. (One wonders now if they all went to the various factory-backed drag teams and racing outfits, but there's no way to prove that, of course. Maybe they simply had trouble making the cars.)

The 300-F would go. They did well at the drags. Car buffs with a desire to talk about the mechanical delights built into their cars once again had some things to talk about. And the body was new. Production for the 300-F?—1160, or darn near double the poor 300-E.

The 300-G was mostly more of the same, with the standard body and some trim added or subtracted, the 413 engine with optional ram tuning. The factory's own stout three-speed replaced the imported and rare four-speed. Ouch. A good thing, actually, as the engine didn't need the help of extra gears and shifting all the time was a pain in town but what does it matter? A three-speed trans was what most of us would give anything to escape. Obviously.

Ah. One other thing. Chrysler got so much hassle, so much mockery from folks offended by the fake continental kit that they took it off. Good for them.

Now we get to the bad stuff. Generalizations aren't fair. One cannot truly say that Germans love to take orders or that Englishmen never speak to strangers. However. If we were to do this with automobile companies, we might dare to say that the big outfits have characteristic flaws.

General Motors is too clever by half, witness the Corvair, the Tempest transaxle, the aluminum-block V-8. Dazzling in the lab, dismal in the marketplace. Ford's good things always arise from the ashes of their previous good thing: The Mustang created a whole new market, the Ponycars. And it killed the Falcon.

What Chrysler does is take their Golden Goose and convert it to a barnyard full of hens. The first 300 was unique. Special body, three colors. Distinct looks. Super engine. Then came extra colors, a convertible, normal or optional engines, standard body. Finally, there was the plain 300 again, only in 1962, the Chrysler 300 was . . . just another car.

Like so: new body, for all the line. The marketing men cashed in their investment. They had spent all that money making the Chrysler 300 series into a special line of car, a line the motoring public knew and liked. Ergo, in their world, the thing to do was let everybody have one. They moved the nameplate from top performance model to the 300 line of sedans, coupes, etc. Replaced the Windsor line, which was the cheapo Chrysler anyway.

Above that, so to speak, was the 300-H. The 300-H had its own medallion and trim, and while the 300's came with a dumb ol' 383 c.i.d. V-8 and a rousing 305 bhp, the 300-H had the 413 and ratings of 380 or 405 bhp, depending on compression ratio, etc. The 300-H also had stiffer suspen-

the rest. The rated power for the 413 was 380. Okay. On the one hand, the manufacturer can claim any power he wants, or he could in those days. Next, the factory always said it ran test after test and the 300-E was just as fast as the 300-D. Stop complaining, they said, you guys still have more power than anybody, and besides when we built racers we got letters from people who wanted calmness. You got calmness and you ask for more power. Be fair, the factory implored.

The buyers, well, the potential market, voted with their checkbooks. The 300-E didn't have what 300's had always had, tests be damned. Total sales of the 300-E: 647.

More major changes for the next 300, the 300-F of 1960. The entire line, all Chryslers, Dodges, etc., that is, got a new unitized body. Nice looking, too. For reasons of cost again, the 300 didn't have too much special work. There was a clean and simple grille and a rather foolish looking fake spare tire shape thing on the trunk lid and that was about it.

Time out for more social comment. When AAA got out of sedan racing, such racing changed from really stock cars with mild cheating into show biz, with rules so relaxed that only big changes, i.e. reshaped bodies and such, made any difference. Stock cars became a business and an entertainment, but they no longer had status as proving ground, or as a means of

sion, better brakes and high-speed tires. Not a bad car at all, mind. The mechanical equipment was there.

What was missing was the magic.

Now then. For what does a person buy a high performance car? Answer: 1) to go fast, 2) in case he or she wants to go fast, 3) so other people will think he or she does go fast.

The Chrysler 300's from A to G fitted right in with markets 1, 2 and 3. They were fast. They could be driven normally and still retain the potential of going fast. And everybody out there knew the 300's were fast, so the buyer whose ego was in need of admiring glances and comments got 'em. In the beginning, all you needed was a lot of money.

Things changed. Drag racing replaced top speed. Power equals speed, but acceleration is a function of power (lots) and weight (as little as possible). The 300's never were light, starting above two tons and going up to 4500 pounds by the Sixties. Power alone worked until the factories began putting big engines in smaller cars. Further, they put their best and most advanced engines into smaller and cheaper cars. In 1963 *Car Life* published an article about all the hot new engines. The story explained the 409 Chevy, the 406 Ford, the 421 Pontiac and the 426 Plymouth and Dodge.

Bitter blow, that. Chrysler used common sense. There were no Dodge, Plymouth and Chrysler engines. Waste of money. Chrysler simply made small, medium and big engines, economy engines and racing engines. All performance models got the 426. The man who wished to cover his competition with rubber dust had a choice of 426 in a light Plymouth or a heavy Chrysler, which is to say, of course, no choice at all. So much for buyers of fast cars.

Buyers who may someday wish to go fast are kidding themselves, and I suspect we know it. It's just as easy to kid yourself in a 421 Pontiac.

Reason 3 aforementioned depends entirely on identification, and the quicker the better. When there was only the real Chrysler 300 and it could be spotted half a mile off, when it was the most powerful car on the road, no problem. When the 300 was more likely to be a stripped sedan than a road-racer coupe thinly disguised, when the owner had to pop the hood to prove he had the 426 rather than the 383, and when he had to forget that the kid down the block also had the 426, well, if you have to talk about how tough you are, you aren't.

We are on our way down hill. In 1963 there was the 300 line and the 300-J, in coupe only, the convertible was no more. For '64, the 300's and the 300-K, which received the stodgy 413 as its claim to high performance.

Once again, one must remember that the letter versions were fine road cars. They had suspension kits, extra comfort items, good tires and all that. In those days, sports car racing was an amateur sport. We all had tow cars. Rich racers used new Chryslers and poor racers used old Chryslers, but all serious racers knew the best way to get from Kansas City to Dallas in time for tech was inside a Chrysler.

Ah, the Hemi. In 1964 Chrysler returned to professional racing, round track and drag. They beefed the 426 block and put improved copies of the old hemi heads atop. They were probably the strongest and most powerful engines ever semi-mass produced. They still are the only engines capable of containing a fuel dragster's 1800-odd horses. The Chrysler line didn't get Hemis, though, because they were really for racing only.

There was the 300 line and the 300-L in 1965.

In 1966 Chrysler Corporation bowed to somebody or something and broke loose with the street Hemi, all the good stuff detuned to be usable if not practical on the street. In that same year, they didn't have a letter 300. Just the plain 300 line. The gentleman's speedy coupe, the powerful car for men willing and able to pay the price, was done. Size no longer equalled power and power was no longer a rich man's delight. The Supercars, Ponycars, budget racers and the like ruled the performance market.

This story has a couple of endings. One is a sad footnote. In 1970 George Hurst, the shifter man who was in the business of producing customized cars also, came out with the Chrysler 300-H. I'm not gonna tell you what the H stood for, as my historian's sense of decorum was offended. The car was a 300 with flossy stuff on it. I drove one, and found it just as good but no better than the normal 300.

The good news is that the lettercars are still out there, being driven. The engine will live forever, most of the parts are available and you can pick up a clean 300-B or F or whatever you fancy for a fair price.

Personally, I was your typical performance-minded buyer. The 300-C was still running good—for me, that is—when Chrysler came out with the thin-wall V-8 in the Valiant. I had sold the slant six Valiant, recall, 'cause it didn't have any suds. The size was perfect. Aha, I said, what I can have now is a Pocket 300. Bought a '64 Valiant convertible, four speed, with a demon 273 V-8. My wife loved it.

Couple years later I saw my old 300-C going down the street. A woman was driving. She had the look of a woman driving a car she fears will not start next time she needs it to.

I know the car is still on the road.

I hope she got home all right. ✿

# ARTIST'S CONCEPTION

## The Novel Cars of a Maverick Named James Scripps-Booth, Who Discovered Being Ahead of One's Time Was Not Enough

The publisher's son was talking horseless carriages again. It was nothing new. Now that the boy's little neighborhood weekly newspaper had become a success—financed by the ads he sold to local businessmen—he spoke mainly of automobiles. In the fashionable family home on Detroit's Trumbull Avenue, George G. Booth listened once again as his son described the wonders of the newest 1904 cars. He looked at the pictures which the energetic and obviously gifted sixteen-year-old had brazenly sketched in the margins of his dull tenth-grade textbooks. And here, handily available, were pictures of a dozen different cars the lad had carefully clipped from various newspapers and magazines.

According to the boy, there was just no longer any way that the family could survive without a motorcar of its own. Just think how much easier it would be to get from Detroit to suburban Cranbrook where their new house was being built! Just look at this engine, this body, this . . . It was under repeated such assaults that George Booth, journalist, essayist, short story writer, sometime author of gardening books, and later president of *The Detroit News,* found himself entering a Winton showroom one day and purchasing a bewildering maroon touring car. That he had no idea of how the machine operated mattered little, for the car disappeared at once into his empty garage where his son began systematically and ferociously to take it to bits. In putting that Winton back together, James Scripps-Booth learned the basics of automotive engineering the only way one could in 1904, with a sore back and greasy hands. He loved every minute of it.

The Winton spent more time being dissected on the garage floor than running on the road. Even when operable, the machine often appeared sans bodywork so James could peer curiously into its churning innards.

Once, perhaps concentrating more on the mechanical symphony he was blissfully directing than on his driving, he passed through Birmingham, Michigan at a speed "greater than a horse could walk" and was accordingly fined ten dollars. It was only after he had exhausted the Winton's capacity to puzzle him that James re-installed the body for good and taught the rest of the family how to drive. The Winton was just a beginning, however, as James' automotive tinkering increased in direct proportion to his increasingly enthusiastic father's car purchases.

All of this was doing nothing to get the young man beyond his sophomore year in high school, of course, and he finally quit after failing the tenth grade three times. Ever afterwards he harbored an open and unremitting suspicion about formal education. James' schooling—or lack of it—was a paradox perhaps considering the substantial endowments made by his father to local educational institutions. But then James Booth was nothing if not a maverick.

In 1908, when he was twenty, James began to think seriously about designing a car of his own and captured his ideas in a neatly executed watercolor. Even with his first design—which he would patent in 1911—James was ahead of his time, a talent that was to keynote, or plague, his entire automotive career. The car was a two-wheeler with a center of gravity so low it obviated the ponderous gyroscope necessary to achieve balance in the two-wheeler Peter Paul Schilovsky built in England—five years later. Instead Booth's low-slung car required only a set of raiseable auxiliary wheels, reminiscent of bicycle training wheels, to maintain an upright position. Above twenty miles per hour, these wheels were lifted, by moving a lever in the cockpit, and the machine was able to

continue balanced only on its two main tires. Booth called his novel-looking invention the Bi-Autogo.

Initially there seemed little hope that it would ever be built and Booth concentrated on his painting—art class had been the only course that had interested him in high school—on learning newspaper reporting at the *News* and on broadening his general automotive background. In 1910, the Hupp company, impressed by his talent, asked James to both write and illustrate their catalogues and instruction manuals. It was good practice.

That project completed, James decided to spend some time studying painting in the very best place he could imagine, Paris. There he was further excited by the variety of automotive machine coursing the Champs-Elysées and other fashionable boulevards, the Mercedes and Renaults, the spindly Bédélia cyclecars. And it was in Paris too that Booth produced the design drawings necessary if the Bi-Autogo were ever to become reality. When he returned to the United States in 1912, the machine James now called a "gentleman's sports car" was completely engineered. With the same charming logic that had led to George Booth's first car purchase, James now persuaded his uncle, William E. Scripps—who produced marine engines—to finance the project.

What emerged from Detroit's Currie Machine Shop later that year was an aluminum-bodied vehicle with an infinite capacity to amaze and looking very much like the original painting. Impressed editors of *The Autocar* labelled it an "Aepyronis Titan among motor bicycles." *Cyclecar and Motorette* called it "something entirely new in the motor world" and astounded pedestrians and motorists around Detroit were agog at the sight of the ponderous-looking Bi-Autogo making test runs.

James declared his creation capable of seventy-five miles per hour and

there seems no reason to doubt this assertion. But the Bi-Autogo's heavy steering seriously hampered its safe use—no power steering units having been invented—and although the 3200-pound machine never came to grief as it banked awesomely through curves, *The Autocar* cautioned that "a skid in a tramline would lead to somewhat serious results."

As unusual as it was in exterior appearance, the Bi-Autogo possessed some more subtle novelties as well, among them the first V-8 engine ever built in Detroit. A 45 hp L-head unit, the powerplant was also designed by Booth and predated the famous Cadillac V-8 by three full years. Cooling the engine was uniquely achieved by 450 feet of copper tubing which swept in golden spaghetti-like bunches along either side of the lift-off hood. The engine was equipped with a compressed air self-starter and drove the rear wheel through a four-speed transmission via a fully-enclosed chain drive—the latter a feature that most modern motorcycles still don't have. The Bi-Autogo also included a patented quickly removeable axle-shaft to facilitate wheel changes.

Despite the vehicle's interesting specifications, it was all too clear that the car would not be commercially feasible. The handbuilt prototype had cost the Booth family some $25,000 and the project was halted after completion of it and a complete set of spare parts. But James didn't brood on the decision to discontinue further work. Instead within a few months, he was busily making sketches for an inexpensive type of vehicle that threatened to take America by storm, the cyclecar. Logically, his impressions of the little vehicles had been formed during his European visit.

Undoubtedly inspired by the Bédélia which had charmed him during his stay in Paris, Booth's prototype cyclecar was a tandem-seater thus keeping frontal area to a minimum and its driver occupied the rear seat and

*On the opening pages: the V-8-powered Bi-Autogo built in 1912. On these pages: the prototype Rocket built in 1913, above left; a production Rocket of 1914, right and below le[f]*

balanced the front-mounted engine's weight. Constructed in a machine shop-equipped garage at the family's Cranbrook estate, it was built with the aid of Booth's enthusiastic brother-in-law, John Batterman. Together, the two young men clambered into the sleek gray-painted machine as soon as it was finished and gave it a thorough road test that carried them through Michigan, Indiana and Ohio at an average speed of seventeen miles per hour. "It caused motorists to marvel," said Batterman of the compact 750-pound car. "Drawing up to the curb, it always drew crowds, at times so large that the driver was asked by an officer to move on so as not to block traffic."

Convinced of the machine's merits and the readiness of Americans to buy cyclecars in great numbers, James discussed the idea of producing the little car with his uncle Will. As usual, his enthusiasm proved infectious. Production of the JB Rocket (James Booth Rocket) commenced near the peak of the cyclecar fad in January 1914. It differed slightly from the prototype, being fitted with vestigial doors, front seat steering, and a tiltable steering wheel that permitted a heavily-bundled driver to more easily enter the narrow car. Besides the roadster, a delivery model labelled the Packet was also produced. Both machines were powered by the same air-cooled V-twin Spacke engine of between 10 and 15 hp, had a top speed in the vicinity of 45 mph, a two-speed gearbox, and drum brakes on the rear wheels. The Rocket sold for $385 and though Booth planned to reduce this figure by selling the car in kit form—the body itself serving as the shipping crate—the idea was never implemented.

Contemporary accounts of the Rocket rated it highly. "The car glided forward and away we went up the street like riding on glass," said a Florida newspaperman after a test ride. "We looked around, we could have sworn there was a bump in the street, and sure enough, there was. But we just rolled over it without a jounce somehow."

The Rocket made something of a name for itself in competition too. In fact, when the first cyclecar contest in the United States was held on June 13th, 1914 at a farm in Teaneck, New Jersey, Rocket owners took first place in every event on the program, defeating a rollicking gaggle of Merzes, Imps and O-We-Go's.

Whatever the Rocket's merits, however, it could not survive the short, hapless life of the American cyclecar industry. About four hundred of the machines had been built when it became apparent that the cyclecar's days were not merely numbered, they were finished. The American public simply was not buying and the fad—such as it was—perished without a whimper. In December 1914, the Scripps-Booth Cyclecar Company was sold to the Puritan Machine Company of Detroit. James Booth was not discouraged. Always brimming with new ideas and energy, he was already planning something new.

What he had in mind now was a new company and a new car, a top quality vehicle he conceived of as a "luxurious light car," a small, well-finished, two-seater that would vie with larger cars for attention and sales. He had actually been harboring a not always secret desire to market such a light car even when the cyclecar company was relatively new. Early in 1914, he had returned to Europe briefly to look over the light cars then being built there and had visited some thirty factories including Singer, Hillman and Peugeot. Upon his return, James again approached his uncle Will Scripps and again proved himself as persuasive as ever. The new Scripps-Booth Company was organized with James' uncle Clarence as president, uncle Will as vice-president and James himself as secretary. To help him design

*It was a four-wheeled motorcycle, so said James Scripps-Booth of his Rocket cyclecar, and "one doesn't even need a garage to keep it in but can shove it under his back porch at night."*

*". . . designed to meet the ideal of drivers of big, expensive family cars who want a light car of equal luxury and equipment," crowed the ads for the Model C, this example built in 1916.*

the new car, James hired a young engineer from the Imp Cyclecar Company of Auburn, Indiana—William Bushnell Stout—and work began. By the end of 1914, Booth was on the threshold of taking his place in the growing ranks of U.S. automakers.

Although announcements and descriptions of the new roadster began appearing in November 1914, the first production examples of the car, called the Scripps-Booth Model C, were not completed until the following February. Engineer Stout was proud. "One innovation of the design was the step-down principle in the frame," he recalled in his autobiography. "It is interesting that the Scripps-Booth car of 1914 had identically the principle hailed in 1949 as the newest advance. . . . For the first time, we also curved the sideline of the body up into the windshield. The body was formed over flat curves without dies. . . . The car was the first sold with five wheels and tires, a spare wheel and tire fitted at the back on the sloping deck. We had the first steering wheel button." Of the latter, *The Auto and Light Car* exclaimed in wonder, "Pressure anywhere on its surface and in any direction suffices to make contact and so sound the warning note."

An undeniably handsome vehicle with glittering German-silver radiator shell, torpedo stern and airy Houk wire wheels, the $775 Model C was powered by a four-cylinder 20 hp Sterling engine. "Here is a car which may be set alongside a $3000 or $5000 motor car and which will show the pleasing lines, the engineering refinements, the luxury and complete equipment of its floormates," the ads crowed.

The Scripps-Booth was, in fact, sometimes sold by the same dealers who traded in such exotica as Isotta Fraschini or Rolls-Royce. The King of Spain and Queen of Holland added a Scripps to their respective royal garages and a 1916 ad in *Vanity Fair* listed one Winston Churchill as a Scripps-Booth owner. Movie stars and celebrities occasionally fell prey to the car's good looks, among them silent screen actress Gertrude Selby, tenor John McCormick, Mrs. Jay Gould and Mrs. Reginald C. Vanderbilt.

But the road to production was not a smooth one. Initially, there were serious delays at the Scripps-Booth factory caused by the difficulty in getting parts—since the Model C was largely an assembled car—from suppliers. James learned of these problems secondhand as, exhausted by the long weeks of design sessions, he had taken a vacation in March and gone to a newly booming U.S. resort, St. Petersburg, Florida.

On March 20th, the company's general manager, R.H. Speare, explained the parts problem to Booth in a letter. "We have been held up all week for fenders and it has been pretty nearly as trying as taking candy from a child. . . . We did our best but simply could not get the fenders." Things didn't improve. A year later in March 1916, Clarence Booth told James: "We will only ship something over 300 cars this month. We have been limited by the production of new motors. They are now coming all right but we are again limited by our axle supply. . . ."

Parts shortages were not the only problems, however. The early Model C's unique electrical door lock system proved impractical and had to be replaced with a more usual one. The first cars had been fitted with a push button device, similar to that used in offices to remotely unlock the door. But when installed on an open automobile and exposed to dust and damp that corroded delicate contacts, the locks failed. Replaced by conventional locks on the Model C roadster, the electrical latches were successfully used on a graceful coupe which soon joined the line.

214

*The four-cylinder Sterling engine of the C was replaced by Chevrolet 490 power late in 1916, and the result was called the G, introduced with high hopes for the 1917 model year.*

As some of the detail problems of the first cars were overcome, a number of Model C's—eventually almost one-third of total production—were exported to England where they were well received. "The Scripps-Booth is a nice car to handle," said *The Autocar*, "its external finish and equipment are excellent, and the car is essentially quiet. . . ." The magazine's editor, S.C.H. Davis, tested one and though the center horn button once malfunctioned in the middle of Picadilly at rush hour, blowing the horn for several minutes until he could disconnect it, Davis enjoyed the car.

A few Model C's also were sold in Cuba. There one of the cars was stripped of its fenders and entered in a road race, finishing third in a field of seventeen cars, defeated only by larger-engined machines, a Chenard et Walcker and a Mercedes.

Racing and sporting machinery was always of interest to James Booth and even as the production of the Model C was getting out of the teething trouble stage, he began work on a new cycle-fendered two-seater to be powered by an engine recently designed by Alanson Brush, the Ferro V-8. Intended as a supplement to the Model C roadster and coupe, the new sports car—the Vitesse—was meticulously planned by Booth and with its 75 mph top speed, it was designed to provide competition for Mercer and Stutz. Knowing he had a potentially popular car on his drawing board, Booth sent a picture and description of the Vitesse to the New York Isotta Fraschini dealer, G.N. Thurber, whom he hoped would market it.

"The appearance of this roadster is certainly most attractive," replied Thurber in November 1915. "I am convinced that we can sell a very considerable number." Thurber did, however, object to the Vitesse's exterior-mounted horn which he thought adversely affected the car's streamlined

look. But James was uncompromising, not interested in a committee-designed sports car. "As to the placing of the klaxon horn under the hood," he rejoindered, "I would say that if that were done, one might as well use any old kind of cheap horn. Psychology undoubtedly plays a big part in the sale of these cars and the pride of ownership I think is more complete if the car looks like money and looks very complete to the man on the street. The severity of the plain lines in general I believe should be broken somewhat and this was my reason for placing the horn as shown."

But if Thurber lost the battle of the horn with the car's young designer, he was adamant about the machine's doors, or rather, its complete lack of them. "This construction would unquestionably be adviseable from the pure speed or racing point of view," he wrote Booth, "but I know the average buyer in New York would want a door. Young men themselves would have no objection to stepping over the side of the body [two steps were provided for just this purpose] . . . however, most young men are unquestionably interested in the fair sex and it has been our experience that women with very few exceptions object to cars without doors. And their influence is strong enough to carry the decision in nearly all cases. For this reason, we unquestionably want doors on any cars we might order."

Before long, however, it became apparent to James Scripps-Booth that all his hopes for the Vitesse had been in vain. Although the prototype Vitesse generated a full twenty percent of the sales prospects for Scripps-Booth cars at the 1916 auto shows, the firm's directors decided not to produce the sports car but a larger four-seater V-8 instead. It was a decision which marked the beginning of James Booth's disaffection with the company that bore his name. Perhaps it marked the beginning of the end

215

*An attractive two-door cloverleaf roadster with a wheelbase of 120 inches, fully ten inches longer than the C, the Scripps-Booth Model D was introduced in the fall of 1916.*

for the company itself. There would be trouble ahead.

Any impending problems were masked, however, by the introduction of the 1916 Model C, a car presented to the public in a catalogue beautifully illustrated by James. The company proved almost snobbishly proud of its new literature, issuing the following statement to the press: "One of the banes of the auto manufacturer is the inveterate catalog collector, the grafter who in reality has no intention of buying a car at any time. . . . The Scripps-Booth catalogs are works of art and they will be handed out solely to prospects entering showrooms with some idea of buying a car . . . and even among such prospects, discrimination is to be made between those who are able to appreciate good work when they see it."

Meanwhile, testing of the new V-8 was commencing slowly. The little company was entering new territory here as, with the exception of Cadillac, most manufacturers were wary of the engine, fearing that the canted cylinders might produce insoluble lubrication problems for the cylinder walls and that mechanics would not be able to cope with the engine's novelty. In fact, it was some time before the engineers at Scripps-Booth could cope with it. After a day's arduous testing in the mountains near Wilkes-Barre, Pennsylvania, a Scripps engineer sent this report about both car and engine to James Booth: "We had the following trouble with the chassis parts: propellor shaft twisted off due to a burst weld, a rear spring seat broke due to a defective casting. . . . The three-inch radiator is insufficient for mountain work in warm weather."

Still, pressure gauges installed on each of the Ferro engine's two main bearings revealed sufficient lubrication under the most trying conditions and removal of the cylinder heads showed "very little" oil had leaked past the pistons into the combustion chambers. One wonders, however, at the meaning of "very little" for according to the report, the V-8 had used "only" one gallon of oil for the 600-mile test. James drew a red line under the figure and incredulously wrote, "Ye Gods" in the report's margin. Subsequent steps were taken to reduce oil consumption along with the addition of a larger fan, radiator and hood louvers to help cool the V-8.

Toward autumn of 1916, with 6000 cars having been built, Scripps-Booth offered America's second production V-8 car for sale. The Model D, called a "light eight" by its makers, was priced at $1175.

At about the time of the D's introduction, Scripps-Booth changed from being a company to a corporation with the purchase of the Sterling Motor Company of Detroit. The decision, which meant public ownership and a new board of directors, did not please James. Since June 1916, he had grown increasingly unhappy with both his company's management decisions and its products. He stated his beliefs in an outspoken though prophetic memo. "Some very great errors have been committed within recent months . . .," he wrote, "and I believe the sooner we allow certain things to dawn on us and penetrate into our systems, the better." He directed himself first to the Model D.

"The present eight does not come under the heading of light cars," he explained. "When the eight was decided upon, the thought was runabout exclusively, imagining that our luxurious light car field called for runabout only. We have thought out and mentioned a slick little four-passenger body on the four-cylinder chassis in past meetings and so forth some months back. Something must have slipped and certain most excellent ideas have never crystallized. However, we find ourselves with an eight-cylinder four passenger car instead of an eight runabout. . . . There is the difference. Eights, exclusively runabouts might still be considered within reason and be included within our field but jump that to a big four-passenger car weighing 2500 pounds ready for the road and business and it's another story entirely." The twenty-eight-year-old was trying to give his elders a lesson in marketing and Scripps-Booth's place in the automotive scheme of things. He cited a trend he'd noted in the contemporary U.S. auto scene.

"One wheelbase leads to a longer wheelbase," he wrote, "and one motor size always to a larger size. . . . We have sinned and better look to our guns and supplies. . . . To my viewpoint, we are possibly paving our way in the direction of the cemetery." But no one was listening. Instead of concentrating on dominating the light car field in the U.S., an area in which it already had a head start, the company was dissipating its efforts, straining its resources, and causing itself the very difficulties James had confidently predicted in his memo.

"Suffice it to say that we have found ourselves burdened with both four and eight cylinder models of widely varying design. . . . The assembly floors are now being handicapped with . . . two types of chassis, two types of motor, three types of body for different chassis and none perfected to the

*s four seats were upholstered in polished black leather and a cloth top was standard—but the company also made available another Scripps-pioneered feature, a removable hardtop.*

point of efficiency and easy handling. . . . We must . . . take the other course and select and produce models that have the least manufacturing friction and overhead cost and if we MUST have different cars to meet the market demand, then have those cars consist of body styles rather than chassis.''

At the same time that Booth saw the company moving away from the light car market in which it had pioneered, he noted that others, notably Briscoe and Biddle—whose cars were larger and more expensive than the Model C—were making inroads into Scripps-Booth sales.

Just as serious as the problems posed by the Model D—which James believed should be built until the supply of parts was used up and then abandoned—were mechanical problems that had become apparent with the four-cylinder cars. "The four-cylinder motor is unfortunately nothing short of a real lemon," he wrote. "Its faults are fundamental and there is little hope of recovery through more careful workmanship or by minor changes in design. We must unquestionably have a good four-cylinder engine. . . . We foolishly aggravated our production problems by adding an eight instead of going after a good four-cylinder motor a year ago."

Besides the reliability problems encountered by some owners once the four had covered appreciable mileage—problems which led some to refer to the car as a "Slips-Loose" or "Scraps-Bolt"—James had also become dissatisfied with the Model C's styling. "While it makes a cute little 5th Avenue or Sheridan Road toy, it does not suggest the get-up-and-go and that red-blooded look that men prefer," he wrote, doubtless still smarting from the decision not to build the Vitesse. "No wonder that I overheard a woman remark, 'Oh Ed, he's riding around the country in his wife's dishpan,' referring to an S-B."

In July 1916, after negotiations with William C. Durant, Scripps-Booth made arrangements to install the four-cylinder Chevrolet 490 engine in the Model C. Though the switch did give the company a more reliable simpler engine—the new car was called the Model G and introduced in 1917—James was not entirely satisfied with the solution. Despite its new valve cover with S-B markings, the engine seemed to James to have changed the character of the car. He couldn't escape the feeling that the Model G was really a Chevy in Scripps clothing. There was only one real solution he felt, an altogether new roadster powered by a Scripps-Booth

designed and built four-cylinder engine, a motorcar whose chassis possessed the length and strength to carry either a V-8 or four and either two or four seats.

James submitted drawings for such a car to his uncle Clarence in the fall of 1916 as the most promising choice for the 1917 model year. Initially approved, the design was later discarded in favor of one by Stout and company chief engineer H.O.C. Isenberg—who had joined S-B from Ferro Machine in Cleveland—both of whom opted to continue with the two-frame policy. For James Booth, his uncle's decision—one made under the auspices of the board of directors—was the final straw. He resigned—and left the factory never to return. Now as the infant Scripps-Booth Corporation faced the New Year without the talents of the young man whose name it carried, all James had feared began to happen.

As problems with parts suppliers continued, Stout was aghast to find that changes were being made on the production line without prior consultation with engineers in order to get the cars out and save money. "A full cantilever spring giving an excellent ride and no trouble was replaced by a stiff quarter elliptical spring on the same frame to save something like fourteen cents per spring on cost," he wrote. "The ride was lost and the frames broke as fast as they went out. Replacements ate up profits." By the fall of 1917, the problems caused by too many different models, too few parts and stories of Scripps unreliability had led to a crisis.

Scripps-Booth Corporation no longer seemed to have much of a future and when William Stout was offered a job at Packard, he accepted. Clarence Booth handed his own resignation to the board of directors in October followed a month later by Will Scripps. The last vestiges of Scripps-Booth family control were thus stripped from the company.

The Scripps-Booth Corporation was absorbed by Chevrolet and the expansionist-minded Billy Durant toward year's end, and the year following when Chevrolet and GM merged, the marque became part of that giant conglomerate. Initially, the future looked promising. "Very little bull was passed," Will Scripps wrote James of a planning meeting he attended in December 1917. But what ultimately resulted were Scripps-Booth cars which were nothing more than GM's Oakland chassis fitted with a 40 hp Northway six-cylinder engine, not light cars at all, and with styling that was thoroughly ordinary. By 1921 Alfred Sloan, who took over  217

*Among the few town cars built on the Model D chassis was this special custom model designed for tennis star and walking champion Eleanor Sears, at a reputed cost of $17,500.*

reorganization of General Motors after Billy Durant's grand dreams had turned into a nightmare, concluded that the company was just so much excess baggage, and in 1922 banished Scripps-Booth from the GM family.

By that time, James Scripps-Booth was living in Pasadena, California. There he had given himself exclusively to painting initially, but some four years after his unhappy experiences in the auto world, the old fascination returned to him one day and James began again to think of car design. He installed a large blackboard on his garage wall and began to draw. What took shape on the board in Booth's precise chalk lines represented a sort of ultimate fusion of his love for painting and his love for cars, the quintessential product of the artist-engineer. "Here as it were, a picture has been painted with tools rather than brushes," he would write when announcing the car. It was a compact 106-inch wheelbase vehicle, a light efficient car jam-packed with innovative features in the Scripps-Booth tradition.

Covered by twenty patents, the design boasted hanging full-adjustable pedals, cable-controlled interior hood latches, a parking brake in the transmission, an Argyll single sleeve valve engine—and most importantly, an underslung worm drive rear axle that permitted a flat nineteen-inch high floor, as opposed to the norm of twenty-five inches. James called his masterpiece by the most appropriate name he could think of: He labelled it the Da Vinci.

Booth did not plan to manufacture the new car himself. He had by now had his fill of the role of automaker and preferred instead to act as industrial designer and sell his complete creation to an established manufac-

turer. Among the first to see his ideas was Walter Chrysler. He was impressed but he was also already planning to bring out a new car bearing his own name and as far as he was concerned, the Da Vinci was too late to be considered. James took his plans elsewhere. He visited Fred Fisher of Fisher Body who was toying with the idea of building a car, the Winton company then in receivership and the builders of the Handley-Knight in Kalamazoo. No one was buying.

Then in September 1924, Booth wrote Stutz's Charlie Schwab. In October he met with Schwab's chief engineer, Charles S. Crawford, and things began to look brighter. Crawford enthusiastically recommended adoption of the advanced Da Vinci. But while Crawford was waxing joyful over the new car, Stutz chairman Eugene Thayer was approached by the redoubtable Frederic Ewan Moskovics who was also trying to sell a new car design to the company. Coincidentally, at least according to later testimony about the whole episode, Moskovics also planned a car with an underslung worm drive.

Not realizing the role Moskovics played behind the scenes, James was informed by Stutz that they would not be able to use the Da Vinci after all. Undaunted, he had a prototype built at a cost of $100,000 and made plans to demonstrate it to prospective buyers in 1926. Then, the New York auto show opened in January and Booth was thunderstruck to see the new car proudly unveiled there by Stutz and named the "Safety Stutz" because of its low-slung frame made possible by its underslung worm drive. Walter Chrysler was shocked too. "Why that's James Booth's car!" he exclaimed

*Ahead of its time in sporting a V-8 engine, the Model D was strictly of its era with its exposed chauffeur's section, and rather imitative in the choice of radiator contour.*

to a friend. James himself was furious. He sued for patent infringement. He lost. He then appealed on grounds of misappropriation and breach of confidence.

While the courts considered his argument's merit, James demonstrated the Da Vinci to more prospects. At Ford, executives showed the car to Henry himself but Ford was not satisfied with the machine, unhappy with—of all things—its low floor. "You tell James it's interesting but people want to sit up high and see over the fences," he said. Others—Graham, Rickenbacker, Dodge, Packard, Hupmobile, Jordan among them—found the vehicle intriguing, but undoubtedly viewed it as an expensive gamble. No one bought the design. The court battle dragged on.

Eventually, in 1935, Booth won his case. By then, however, Stutz had fallen on hard times and was nearly bankrupt. James Scripps-Booth realized $40,000 out of the case and his dream car. The money was just enough to pay his attorneys.

Although the Da Vinci affair forever decided Booth against reentering the automobile business in any form, his imagination was just too fertile not to be again exercised on a car. In 1930 he had returned to one of his favorite automotive genres, the cyclecar, and constructed what is probably the ultimate such vehicle, a sleek super variation he called the Da Vinci Pup. It featured a wood-aluminum body frame unit and was initially powered by a four-cylinder Henderson motorcycle engine, later by an all-aluminum Van Blerck marine engine with overhead cams delivering 35 bhp. The Pup could achieve 90 mph. Belt driven like the Rocket of 1914,

the car incorporated a new steel-core drive belt—one per side—which James felt would eliminate much of the earlier cyclecar's belt-stretching and breaking problems. He proved this theory by making extensive trips in the car and took delight in humiliating the drivers of more conventional cars by leaving them far behind.

The Pup was Booth's last complete design and after it was built—at a cost of $30,000—he spent his time primarily in his studio painting, and doing some writing. He died suddenly in 1955 at the age of sixty-six. It was something neither James nor anyone else had expected and there had been a lot more that he'd wanted to do.

Among his various projects, James had been planning—just for fun—to re-engine the Pup. At the time of his death, a local machinist was at work on a new bell housing that would join an Austin engine to a Booth gearbox. Having always kept abreast of the latest trends in the auto world, perhaps Booth planned to test the Pup against the new small English sports cars which were gaining popularity. Then too, had he lived to see the huge growth of the small car market in the United States, Booth would probably have nodded his head in recognition and understanding. After all, he could rightly have claimed to have had the same idea some forty years earlier. As he had learned, however, it took more than good ideas, more than being ahead of one's time, to become a successful auto manufacturer. It took capital and unerring business sense. Still, of the thousands who made the effort and failed, the legacy left by James Scripps-Booth has proved more enduring—if not always as well recognized—than many.✤

# STURM UND DRANG

*Auto Union versus Mercedes
For the Glory of Germany, Scenes
of a Thundering Era
Painted by Walter Gotschke*

May 27th, 1934: A.V.U.S.

von Klinger in 1776, and the name soon came to be given to the German literary movement that followed for which Goethe, Schiller and Herder, among others, created characters and plots of monumental passion and tumult. But the phrase might just as appropriately have been coined a century and a half later to describe larger-than-life theatrics in another setting altogether. *Sturm und Drang.* Auto Union and Mercedes-Benz.

Looking back, it all seemed quite prosaic in the beginning, as if nothing truly extraordinary would ensue. "This was the first race of the new German cars against the Maseratis and Alfas that have long ago left behind them all trace of teething trouble," the press said, "and in effect the two German teams were merely trying out their cars . . . ."

It was early summer 1934—and the event reported was the May 27th race at A.V.U.S. (Automobil Verkehrs and Übungs Strasse—Traffic and Practice Road) near Berlin. Rudi Caracciola and his Mercedes were, truly, simply testing each other; the car was brand-new, having being wrung out two months previous at Monza; its driver had earlier been wrung out as well, emotionally and physically—the death of his wife, and an automobile accident from which he had painfully and slowly convalesced.

He had to drive again—"It was the only way to endure life"—he took the Mercedes out for seven laps during practice and proved he could do it.

team manager Alfred Neubauer decided that was enough for both car and driver for one day.

Alone, the other new German car would challenge Alfa supremacy in the race itself. There were three of the mysterious P-wagen Auto Unions on the starting line, strange long-tailed silver things. Two of them retired midrace; August Momberger in the third managed to stay the distance, finishing behind two Alfas. The Italians didn't appear worried.

Two hundred thousand spectators had been at A.V.U.S. There were Brownshirts by the thousands, high ranking Nazi officials. And Adolf Hitler. He had a lot of surprises in store for a watching—if not watchful—world. Utter domination in motor racing was but one of them.

A State-supported, money-no-object program for the new 750 kg Grand Prix Formula—and a grand prize of several hundred thousand dollars for the manufacturer which provided Germany with the most glory in 1934's racing season, that was the Führer's idea. The idea behind the new Formula, as tradition would have it, had been to reduce speed. It had precisely the opposite effect. Technology advanced to realms hitherto undreamed. For Mercedes, initially the W.25 designed by Dr. Hans Nibel, a dohc 3.4-liter 354 bhp straight-eight, box girder frame, independent four-wheel suspension, aerodynamic body; by 1937 the remarkable W.125 with 646 bhp, twin tube frame and yet more sophisticated suspension. For Auto

*August 23rd, 1936: Swiss Grand Prix*

Union, the gospel according to Ferdinand Porsche, a supercharged sohc V-16 of narrow 45 degree angle, 4.4 liters and nearly 300 bhp, and mounted behind the driver; chassis of steel tubing; all independent suspension with torsion bars and trailing links at the front, transverse leaf spring and swing axles at the rear (soon refined to torsion bars carried in the frame tubes); aluminum body with side panels of doped fabric over aluminum framing (subsequently to be replaced by light alloy sheet). And refinements, always the refinements, as they were needed, and as they are possible when the cash never stops flowing. Nobody else had a chance. They just didn't know it right away.

Alfa Romeo, under the tutelage of Scuderia Ferrari, increased engine capacity of the P3 to 2.9 liters; Maserati was already at 2.9, quite sufficient, it was thought; Bugatti had its new Type 59 with 3.3 liters and 240 bhp, a split front axle and a rather troublesome transmission. It was scarcely enough.

The French Grand Prix at Montlhéry later that summer of '34 saw both

Mercedes and Auto Union falter. They were blisteringly fast, but they were still teething. Alfa Romeo finished a commanding one-two-three. It wouldn't happen again. The German cars sorted themselves out for the remainder of the season, and won while doing it: Auto Union thrice, Mercedes thrice.

For 1935 Mercedes had 430 bhp, Auto Union 375—and Alfa bored out the P3 as far as possible, 3.2 liters . . . for 270 bhp. For the rest of a troubled decade, motor sport would be *Deutschland Über Alles.* The German anthem would be booed—on foreign soil—but it would be played with almost monotonous regularity as Grand Prix followed Grand Prix. An occasional super-human effort by a Nuvolari at the Nürburgring or a Dreyfus at Pau might see an Alfa or privately entered Delahaye take the checkered flag, but this happened rarely. Generally, Auto Union and Mercedes were simply fighting each other.

Caracciola won six races—four of them major GP events—for Mercedes in 1935, and the Auto Union team had the services, the talent and the long-

*September 12th, 1937: Italian Grand Prix*

time experience of Achille Varzi at its command. He won at Tunis. But it was a former motorcycle racer newly recruited to Grand Prix car competition who provided the thrills—losing by only two seconds to Caracciola at the Eifelrennen—and the portent of things to come. His name was Bernd Rosemeyer.

For 1936 Auto Union had 520 bhp, Mercedes 500 bhp and a new chassis, which wasn't a blessing. Alfa had an eight and a twelve, for 300 and 360 bhp. The Bugatti and Maserati factories had given up.

Bernd Rosemeyer won three major Grands Prix for Auto Union in '36; eliminated by a fire in a fourth, Varzi took that one for the cars with the four-ring emblem. Most spectacular of the lot had been the Swiss GP at Berne on August 23rd where Rudi Caracciola in the No. 12 Mercedes and Rosemeyer in the No. 4 Auto Union had seemed settled into a moderately hot struggle early on. Then the latter was given a go-faster signal from the pits and stepped up the pace, until on lap fifteen Rosemeyer put up an astounding 105.42 mph round, a record not since broken in a race on the

Berne circuit. Rosemeyer's daring was Caracciola's undoing; a bracing in the rear suspension of his Mercedes broke, and the car was finished for the day. Afterwards Bernd repeated to Rudi the words Rudi had said to him the year before: "Well done, my dear fellow. But in the future don't just drive round and round the circuit; use your head."

But it was Rosemeyer's foot that had devastated the field at Berne. The circuit was nearly deserted near the finish. The Alfas, the Maseratis, the Bugattis . . . they were all out. Only the entire Auto Union team remained, finishing first, second, third and fifth—and one lone Mercedes which slipped into fourth. That car's driving had been shared by Hermann Lang and Luigi Fagioli; some weeks before, Lang had broken a finger at the Nürburgring—that, and Rosemeyer's frantic pace, had seen to the wisdom of his replacement at the wheel mid-race.

On May 30th the year following, Lang was back in form—and so was Mercedes. The occasion was a Sunday afternoon outing at A.V.U.S., newly banked at its north curve—"like an oversize wall of death," Neubauer    225

stand completed. Marshalled by thousands of the Führer's men—"trying not to appear uncomfortable in the heat of their heavy uniforms," one journalist noted—the spectators numbered 380,000. What they saw was "ultra streamlining . . . and the fastest automobile race ever run." In the first heat, Caracciola won over Rosemeyer—by seven-tenths of a second—at 155.59 mph. In the second, the Manfred von Brauchitsch Mercedes triumphed over the Rudi Hasse Auto Union, at 160.37 mph. In the third, Hermann Lang in Mercedes No. 37—plagued by tire trouble in the earlier heats—came into his own, overtaking Hasse in Auto Union No. 34, and winning at 162.61 mph. But Auto Union did one thing better than Mercedes that afternoon—one lap, the fastest of the day, at a blistering 171.74 mph. Exclamation points riddled press reports of that fact—though no one was particularly surprised at the gentleman who accomplished it. It was Bernd Rosemeyer.

Achille Varzi was the forgotten man of Auto Union. Dick Seaman had joined the team. Varzi's contract had not been renewed for '37. His hair was grey now, his eyes were expressionless, deep lines etched his face—he

September—when he appeared one day amidst the Auto Union team just as preparations were under way for the Italian Grand Prix. The event was not to be held at Monza this year, its traditional site, but at Leghorn instead, this the ruling of the Royal Automobile Club of Italy. The latter circuit would, it was hoped, work to the advantage of the less swift but more manageable Italian cars.

Varzi asked for an Auto Union to drive. His problems were behind him, he said, "I won't let you down." In practice he didn't. He lapped the circuit at 3 minutes 13 seconds, faster than Nuvolari, faster than von Brauchitsch, than Lang, than Stuck, than Seaman, than Rosemeyer—only Caracciola bettered Varzi's time, and he had to press to do it.

The crowd on race day was ferociously nationalistic. Varzi, a native of northern Italy, was driving a German car. All eyes were focused upon and all cheers directed toward Tazio Nuvolari and his red Alfa Romeo. In one beautiful moment early on, while both were in contending position and after von Brauchitsch spun out his Mercedes, Varzi closed in on Nuvolari, and it looked like the beginning of a splendid duel. But it was not to be.

*October 25th-27th, 1937: German Record Week*

moded to be a winner. Tazio became bored after a while, and more than a little disgruntled, and halfway through the race gave up the chase and handed his car over to teammate Farina. Von Brauchitsch retired. Caracciola was an easy victor, Lang was a comfortable second, Rosemeyer a facile third. Varzi's sixth place was agonizingly won. Utterly exhausted at the finish, he had to be lifted from his car by mechanics. He was told by team manager Feuereissen, as gently as possible, that Grand Prix competition was not a sport for convalescents. It was his last race for Auto Union.

Rudi Caracciola won the European drivers' championship for Mercedes in '37. And Auto Union took the German Record Week in October. Bernd Rosemeyer again. And again there were the exclamation points. "Over 252 M.P.H.!"—252.47 to be exact, in the flying kilometer. Next to the giant hangar housing the *Graf Zeppelin*, the timekeepers had gathered, with a section of the nearby Frankfurt-Darmstadt-Heidelberg autobahn closed to traffic for the event. There were two Auto Unions for Bernd, the aerodynamic A.V.U.S. C-Type with a specially built 6.3-liter V-16 of some 545 hp for the more flamboyant records and a smaller car for 3000-5000 cc

class mark attempts. In all, Bernd Rosemeyer captured no fewer than seventeen new records.

Mercedes had been there too, with a new streamlined twelve-cylinder car around which everybody crowded, including as veteran journalist John Dugdale observed, many "investigators . . . from the Auto Union camp." Caracciola wasn't too happy with the car that day. A little more work was done. In January of '38, he was back on the Frankfurt autobahn early one morning—and broke Bernd's record, 268.86 mph for the kilometer. Then he returned to his hotel with von Brauchitsch and Alfred Neubauer for breakfast. Neubauer received a phone call. "The Auto Union gang is out there! With their record car. With Rosemeyer and the whole bunch." Caracciola was speechless: "Who ever heard of records being run like races?" The Mercedes contingent returned to the autobahn to see what was happening.

This Auto Union carried the 545 hp engine in a revised body with a new straight-through, fender line which reduced resistance—but also high speed stability. Bernd Rosemeyer was seated in it, with Auto Union people all round him. It was late morning, the calm of dawn had given way to

*January 11th, 1938: Frankfurt Autobahn*

breezes threatening to become gusts. "Don't worry," the Auto Union driver said when Caracciola suggested he postpone the attempt. "I'll be all right. I'm one of the lucky ones." After a practice run, Bernd Rosemeyer was sent off. Moments later, a wicked cross-wind, a crash. Everyone ran down the road. Except von Brauchitsch and Caracciola. "I don't want to go there," Rudi said evenly. Bernd Rosemeyer was dead. There would be no exclamation points in the press reports about record breaking at Frankfurt this time.

Hill climbing. Not as spectacular, not as headline-grabbing, not as tragic—but as fiercely contested between Auto Union and Mercedes as a record attempt or a Grand Prix. In August of 1938, Auto Union had the C-Type Grand Prix car, suitably lightened and with a shorter wheelbase and two extra rear wheels. And Auto Union also had Hans Stuck, *bergmeister* nonpareil. The German Hill Climb Championship this year saw the venue changed from Schauinsland at Freiburg to the Austrian Alps, the Grossglockner pass and a circuit rising from 3900 to 7900 serpentine feet. The relocating didn't bother Hans Stuck at all, any more than did his age. No one knew exactly how old he was. Reportedly German racing of-

ficialdom, desirous of young heroes, took to shaving off a few years from his birth date in competition programs. But regardless of what side of forty he was on that dreary August 28th, he took the Grossglockner with ease, fastest time of the day and the championship—as he had the year previous, and so many times before. The word was that hill climbing officials thought it might be easier to simply give him the key to the trophy warehouse.

Things were not so easy for Auto Union in '38. With the new 3-liter Formula in effect, Mercedes had answered with its supercharged four overhead-cam V-12 of 420 bhp, Auto Union's reply being the three camshaft twelve-cylinder, 400 bhp D-Type, also supercharged. Mercedes had won the Tripoli Grand Prix (Lang), the French Grand Prix (von Brauchitsch), the German Grand Prix (Seaman), the Ciano Cup (Lang), the Acerbo Cup (Caracciola), the Swiss Grand Prix (Caracciola)—and Auto Union had won nothing at all. But Tazio Nuvolari was with Auto Union now. Fortunes would change.

Two factors had determined the Flying Mantuan's presence on the German team. From Auto Union's side, the death of Bernd Rosemeyer. From

*October 22nd, 1938: Donington Grand Prix*

Tazio's, a practice accident at Pau in '38 when the fuel tank of his Alfa inexplicably caught fire. Since accidents rarely nettled him, Rudi Caracciola had even jokingly asked him afterward why he hadn't driven "the car into the lake just to cool it off." But Tazio was furious, the accident had been an inexcusable one, and he vowed never to race again for Alfa Romeo. And he was weary in any case of seeing silver ahead of him in so many races as he vainly struggled to be competitive in a car that so obviously was not.

After he recovered from his burns, he took his place at the head of the Auto Union team in July. He didn't win the first time out, nor the second, nor the third. Journalists began asking themselves if perhaps he wasn't too old. He was, after all, forty-six, and he admitted it. They stopped asking in September after the Italian Grand Prix, and Tazio's spectacular win there.

And any lingering doubts were dispelled the following month in England at the Donington Grand Prix. The political situation had threatened its cancellation, but resulted only in postponement until the 22nd, and on that day British spectators were treated to a performance for which virtuoso seems scant praise indeed. "The car went faster and faster, yet it cornered as though on rails," one reporter commented. In his yellow sweater

Tazio positively charged to victory, with Lang's and Seaman's Mercedes trailing far behind.

At the post-race party, an impish Nuvolari apologized to Mercedes, allowing, however, that they had really won quite enough already—and suggested they might do better next year—if they built some new cars. The rotund Neubauer nearly laughed himself to the floor. Amid the gaiety, Mercedes designer Rudi Uhlenhaut whispered to Dick Seaman, "Somehow we always have the best parties when we lose." The fun would stop soon.

Nineteen thirty-nine. Lang took the Belgian Grand Prix for Mercedes. Dick Seaman died there. Müller took the French Grand Prix for Auto Union. No Mercedes lasted the race. Caracciola took the German Grand Prix, the only Mercedes to finish; Müller finished second, the only Auto Union to complete the distance. At the Swiss Grand Prix, it was Lang, Caracciola and von Brauchitsch for Mercedes, Auto Union fourth and fifth. At Belgrade, Nuvolari captured the Yugoslav Grand Prix, with von Brauchitsch second, Müller third. It would be the last such event for quite a while. It was September 3rd. War had been declared that morning ✪ 227

# A PACKARD HEXAD

*Six of One Was Not
a Half Dozen of Another
When the Cars Came
From East Grand Boulevard
During the Company's Good Years*

The prototype was nicknamed "Gasoline Gus" and when its appointed testing duties were served, it was given a delivery wagon body and further work as a mail truck between the plant and downtown Detroit. Henry Joy had a prairie schooner devised of one for "roughing it in the sparsely settled sections of the far West." Not that he would find the time often—for the car was a Model Thirty and it was the Model Thirty which more than any Packard previous or subsequent firmly established the company's reputation for quality, and kept things very busy at the factory from 1907 into 1912.

Designed by Russell Huff to be "bigger and more speed-daring than any of its forebears" (a 5 by 5½ four, rated at 30 hp, though actual was probably closer to 60), it was quite a car. There were others more expensive, but few could match its stamina. Packard was really going places now—and so was the Model Thirty.

In a carefully orchestrated series of endurance runs—all evocatively recalled by their participants in lengthy articles in the motoring journals of the day—the Packard prowess was promoted. Sales manager S.D. Waldon was in charge, beginning in 1906 with a Detroit-Chicago run and a record-breaking 606 miles in less than a day along Michigan's sandy roads ("We glance and scoot away. For the road is good here and there are no teams in sight. We can run the little tell-tale up to sixty and improve the 'average!' ")—and next year to a less hospitable New York-Philadelphia ("Zig-zagging from right to left, the car crossed [the thank-you-m'ams] obliquely, with the passengers in the tonneau on their feet and holding to the back of the driver's seat.")—and yet another Detroit-Chicago, this one mid-winter, Waldon again driving, with "four of us of the proletariat [constituting] the ballast-pneumatic-tire Red Cross corps [who] divided the task of record-keeping into looking at the speedometer, at a watch, and at making marks on a 5-cent note book . . . . I lost a mitten trying to write Ypsilanti . . . as we jostled along about 55 miles an hour." By 1910, when Waldon broke the Pittsburgh-Philadelphia record, he had been promoted; in Philadelphia he confided to a reporter that he was "vice-president of the Packard Motor Car Company when he is washed."

There had been many other changes at Packard by that time too. Behind most of them was the storied success of the Model Thirty. It broke the thousand-car-a-year mark for Packard in 1907 and, with its companion Model Eighteen, was produced in nearly 12,000 units through 1911. And behind it was the ebullient Mr. Joy, who had mushroomed the factory space at Detroit during the Thirty's years from 10.0 acres to 37.7, its employee rolls from 2500 to 7575. And with a splendid net profit for fiscal year 1911 of $1,406,410.71. All of which was a bit too much for James Ward Packard who had started the whole Packard automobile idea the century previous. Ward, who preferred single cylinders and a little peace to the frantic activity Henry Joy was generating, turned over the company presidency to the latter in 1909. Henry Joy brought in one Alvan Macauley to take over his (Joy's) general manager duties in 1910, and Macauley brought with him an engineering fellow by the name of Jesse Vincent. For 1912 the Thirty would be joined on the production line by a new six . . . .

Vice-president Waldon was on the road to Chicago in the late summer of 1912, clipping about an hour off his previous record with the Thirty—and, as the orders poured in by the hundreds, the Packard company in mock

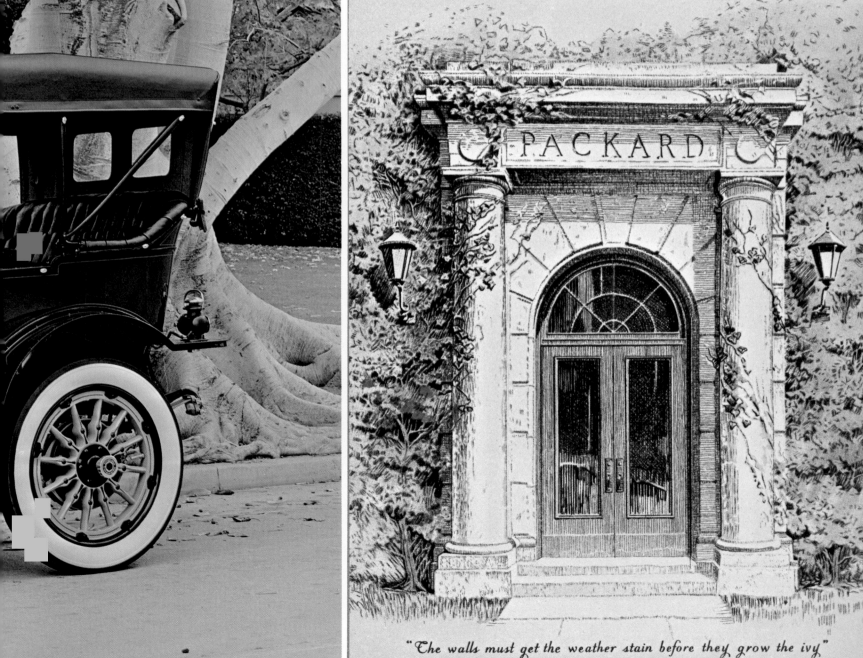

"The walls must get the weather stain before they grow the ivy"
ELIZABETH BARRETT BROWNING

horror cried out in its splendidly edited house publication, "will someone please sit on the lid." The Packard sixes, numbered 38 and 48, were on their way—and the company, as the cliché goes, couldn't build them fast enough.

With Russell Huff, who developed the new cars, now departing the engineering center stage for consulting from the wings, Jesse Vincent stepped front and center. The two individual sixes would become his babies too. Though the factory men building the 38's might trounce the 48's in a company baseball game (44-0 was the score), on the road the 48 series obviously had the legs of its kid brother—the former a 4½ by 5½ T-head (by 1914 L-head) of 525 cubic inches and 82 hp, the latter a 4 by 5½ L-head of 415 cubic inches and 60 hp. "Chief engineerial vibes of the Vincent voltage were sent hurtling into the assembled Packardiers" crowed *The Packard* magazine after one of the enthusiastic Jesse's visits to a sales meeting. The new Packards provided the same.

In mid-June 1914 at Indy, the larger six was sent round the speedway at 70.4 mph, the smaller 62.4, "settling definitely," *Motor Age* reported, "the ancient contention that no stock touring car is capable of the speed of a mile a minute." Harry K. Thaw, incidentally, had unofficially confirmed that the year previous when he made his legendary escape from the Mattewan State Asylum for the Criminal Insane in a Packard six. ("When a fast getaway is absolutely imperative, ask the man who . . . " winked *The Packard.*)

But the Packard sixes did much more for the company than perform heroically on the road. In the marketplace, they positioned the company squarely in league with Pierce-Arrow and Peerless. Though the Three P's might have been talked of during the Thirty's years, the four-cylinder Packards weren't quite on the same rarefied plane with the smooth sixes of Pierce and Peerless. The new Packards changed that—and with their body styles numbering into the dozens and their pleasantly indulgent price tags, they even managed to outsell the other two P's to boot. That was precisely what Henry Joy had in mind.

When a fellow from Maryland wrote him he had heard from a Pierce-Arrow agent that Packard was forthwith going to drop down a notch, compete instead on the level of "Caddilac (sic), Cole and several others," and build an assembled car, Henry Joy replied with a two-page letter politely saying no—and circulated both missives to *his* dealers admonishing them to "stand squarely on your Packard feet." The company was now absolutely where he wished it to be. "Let Joy Be Unconfined" chortled *Harper's Weekly* the year following when Packard's president publicly urged all advertisers to boycott publications that spoke well of President Wilson—Henry Joy's political opinions, like all views he had, were pronounced.

But Henry Joy, and Jesse Vincent, were by now becoming convinced that even six cylinders were too confining for their Packard. The company was about to provide a new car and a new engine for the Men Who Owned One who had declared the six perfection, like the chap who testimonially wrote that "the only man who could get it away from me would be the Sheriff." It would be a car that, the following year, would prompt the powers-that-be of Pierce-Arrow in Buffalo to declare smugly, if a bit

*"Straight as an arrow through ten years of consistent progress can be traced the ceaseless pursuit of Perfection to its culmination" exulted Packard when the car was introduced in 1907. Five years later, the Model Thirty (on the opening pages) was built, as the venerable four-cylinder's place on the production line was gradually being taken over by the company's latest "ceaseless pursuit of Perfection," the new six. The six-cylinder Model 4-48 (above left)—the second 48 series for model year 1914— was, with its 144-inch wheelbase, the biggest Packard built to date, and designed to compete with Pierce-Arrow's mighty 66. The sidelamps from the previous Model 14-48 had been fitted on the car by the factory at the request of its original owner. Indicative of how independent coachbuilders influenced Packard design is the Twin Six Town Car by Fleetwood (below left). Ordered by the Atwater Kent family of radio renown in 1919, delivered in '20 and seen thereafter in only the best places, chauffeur and footman aboard, it was probably the haughtiest car in all Philadelphia. It was special, from its wheelbase (145 inches, a specially prepared chassis nine inches longer than standard) to its hood (again higher, longer than standard) to its bumpers (steel completely rubber encased) to its collapsible top (converting it to a touring car) to its sparkling varnish finish and its drum headlamps and disc wheels. The latter two features were incorporated on a 335 Special Packard built later in 1920 to show what the company could do in the way of distinctive coachwork. And the headlamps, of course, would subsequently become standard equipment for the entire Packard line.*

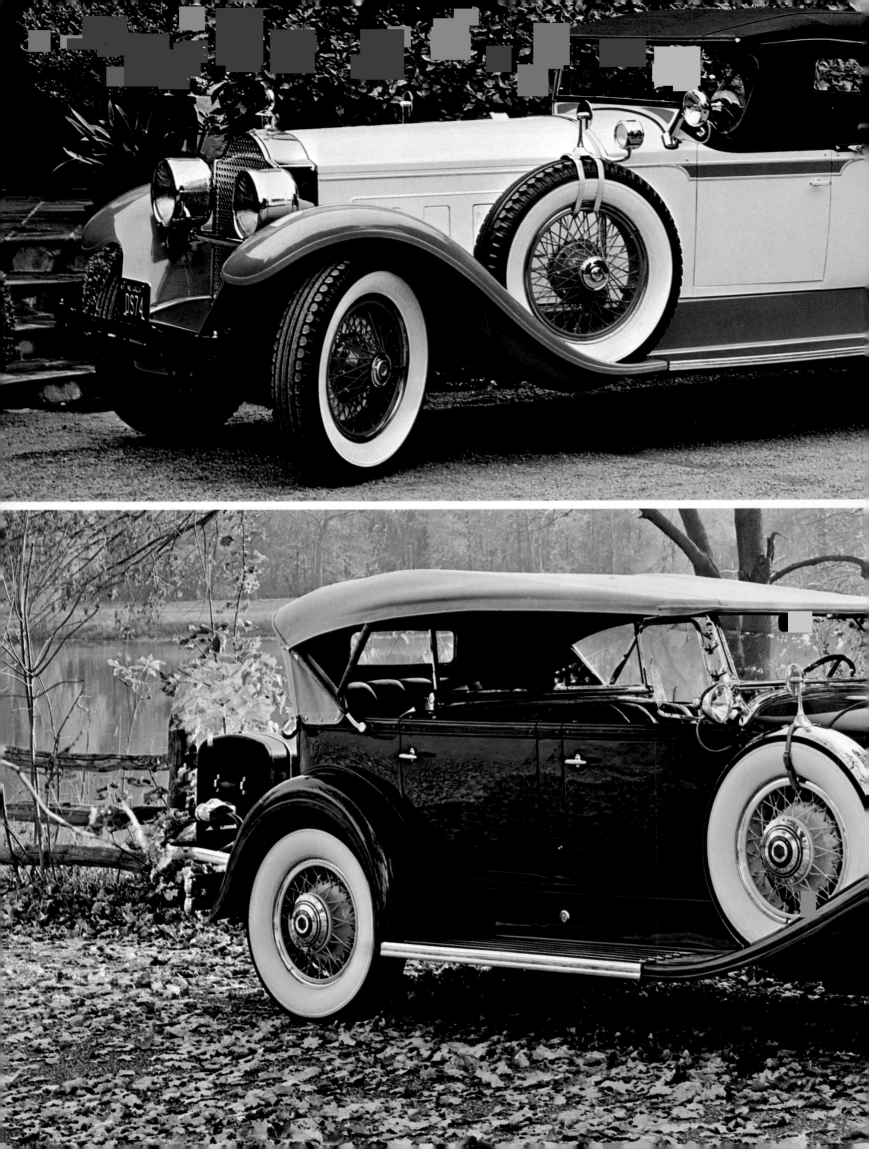

apologetically, in announcing that company's continuing loyalty to the six, that multi-cylinder cars were "merely novelties introduced for a more spectacular selling argument." It would debut in May of 1915 . . . .

Humorist George Ade, writing of motoring in the *American Magazine*, said it best: "The joys of life may be made to increase with the multiplication of the cylinders." That was a few years after the Twin Six was introduced. That May day of its debut, however, the wonder was how Jesse Vincent had done it. A twelve-cylinder engine under a hood that was no wider and even a half foot shorter than that under which the sixes rode before? Impossible! But a V angle of sixty degrees and a three-inch bore (by five stroke) resulting in an engine less lengthy than the six-cylinder had seen to it. Its cubic inches (424) were comparable to the smaller six, the horses extracted (85, later upped to 90) comparable to the larger. Brute power wasn't the aim but the sort of gentility that would lead Packard to exquisitely understate that "The home that is served by the Packard Car continually enjoys the utmost in agreeable automobile travel."

Thirty-six hundred Twin Sixes were produced in 1915, some 10,645 in 1916—and soon after Jesse Vincent and Alvan Macauley took Packard to war for a while. Henry Joy was gone by now—in 1916 he resigned in a fit of pique after a Charles Nash/James Storrow try at buying Packard fell

*"Fast or slow, flashing through the maze of metropolitan congestion, or smoothly annihilating distance at almost aircraft speed in the open . . ." With phrases like that ringing in their ears, more than ten thousand motorists rushed out to buy the new Fourth Series Model 443 Packards introduced for 1928 in nineteen body styles. Just under four thousand dollars would have bought the winsome Raceabout (left). "Trim and sleek . . . offered to those who live in fine and sunny climes or who can afford the pleasures of both open and closed cars" was the Packard advertising rationale for the splendid Eighth Series Model 840 Custom Phaeton (below) introduced for the 1930 model year. Of the 3345 Eighth Series cars produced, some 114 were phaetons. And at least six were Four-Door Convertible Sedans by Dietrich (pages following), produced by the independent designer for automobile show appearances and special clients.*

through. So incensed was he, legend has it, that not only did he sell his stock but he also procured a Cadillac which he drove, honking all the while, back and forth in front of the Packard plant. Indeed. The implied comparison, to the men of Packard, was silly. They were, by their own estimation, building the best car in America. And others agreed. When "Sir Hubert" writing in the *Illustrated London News* noted that Packard was to America what Rolls-Royce was to England and commented regarding the Twin Six that "so smooth is the running that the car does not appear to be moving. It is simply that the road is winding under the wheels . . ." —Packard public relations graciously thanked him, adding, "Perhaps you don't know that we operate a Rolls-Royce occasionally just to make sure that we aren't outdone."

About 35,000 Twin Sixes were built during its near decade of production. Some people who've been delighted to ride in one since wonder betimes if it should not have gone on forever. A rather pleasant idea. But at the time, back at Packard, Jesse Vincent had yet another one . . . .

Actually there were two ideas—the first borne of facts made abundantly clear by the close of World War I, viz, that the automobile had proved itself sufficiently practical to appeal to virtually all segments of the traveling public, and one in particular that Packard was especially anxious to woo—the one, as Alvan Macauley explained, that would find attractive and attainable "a moderate-priced, high grade car, particularly suitable for the owner-driver." Packard was aiming at the well-to-do motorist, a financial step removed from the supra-moneyed class which had largely been the Twin Six's clientele.

For them the company would provide—amidst a flourish of promotional trumpets—the Single Six. A V-8 was rejected, Jesse Vincent said, because "it is not inherently balanced." One might suspect some marketing politics was involved in the decision too. Cadillac, after all, had a V-8 already, brought out even before Packard's Twin Six. That wouldn't do. The Single Six was introduced in 1920, and back to the drawing board went Jesse for his second idea, a replacement for the esteemed Twin Six. He was still thinking in-line. He emerged with the Single Eight in 1923.

It was the first volume-produced American car to carry a straight-eight engine, the first too to have four wheel brakes. Refinements would come, and horsepower would rise over the years from the initial eighty-four (from 358 cubic inches) to well over the hundred mark. For more than a decade and a half, the Single Eight would serve as Packard's mainstay, and in-

deed, in a less costly variation, would replace the six in 1928.

From the very day of the Single Eight's debut, Packard was sure it had a winner. So, it seemed, did a lot of other people. By the end of the decade, Packard was outselling every other prestige car in the world. And the garages in which Packards began finding themselves were as estimable as the cars themselves. In Washington, D.C., there was Chief Justice William Howard Taft, associate justices numbering four, Secretary of State Frank B. Kellogg, Speaker of the House Nicholas Longworth, among many others. Better than one of five governors of the States were Packard owners, a dozen ambassadors took Packards with them to their embassy posts, scores of college presidents to their campuses, and locomotive officials to their trains. The car was ubiquitous in Hollywood. Even Howard Hughes liked it. And on the East Coast, Cornelius Vanderbilt, Jr. was so pleased he wrote Packard a lavish thank-you, noting that his car had suffered no mechanical trouble that he couldn't fix himself, though he retained two chauffeurs, one of them an ex-Packard factory man, to keep it in first class shape. Minions of polishers and mechanics provided the same service in the many royal garages of Europe that housed the cars from East Grand Boulevard, Detroit.

The Twenties were good years for Packard. In the seventh year of the decade, the company opened its Packard Proving Grounds at Utica, and when Colonel Lindbergh motored down the streets of New York in ticker tape triumph, he rode in a Packard. That year Packard sold more than 36,-000 cars, the year following more than 50,000. And in the summer President Macauley, in response to widespread rumor mongering, announced, "We have made our own way from the beginning . . . . we do not intend to lose our identity through any merger, combination, or consolidation, now or hereafter." It was 1928, Pierce-Arrow had just merged with Studebaker.

In 1931, when Hampshire House on Central Park South in New York City was erected, into the cornerstone were placed representations of the American "creative spirit" in the arts and sciences; poetry by Benet, a novel by Hemingway, a play by O'Neill, a mural by Benton—and a photograph of a town car by Packard. Betweentimes came the crash and depression. And there would be *autre temps, autre pensées*, a fabulous twelve as Packard's entry in the super-car race and a low-priced companion for the other end of the market—and lots of controversy since as to whether Packard had taken the right road. Using the wrong fork would have been unthinkable for Packard during the good years. ✪ 235

# Bibliography of Stories

*The articles in this book were adapted from or inspired by articles published in* AUTOMOBILE Quarterly. *Their derivation is shown below. Data given include the authors and titles of the original articles and the volume and number of the* AUTOMOBILE Quarterly *issue in which they appeared, as well as further research and source material when relevant.*

### THE MASCOT

Adapted from "Mascots: The Automobile's Grand Afterthought," by W.C. Williams, Volume XIII, Number 3 and "Hood Ornaments by Lalique," Volume V, Number 3.

### MIGHTY MODEL J

Adapted from "The Mighty Model J: An Appreciation," and accompanying articles, by Don Vorderman, Volume X, Number 2.

### PIONEERING FROM PAWTUCKET, R.I. TO PUTEAUX ON THE SEINE

Adapted from "A Castle Full of Cars: Antiques from the Filipinetti Collection," Volume XIII, Number 4, with additional research in marque literature, motoring journals and other references from the period.

### THE SPORTING RILEYS

Adapted from "The Sporting Rileys," by Dennis May, Volume IX, Number 1.

### PROMOTING THE PIERCE-ARROW

Adapted from "The Artists Who Painted for Pierce-Arrow: Automobile Advertising's Grandest Era" and "The Elegant Notions of Adolph Treidler: An Artist Remembers His Pierce-Arrow Days," Volume XIV, Number 3.

### IT'S THE BMW TURBO

Adapted from "BMW Turbo: A Wild New Münchener," by Don Vorderman, Volume XI, Number 1, with research updated to 1976.

### THE CAR CALLED E.R.A.

Adapted from "The Upright and Proper Champion: E.R.A.," by Simon Read, Volume XIII, Number 3.

### THE HUDSON MOTOR CAR COMPANY STORY

Adapted from "Hudson: The Car Named for Jackson's Wife's Uncle," by Maurice D. Hendry, Volume IX, Number 4.

### AND NOW . . . FOR MY NEXT NUMBER

Adapted from "And Now . . . For My Next Number," by Arthur W. Einstein, Jr., Volume II, Number 1.

### TALES OF THE 300 SL

Adapted from "Stuttgart's Immortal 300 SL," by Simon Read, Volume XIII, Number 2.

### A LITTLE ON THE BIDDLE FROM PHILADELPHIA

Adapted from "A Little on the Biddle," by Beverly Rae Kimes, Volume XI, Number 3, with further research on the marque in Biddle literature and motoring periodicals of the era.

### THE BENTLEYS BUILT BY ROLLS-ROYCE

Adapted from "The Rolls Bentley: The Song Is Ended, But the Melody Lingers On," by Don Vorderman, Volume XII, Number 2.

## THE HEROIC AGE

Adapted from "Peter Helck Goes Racing: A Portfolio
of the Artist's Paintings with his Notes,"
Volume IX, Number 3; "The Vanderbilt Cup: 1904-1910,"
by Beverly Rae Kimes, Volume VI, Number 2;
"A Portfolio of Famous Road Races," by Peter Helck,
Volume III, Number 1; with additional references
from contemporary press reports of the various races.

## THE HOUSE VINCENZO LANCIA BUILT SO WELL

Adapted from "Lancia—Part I: The Vincenzo Years [and]
Part II: Carrying On—New Cars, Old Traditions,"
by David Owen, Volume XII, Number 4.

## KELSEY'S MOTORETTE

Adapted from "Cadwallader Washburn Kelsey:
The Spirited Career of an American Pioneer,"
by Beverly Rae Kimes, Volume XIII, Number 2.

## NOW AND FOREVER, THE COBRA STORY

Adapted from "The Now and Forever Cobra,"
by Allan Girdler, Volume XIV, Number 3.

## THE TOSS OF A HAT-IN-THE-RING: RICKENBACKER

Adapted from "Hat in the Ring: The Rickenbacker,"
by Beverly Rae Kimes, Volume XIII, Number 4.

## AMILCAR OF ST. DENIS

Adapted from "Red Ones and Blue Ones, Black Ones
and Tooled Aluminum Jobs—The Amilcar,"
by Stan Grayson, Volume XIII, Number 1.

## THE FOOL THINGS

Adapted from "The Meticulous Art of Leslie Saalburg,"
Volume X, Number 2, with story inspired by and created from
marque literature, automotive or motoring journals and
other references from turn of the century literature.

## THE GLORIOUS DELAGE, A BITTERSWEET STORY

Adapted from "Empire and Elegance, Ferment and Faith:
The Story of Delage," by Griffith Borgeson,
Volume XIV, Number 3, with additional references from marque
literature and motoring journals pursuant to the era.

## CHRYSLER'S ALPHABET FROM C TO B TO L—
THE 300 LETTERCARS

Adapted from "The Chrysler Lettercars," by Allan Girdler,
Volume XIII, Number 4.

## ARTIST'S CONCEPTION

Adapted from "Artist's Conception: The Novel Cars of
James Scripps-Booth," by Sam Medway, Volume XIII, Number 3.

## STURM UND DRANG

Adapted from "Auto Union Rennwagen," Volume VIII, Number 1,
with research from "I Remember Rudi," by Alfred Neubauer,
Volume VII, Number 1; "Man on Fire: The Incredible
Tazio Nuvolari," by Beverly Rae Kimes, Volume XI, Number 1;
contemporary references to the events and other research.

## A PACKARD HEXAD

Adapted from "Five Great Packards," by Beverly Rae Kimes,
Volume XIII, Number 3.

# Photography & Owner Credits

*The logistics involved in locating rare cars and arranging for them to be photographed for* AUTOMOBILE *Quarterly publications are, of necessity, complicated. The photographs of cars featured in this book are the result of more than ten years of research and better than sixty-five individual photographic assignments. Credit is given below to the photographer who took each picture and to the owner of each automobile shown, as of the time when it was photographed. Artwork is credited as well to the owner's collection. When no credit is given, the painting is from the artist's personal archives or was the result of special assignment by* AUTOMOBILE *Quarterly for specific illustration of the story involved.*

### THE MASCOT
Page 11: the devilish creature from a 1912 Léon Bollée courtesy of the Henri Malartre Collection, Musée Français de l'Automobile, photograph by Vanni Belli. All other mascots courtesy of the Allen R. Thurn Collection, photographs by Stanley Rosenthall.

### MIGHTY MODEL J
Title pages: SJ engine from 1935 Convertible Coupe by Walker-LaGrande courtesy of Leo Gephart, photograph by Don Vorderman. Pages 18-19: 1929 Dual Cowl Phaeton by LeBaron courtesy of M.H. Gould, photograph by L. Scott Bailey. Pages 20-21: 1929 Dual Cowl Phaeton by Derham courtesy of Homer Fitterling, photograph by Don Vorderman. Page 22: 1933 Tourster by Derham courtesy of Dr. Carl Elsner, photograph by Don Vorderman. Page 23: 1936 Convertible Coupe by Walker-LaGrande courtesy of William Goodwin, photograph by Rick Lenz; 1930 Two-Door Coupe by Bohman & Schwartz courtesy of S.W. Mudd, photograph by Rick Lenz. Pages 24-25: 1935 Roadster by Gurney Nutting courtesy of Harry Resnick, photographs by Don Vorderman. Pages 26-27: 1935 Convertible Coupe by Rollston courtesy of T.E. Adderley, photograph by Don Vorderman; 1935 Speedster by LaGrande courtesy of Alfred Ferrara, photograph by Don Vorderman; 1936 Convertible Coupe by Rollston courtesy of Harrah's Automobile Collection, photograph by Rick Lenz. Page 28: 1930 Boattail Speedster by Murphy courtesy of Erle M. Heath, photograph by Don Vorderman. Page 29: 1934 Convertible Sedan by Brunn courtesy of B.C. Hartline, photograph by Don Vorderman.

### PIONEERING FROM PAWTUCKET, R.I. TO PUTEAUX ON THE SEINE
All cars courtesy of the Chateau de Grandson, photographs by Vanni Belli.

### THE SPORTING RILEYS
Page 36: Redwing courtesy of G.B. Sherratt. Page 37: Imp courtesy of W.D.J. Lamb. Pages 38-39: Dixon Nine courtesy of G. Dick; Brooklands Nine courtesy of F.E. Marriott. Pages 40-41: Brooklands Nine courtesy of R. Melville-Smith; M.P.H. courtesy of F.J. Rolph. Page 42: Ulster Imp courtesy of H. Geary. Page 43: Grebe Replica courtesy of W.A. Alderton. Pages 44-45: Appleton Special courtesy of R.P. Cook; Dixon Nine courtesy of N. Farquhar. Pages 46-47: Sprite courtesy of G.R. Middleton. All photographs by John F. Hughes.

### PROMOTING THE PIERCE-ARROW
Pages 48, 49, 51 below, 56 above left and below: advertisements courtesy of the National Automotive History Collection, the Detroit Public Library. Pages 50 left, 51 above, 52 above and below, 53 below, 54 above left and below, 54-55 above center, 55 above and below, 56 above right, 57 above left and right and below: advertisements courtesy of the Peter Helck Collection. Pages 50-51 center, 53 above: advertisements courtesy of the Frederick C. Crawford Auto-Aviation Museum.

### IT'S THE BMW TURBO
Pages 58-63: all photographs by Don Vorderman.

### THE CAR CALLED E.R.A.
Pages 64-65: R3A courtesy of N. Arnold-Forster and H.F. Moffatt. Pages 66-69: R1B courtesy of C.P. Marsh. All photographs by Neill Bruce.

### THE HUDSON MOTOR CAR COMPANY STORY
Page 70: 1910 '20' Roadster courtesy of the Long Island Automotive Museum; 1911 '33' Torpedo courtesy of Wesley Carlson; photographs by Henry Austin Clark, Jr.

Pages 72-73: 1915 6-40 Coupe courtesy of the Henry Ford Museum and Greenfield Village, photograph by Charles Miller; 1911 Super Six Four-Passenger Phaeton and 1918 Super Six Limousine courtesy of Harrah's Automobile Collection, photographs by L. Scott Bailey; 1926 Super Six Four-Door Brougham courtesy of Carroll Kerchner, Jr., photograph by Don Vorderman; 1916 Super Six Seven-Passenger Touring, photograph by Rick Lenz; 1922 Essex Coach courtesy of William Cuthbert, photograph by Rick Lenz. Pages 74-75: 1929 Dual Cowl Phaeton by Biddle and Smart courtesy of the A.N. Rodway Collection, photographs by L. Scott Bailey. Page 76: 1929 Two-Passenger Coupe, photograph by Rick Lenz; 1929 Greater Special Sport Sedan and Sport Phaeton by Biddle and Smart courtesy of Harrah's Automobile Collection, photographs by L. Scott Bailey; 1927 Essex Six Roadster by Biddle and Smart courtesy of the A.N. Rodway Collection, photograph by Russel Berry. Page 77: 1931 Great Eight Boattail Speedster by Murray courtesy of the A.N. Rodway Collection, photograph by Russel Berry. Pages 78-79: 1932 Indy Special courtesy of M.H. Gould, photograph by Richard Langworth; 1931 Greater Eight Phaeton and 1930 Greater Eight Roadster courtesy of Harrah's Automobile Collection, photographs by L. Scott Bailey; 1933 Essex Terraplane courtesy of Harold Reimensnyder, photograph by Richard Langworth; 1932 Major Series Brougham courtesy of Pete Booz, photograph by Rick Lenz. Pages 80-81: 1936 Six Sedan courtesy of Roger W. Mease; 1939 Six Coupe courtesy of Loring Craymer; 1941 Traveler Sedan courtesy of Robert Kerchner; 1947 Commodore Six Sedan courtesy of Richard Royer; photographs by Don Vorderman. Page 82: 1949 Commodore Six courtesy of Cliff Crouse, photograph by Don Vorderman. Page 83: 1953 Hornet courtesy of Raymond R. Robinson, 1954 Jet Liner courtesy of Duchin Wukelic; 1957 Hornet courtesy of Russell Pierce; photographs by Don Vorderman. Pages 84-85: X-161 courtesy of Hal Denman; Italia courtesy of Raymond R. Robinson; photographs by Don Vorderman.

### TALES OF THE 300 SL
Pages 90-91: 1955 Coupe courtesy of Edward John Boyd V. Pages 94-95: 1957 Roadster courtesy of Stan Tarnopol. Pages 96-97: 1961 Roadster courtesy of Edward John Boyd V. All photographs by Stan Grayson.

### A LITTLE ON THE BIDDLE FROM PHILADELPHIA
Page 99: 1918 Series H Town Car courtesy of the Long Island Automotive Museum, photograph by Henry Austin Clark, Jr. Pages 100-101: 1916 Series D Four-Passenger Touring Car courtesy of Harry Resnick, photograph by Don Vorderman. Pages 102-103: 1920 Model B1 Roadster courtesy of Harrah's Automobile Collection, photographs by Don Vorderman.

### THE HEROIC AGE
Pages 104-105: 1906 Vanderbilt Cup painting courtesy of the Long Island Automotive Museum; 1908 Vanderbilt Cup painting courtesy of Richard M. Roy. Pages 106-107: Briarcliff painting courtesy of the New Britain Museum of American Art. Pages 108-109: Indianapolis paintings courtesy of Tony Hulman. Pages 110-111: Grand Prize painting courtesy of the George H. Waterman, Jr. Collection.

### THE HOUSE VINCENZO LANCIA BUILT SO WELL
Pages 112-115: 1908 Alfas, 1909 Beta courtesy of the Museo Vincenzo Lancia, photographs by Centro Storico Fiat; 1914 Theta courtesy of the Museo dell' Automobile Carlo Biscaretti di Ruffia, photograph by Josip Ciganovic. Pages 116-117: 1925 Lambda courtesy of the Museo Vincenzo Lancia, photograph by Don Vorderman; 1925 Lambda by Casaro courtesy of Kent L. Wakeford, photograph by Alexandre Georges. Pages 118-119: 1925 Lambda by Casaro courtesy of Mark Shetler, photograph by Rick Lenz; 1927 Lambda by Pininfarina courtesy of Fred S. Sherman, photograph by Rick Lenz; 1930 Dilambda by Mulliner courtesy of the Museo Vincenzo Lancia, photograph by Don Vorderman. Pages 120-121: 1931 Dilambda by Castagna courtesy of Harrah's Automobile Collection, photograph by Don Vorderman; 1933 Astura by Castagna courtesy of L. Scott Bailey, photograph by L. Scott Bailey; 1934 Augusta by Earl of March courtesy of M.L. Bud Cohn, photograph by Rick Lenz. Page 122: 1935 Astura courtesy of the Aalholm Automobilmuseum; 1938 Astura courtesy of the Henri Malartre Collection, Musée Français de l'Automobile, photograph by Tom Burnside. Page 123: 1938 Aprilia courtesy of Anna Bulgari, photograph by Josip Ciganovic. Page 124: 1958 Aurelia B 20 GT by Pininfarina courtesy of Francesco Burgisser, photograph by Don Vorder-

man. Page 125: 1959 Aurelia B 24 by Pininfarina courtesy of James Harvey, photograph by Don Vorderman. Page 126: 1961 Appia GTE by Zagato courtesy of Cesare De Feo, photograph by Don Vorderman; 1963 Flaminia show car by Pininfarina courtesy of Richard E. Buckingham, Jr.; 1964 Flaminia by Pininfarina courtesy of James E. Dillard, photograph by Don Vorderman. Page 127: 1963 Flavia by Pininfarina, photograph by Emilio Chiesa. Page 128: 1963 Flavia by Vignale courtesy of Herman Redden; 1967 Fulvia courtesy of James Adams; photographs by Don Vorderman. Page 129: 1967 Fulvia Sport by Zagato courtesy of Larry Menser, photograph by Rick Lenz; 1975 Beta, photograph by Stan Grayson.

### KELSEY'S MOTORETTE
Pages 131-133: Motorette courtesy of Robert Zlotoff, photographs by Stan Grayson. Page 132: advertisement courtesy of the Keith Marvin Collection.

### NOW AND FOREVER, THE COBRA STORY
Pages 134-135 and 138-139: 289 Roadster and Daytona Coupe, photographs by Stan Grayson. Pages 136-137: 427 Roadster courtesy of Tom Boffo, photograph by Don Vorderman. Pages 140-141: 427 Roadster courtesy of Davide R. Ruocco, photographs by Stan Grayson. Pages 142-143: 427 S/C Roadster courtesy of Geoffrey Howard, photograph by Stan Grayson.

### THE TOSS OF A HAT-IN-THE-RING: RICKENBACKER
Page 145: 1923 Model B Touring Phaeton courtesy of Darrell Mitchell, photographs by Rick Lenz. Page 146: 1924 Model C Opera Coupe courtesy of Bob Hendricks, photograph by L. Scott Bailey. Page 147: 1925 Model D Coach-Brougham courtesy of Mike McBride, photograph by L. Scott Bailey. Page 148: 1925 Model D Roadster courtesy of Howard Henderson, Jr., photographs by Richard A. Brown. Page 150: 1925 Model D Coach-Brougham courtesy of C.L. Bailey, photograph by L. Scott Bailey; 1926 Vertical-8 Superfine Coupe courtesy of Harrah's Automobile Collection, photograph by Rick Lenz. Page 152: 1926 Model E Brougham courtesy of Bellm Cars & Music of Yesterday, photograph by Joseph Janney Steinmetz; 1926 Model E Roadster courtesy of C. Creighton Evans, Jr., photograph by Richard A. Brown. Page 153: Super Sport illustration courtesy of Charles W. Schaub.

### AMILCAR OF ST. DENIS
Page 154: circa 1922 C4, photograph by L. Scott Bailey. Page 155: 1924 CGS3, photograph by Henry Austin Clark, Jr. Pages 156-157: 1926 CGSs Italiana courtesy of Bryan K. Goodman, photographs by Neill Bruce. Page 158: 1926 C6 courtesy of Desmond Peacock and Guy Weightman, photograph by Neill Bruce. Page 159: 1927 CGSs courtesy of Elaine Drake, photograph by Neill Bruce. Pages 160-161: 1930 M2 faux cabriolet courtesy of I. Irving Silverman, photographs by Stan Grayson. Page 162: 1926 CGS courtesy of Christopher Leydon, photograph by Stan Grayson. Page 163: 1929 CGSs courtesy of Christopher Leydon, photograph by Richard Langworth.

### THE BENTLEYS BUILT BY ROLLS-ROYCE
Page 164: 1934 3½ Litre Tourer by Vanden Plas courtesy of T.K. Wilyman, photograph by Don Vorderman. Page 165: 1936 4¼ Litre Drophead Coupe by Park Ward courtesy of Richard Broster, photograph by Don Vorderman; 1936 4¼ Litre Sport Coupe by Gurney Nutting courtesy of Charles Mulhern, photograph by L. Scott Bailey. Page 166: Eddie Hall Tourist Trophy Bentley courtesy of the Briggs Cunningham Automotive Museum, photograph by Rick Lenz. Page 167: Nicky Embiricos Bentley courtesy of Christopher Soames; 1938 4¼ Litre Coupe by Van Vooren courtesy of Al Garthwaite; photographs by Don Vorderman. Pages 168-169: 1937 4¼ Litre Tourer by Vanden Plas courtesy of David John Thornton, photograph by L. Scott Bailey; 1939 4¼ Litre Sedanca de Ville by Gurney Nutting courtesy of Bob Hicks, photograph by Rick Lenz; 1936 4¼ Litre All Weather Tourer by Vanden Plas courtesy of George Russell, photograph by Rick Lenz. Pages 170-171: 1939 4¼ Litre Saloon by Park Ward courtesy of W.J. Snook; 1939 4¼ Litre Tourer by Vanden Plas courtesy of Johnnie Green; 1949 Mark VI Drophead Coupe by Mulliner courtesy of R. Carpenter; photographs by Don Vorderman. Page 172: 1951 "Olga" R-Type Continental by Mulliner courtesy of Stanley Sedgwick, photograph by Don Vorderman. Page 173: 1955 R-Type Stan-

dard Saloon courtesy of George Strong; 1959 Series S Standard Saloon courtesy of Alexander Cameron III; photographs by Don Vorderman. Page 174-175: 1962 S.2 Continental Flying Spur by Mulliner courtesy of H.C. Green, photograph by Don Vorderman; 1971 Series T Saloon courtesy of the Vintage Car Store.

### THE FOOL THINGS
Pages 176-183: Paintings courtesy of the Long Island Automotive Museum.

### THE GLORIOUS DELAGE, A BITTERSWEET STORY
Page 184: 1910 Type F Runabout courtesy of the Chateau de Grandson, photograph by Vanni Belli; 1914 Type R4 Runabout courtesy of W. Darcy Read. Page 185: 1913 Type R4 Runabout courtesy of Austin B. Pooley, photograph by Neill Bruce. Page 186: 1925 Type DI Formal Limousine by Castraise courtesy of Gaston Natoly, photograph by Don Vorderman. Page 187: 1927 Type DIS Torpedo by Kelsch, photograph by Neill Bruce. Pages 188-189: 1930 Type D8N Coach by Chapron and 1933 Type D8S Drophead de Ville by Pourtout courtesy of the André Surmain Collection, photographs by Don Vorderman. Pages 190-191: 1932 Type D8 Coupe de Ville by Fernandez courtesy of Michel Seydoux, photographs by Vanni Belli. Pages 192-193: 1933 Type D8 Drophead de Ville by Fernandez & Darrin courtesy of the Adrien Maeght Collection, formerly Antony G. Newell, photograph by Don Vorderman; 1936 Type D6 70 Drophead de Ville by Coachcraft courtesy of Joe Philp, photograph by Don Vorderman; 1937 Type D8 100 Seven-Passenger Town Car by Franay courtesy of Frederick Z. Tycher, photograph by Hubert and Betty Cook. Pages 194-195: 1934 Type D6 11 Coach by Letourneur et Marchand courtesy of André Taminau, photographs by Vanni Belli. Page 196: 1938 Type D6 Convertible Victoria by University Coach Works Ltd. courtesy of Ernest H. Rice, Jr. and Walter C. Binder, photograph by Stan Grayson. Page 197: 1939 Type D8 120 Torpedo by de Villars courtesy of Alberta Berndt, photograph by Henry Austin Clark, Jr.; 1939 Deltasport by Letourneur et Marchand courtesy of Harrah's Automobile Collection, photograph by Rick Lenz.

### CHRYSLER'S ALPHABET FROM C TO B TO L—THE 300 LETTERCARS
Pages 198-199: 1955 C300 courtesy of Harrah's Automobile Collection, photograph by L. Scott Bailey. Pages 200-201: 1956 300-B courtesy of Dan McFall, photograph by Rick Lenz. Pages 202-203: 1957 300-C courtesy of Ken Heagy, photograph by Rick Lenz; 1958 300-D courtesy of Harrah's Automobile Collection, photograph by L. Scott Bailey; 1959 300-E courtesy of Neil Rasmussen, photograph by Rick Lenz. Pages 204-205: 1960 300-F courtesy of John Characky; 1961 300-G courtesy of A.C. Baumgartner; photographs by Rick Lenz. Pages 206-207: 1962 300-H courtesy of J. Horstmeier, photograph by Rick Lenz. Pages 208-209: 1963 300-J courtesy of Charles S. Hill; 1964 300-K courtesy of Bill Fulford; 1965 300-L courtesy of Bill Arnold; photographs by Rick Lenz.

### ARTIST'S CONCEPTION
Pages 210-211: Bi-Autogo courtesy of the Detroit Historical Museum, photograph by Stan Grayson. Pages 212-213: Rocket prototype courtesy of the Henry Ford Museum and Greenfield Village; 1914 production Rocket courtesy of the Detroit Historical Museum; photographs by Stan Grayson. Page 214: 1916 Scripps-Booth Model C courtesy of Harrah's Automobile Collection, photograph by Rick Lenz. Page 215: 1916 Scripps-Booth Model G courtesy of the Zimmerman Collection, photograph by Stan Grayson. Pages 216-217: 1917 Scripps-Booth Model D Roadster courtesy of Gary D. Leuthauser, photographs by Stan Grayson. Pages 218-219: 1917 Scripps-Booth Model D Town Car courtesy of the Swigart Museum, photographs by Stan Grayson.

### A PACKARD HEXAD
Page 228: 1912 Model Thirty Touring Car courtesy of Phil Hill, photograph by Rick Lenz. Page 229: Packard gate illustration courtesy of Richard Teague. Pages 230-231: 1914 Model 4-48 Touring Car and 1920 Twin Six Town Car by Fleetwood courtesy of Stan Tarnopol, photographs by Richard Langworth. Pages 232-233: 1928 Model 443 Raceabout courtesy of Ted Bacon and the Minden Automotive Museum, photograph by Rick Lenz; 1931 Model 840 Custom Phaeton courtesy of Art Schreiber, photograph by Stan Grayson. Pages 234-235: 1931 Model 840 Four-Door Convertible Sedan by Dietrich courtesy of Robert Turnquist, photograph by Don Vorderman.